THE DOMESTICATION OF HUMAN TRAFFICKING

Law, Policing, and Prosecution in Canada

Human trafficking has emerged as one of the top international and domestic policy concerns, and is well covered and often sensationalized by the media. The nature of the topic combined with various international pressures has resulted in an array of government-led mandates to combat the issue.

The Domestication of Human Trafficking examines Canada's criminal justice approaches to human trafficking, with a particular focus on the ways in which the intersecting factors of race, class, gender, and sexuality impact practice. Using a wide range of qualitative and empirically grounded research methods, including extensive analysis of court documents, trial transcripts, and interviews with criminal justice actors, this book contributes to much-needed research that examines, specifies, and sometimes complicates the narratives of how trafficking works as a criminal offence. *The Domestication of Human Trafficking* turns our attention to the ways in which the offence of human trafficking is made on the front lines of criminal justice efforts in Canada.

KATRIN ROOTS is an assistant professor in the Department of Criminology at Wilfrid Laurier University.

The Domestication of Human Trafficking

Law, Policing, and Prosecution in Canada

KATRIN ROOTS

UNIVERSITY OF TORONTO PRESS
Toronto Buffalo London

ISBN 978-1-4875-0697-1 (cloth)
ISBN 978-1-4875-2471-5 (paper)
ISBN 978-1-4875-3535-3 (EPUB)
ISBN 978-1-4875-3534-6 (PDF)

Library and Archives Canada Cataloguing in Publication

Title: The domestication of human trafficking : law, policing,
and prosecution in Canada / Katrin Roots.
Names: Roots, Katrin, author.
Description: Includes bibliographical references and index.
Identifiers: Canadiana (print) 20220251401 |
Canadiana (ebook) 20220251460 | ISBN 9781487506971 (hardcover) |
ISBN 9781487524715 (softcover) | ISBN 9781487535353 (EPUB) |
ISBN 9781487535346 (PDF)
Subjects: LCSH: Human trafficking – Law and legislation – Canada.
Classification: LCC KE9059 .R55 2022 | LCC KF9449 .R66 2022 kfmod |
DDC 345/.7102551 – dc23

We wish to acknowledge the land on which the University of Toronto
Press operates. This land is the traditional territory of the Wendat,
the Anishnaabeg, the Haudenosaunee, the Métis, and
the Mississaugas of the Credit First Nation.

This book has been published with the help of a grant from the Federation
for the Humanities and Social Sciences, through the Awards to Scholarly
Publications Program, using funds provided by the Social Sciences and
Humanities Research Council of Canada.

University of Toronto Press acknowledges the financial support of the
Government of Canada, the Canada Council for the Arts, and the Ontario Arts
Council, an agency of the Government of Ontario, for its publishing activities.

Contents

THE DOMESTICATION OF
HUMAN TRAFFICKING

Introduction

Gregory Salmon is a young man who was charged with human trafficking in Ontario in 2014. According to the evidence at trial, Salmon developed an online friendship with the complainant – a young woman[1] from Manitoba. After several months of communicating online, the complainant travelled to visit Salmon in Ontario. The two began a romantic relationship, and she stayed to live with him. Soon after her arrival, however, Salmon lost his job and the young woman started working in the sex trade to provide financial support. The relationship was a troubled one, and Salmon was frequently violent and abusive, escalating to the point that the complainant called the police. Because she was working in the sex trade and shared her income with him, the police charged Salmon with human trafficking, in addition to domestic violence–related offences (*R. v. [Gregory] Salmon* 2014).

Despite the complainant's testimony in court that she freely chose to enter the sex trade, the Crown attorney[2] argued that Salmon coerced her and that she was therefore a victim of trafficking. While there was no question that Salmon physically abused the complainant during their relationship, the Crown provided no evidence to demonstrate that violence was used to force her into the sex trade. In fact, the Crown himself acknowledged that the complainant had entered the trade on her own accord: "I'm not saying that he be convicted because he pushed her into prostitution, that was a choice she made." But the Crown was inconsistent on this key point, arguing later that the violence inflicted on the complainant by the accused was used to force her into the sex trade to "put her down and in her place" (*R. v. [Gregory] Salmon*, audio of trial, 25 May 2014). In the end, the judge rejected this argument and acquitted the accused of trafficking charges.

While some may dismiss this incident as routine over-charging corrected by judicial oversight, the case raises several important questions about how human trafficking is characterized and mobilized by police and prosecutors. In particular, how does a case where the complainant acknowledges entering and staying in the sex trade *voluntarily* and with full control over the money produced from services rendered come to be seen as a case of trafficking? How are the constituent elements of the trafficking offence construed and enacted by Crown and defence attorneys, judges, and police officers? And, in this case, how did domestic violence become re-framed as human trafficking? These questions highlight a critical gap in literature around the operationalization of anti-trafficking laws on the ground. To understand these specific questions, it is necessary to consider them in the broader sociohistorical and legal context of international and national anti-trafficking regimes.

Using an empirically grounded examination of front-line policing prosecution and defence efforts in Ontario, as well as court decisions, policy and legal documents, police and non-governmental organization (NGO) reports, and media outputs from across Canada, this book examines how international trafficking discourses become domesticated in Canada. I endeavour to explore in rich empirical detail how, in the presence of confusion around the meaning of the term "human trafficking," the front-line day-to-day anti-trafficking policing and legal activities work to shape the offence of trafficking. In particular, the book demonstrates that, while at the level of international and, to some extent, domestic policy, the guiding preoccupations revolve centrally around organized crime threats to public safety and national security, on the front line, things are decidedly more complicated. This is because anti-trafficking efforts in local police departments and courtrooms are shaped by a host of influences, practices, and justifications and entail a variety of diverse effects. This book is less about the cases that are brought to court and final verdicts and more about how the various intersecting discourses reify complex relationships and power dynamics through the heavy-handed concept of human trafficking.

At the local level, criminal justice authorities remain guided by the historically longstanding aim to protect women and children from the threats of physical and sexual assault, particularly in relation to the sex trade. These motivations are fuelled by systemic race, class, gender, and age biases that emphasize the need to protect some women, and in particular white, middle-class women, while punishing and criminalizing all others. In the context of Canada's anti-trafficking efforts, Elya Durisin rightly points out that "fears about victimized white femininity and foreign threats present in government discourse gesture to the importance of white female bodies to the stability of national boundaries" (2017, 13). This victimized, female figure is represented by the category of the "ideal victim," which, in Canada's anti-trafficking discourses, presents as the white, young, and innocent daughter of middle-class families – "the girl next door." The protection of this group in a white settler-colonial Canada is particularly important since these women are seen to be responsible for the well-being of Canadian families and establishing the country's moral purity and superiority over others (Doezema 2000, 2010; Durisin 2017; Kaye 2017). The need of the white settler state to protect the "girl next door" serves to legitimatize law and policy expansions, increased funding for anti-trafficking efforts, and supports the overall need to "do more" to combat human trafficking. These concerns are not new, as a wave of fears over "white slavery" – the historical version of human trafficking – also took place at the end of the nineteenth century and bears a striking resemblance to the current panics over trafficking.

Fear over white slavery emerged first in Britain and focused on the sexual exploitation of white women travelling abroad for work (Bullough and Bullough 1987; Cordasco 1981; Doezema 2000, 2010; Donovan 2006; Gallagher 2010; McLaren 1990; Valverde 2008; Walkowitz 1980). Although there was insufficient evidence that a large-scale traffic of women was taking place, these concerns were fuelled by broader anxieties around sex, class, and race relations (Chapkins 1997, 42). And, despite an absence of evidence to support the panic, the issue of white slavery became used as a justification for the need to eliminate the sex trade. Religious missionaries, and later abolitionist feminists, insisted that adult women working in the trade were there against their will and called on lawmakers and politicians to denounce the sex trade. Contemporary concerns over human trafficking borrow significantly from the white slavery panics, including concerns over the safety and well-being of white women and girls, the moral positioning of sex work as evil and the suppression of sex workers' efforts for self-determination through a focus on their victimhood and need for rescue.

Alongside the girl next door, who is always seen as an innocent victim of trafficking, marginalized and Indigenous women and girls who are involved in the sex trade are paradoxically constructed along a criminalization/victimization continuum. These categories are shaped not only through historic concerns around white slavery but also sexual violence against women and children that emerged in the 1970s and were animated by the panics that took hold in the 1980s and 1990s over youth in the sex trade. The Indigenous victim of trafficking category is also structured through colonial discourses that construct Indigenous women in pathologized, criminalized, and infantilized terms. In the context of current anti-trafficking efforts, this longstanding aim of protection re-emerges in anti-trafficking regimes and is operationalized through the key concept of exploitation.

Anti-trafficking protectionist discourses are also shaped by the historical and racialized legacy of concerns over "pimps," and especially their targeting of white women and girls. Indeed, as my empirical research shows, the targets of anti-trafficking efforts are overwhelmingly young, poor, and racialized – particularly Black – men. The criminalization of this demographic through anti-trafficking efforts reflects the extent to which systemic racism is embedded into our cultural fabric and through which Black men are seen as inherently criminogenic and pathological (Alexander 2012; Davis 2017; Hill Collins 2004; Maynard 2017; Walker 2010). Black men's perceived violence and hypersexuality are seen as particularly threatening to the safety and well-being of white women. Although in Canada there is a desire "to avoid the appearance of American-style racism, state officials and powerful white settler groups [in Canada] mobilize around the image of Black men as dangerous sexual predators" (Maynard 2017, 42). In this context, knowledges and practices aimed at combating trafficking have become extensions of systemic forms of race, class, gender, and age discrimination intended to save white women from Black men (Bernstein 2010; Doezema 2000, 2010; Horning and Marcus 2017 Kempadoo 2005; Kempadoo and Doezema 1998; Valverde 2008; Williamson and Marcus 2017).

This book turns our attention to the ways in which the offence of human trafficking is continually made on the front line of legal and criminal justice efforts in Canada. By mapping the numerous, complex, and varied effects of anti-trafficking regimes through grounded and detailed empirical findings, I seek to complicate dominant narratives about the definition and nature of trafficking. The heightened political and popular focus on the threats of human trafficking has indeed produced a number of notable effects. For example, police departments across Canada are competing for the expanding federal and provincial resources being made available for anti-trafficking efforts, and subsequently forming specialized anti-trafficking units. These units and, more recently, specialized prosecutorial teams have produced a climate favouring increased arrests and convictions for trafficking offences. Together, they have also implemented new forms of knowledge and expertise, including what constitutes human trafficking and the role played by technology in facilitating trafficking. The evolving legal tactics and strategies used in trafficking trials have additionally played a role in shaping trafficking victims and offenders as well as the meaning of trafficking itself.

To make sense of the complex empirical data, I developed a concept I call the "human trafficking matrix." The matrix refers to the dynamic and shifting web of diverse intersecting historical and contemporary discourses, specialized forms of expertise, technologies, and strategies of application that have come together to govern human trafficking. These include turn-of-the-twentieth-century concerns about white slavery, the 1970s feminist movement against sexual violence, and the 1980s and 1990s panics over youth in the sex trade. Within the matrix, these discourses, specialized knowledges, technologies, and strategies of application intersect with concerns over organized crime and threats to national security and are further impacted by intersecting fears over terrorism. For example, recent findings by the UN Security Council suggest that proceeds from human trafficking are used to support terrorist activities (UNODC 2015a). The discursive linking of trafficking with terrorism, organized crime, and national security threats has the effect of increasing the perceived urgency, severity, and danger posed by trafficking activities. The intersection of these fears with domestic concerns over sexual violence, child sexual exploitation, and youth involvement in the sex trade shapes not only the understanding of human trafficking but also the indicators and characteristics that constitute a trafficker and a victim. It further impacts the strategies required to combat it, including on-the-ground enforcement and prosecutorial efforts and the motivations, decisions, and actions of criminal justice and legal actors. The trafficking matrix, then, captures the intersection and effects of the various complex, overlapping, and, at times, contradictory developments in the anti-trafficking terrain.

Law is one important factor within the trafficking matrix. The current international law against human trafficking, The Protocol to Prevent, Suppress and Punish Trafficking in Persons, Especially Women and Children (henceforth Trafficking Protocol) (2000), was developed in response to contemporary concerns over human trafficking that rose to the forefront of political interest in the aftermath of the collapse of the Soviet Union and the increased migration, particularly of women, out of the Eastern Bloc nations that took place following the end of the Cold War (Ferguson 2012; Gallagher 2010; Kempadoo 2005). As Kamala Kempadoo notes (2005), the potential for women's independence through newfound job opportunities was seen as threatening to the patriarchal order. The "image of the duped and violated 'Natasha'" came to act as the fear factor intended to deter women from migrating and to "replace the threat of communism as the global specter of abjection" (Suchland 2015, 1).

While the Trafficking Protocol (2000) has certainly not been the first international legislation of this nature, as legal frameworks governing trafficking date back to the late nineteenth and early twentieth centuries (Cordasco 1981, 5; Doezema 2002; Gallagher 2010), it has been the most impactful of the anti-trafficking legislations thus far. Indeed, it was the enactment of the Trafficking Protocol that led politicians, the media, international organizations, state governments, and more recently, police and the criminal justice system paying much attention to the issue. Unlike its predecessors, the current UN Trafficking Protocol has gained significant traction within the international community, with 117 signatories and 175 parties at the time of writing in 2021.[3] Anne Gallagher (2006) argues that this increased interest in and urgency surrounding trafficking stems from a shift that took place during the process of drafting the Trafficking Protocol, from human rights to a criminal law framework, which linked trafficking to international threats posed by the involvement of transnational organized crime in migrant smuggling. In this process, the protocol became one part of the Convention against Transnational Organized Crime (2000), which also includes the Protocol against Illicit Manufacturing of and Trafficking in Firearms, Their Parts and Components and Ammunition, and the Protocol against the Smuggling of Migrants by Land, Sea and Air. To ratify any of the protocols, states must first ratify the Convention itself since the protocols were not intended as stand-alone treaties but were meant to be interpreted together with the Convention (Gallagher 2010, 73). Any modifications to the interpretation of the protocols must also be made in light of the simultaneous application of the Convention (ibid.). Therefore, the definition of human trafficking under the Trafficking Protocol – which was the first international definition of human trafficking developed and is one of the key contributions of this protocol – must adopt the characteristics of legal norms surrounding transnationalism and organized crime, which inform the Convention. The Trafficking Protocol, with its emphasis on organized crime and transnationalism, is the basis on which contemporary international discourses around trafficking have formed.

Canada's ratification of the Trafficking Protocol in 2002 was followed by numerous legal reforms, as seen by the series of amendments to trafficking laws. In 2002, the government enacted the Immigration and Refugee Protection Act (IRPA) and with it, section 118, which governs cross-border trafficking of persons. In 2005, sections 279.01–.04 were added to the Criminal Code to criminalize domestic human trafficking. Since then, the trafficking provisions within the Criminal Code have been amended four times. With each amendment the definition of trafficking was expanded in ways that allowed for a broader range of activities to be categorized as trafficking. As I detail in chapter one, Canada's adaptation of the international trafficking law stripped large portions of the definition of trafficking provided by the United Nations.

Despite this, the initial focus was on transnational trafficking where the activity imagined involved the kidnapping, deception, and transportation across transnational boundaries of victims by organized crime rings primarily from Eastern and Central Europe. This was seen as resulting from the global collapse of economies, particularly following the breakdown of the Soviet Union. In more recent years, however, these discourses, along with policy and criminal justice efforts, have shifted to focus on domestic trafficking, with concerns fuelled largely by the possibility of the "girl next door" becoming a victim (see also De Shalit et al. 2021; Durisin and van der Meulen 2020). Throughout this book I explore a number of trafficking cases in detail to understand how this domestic trafficking "problem" has come to be.

Despite the extensive legal developments to support anti-trafficking efforts, this book suggests that there is ongoing ambiguity around the meaning of human trafficking among criminal justice actors. Crown and defence attorneys, judges, and police have notably different, and sometimes contradictory understandings of the meaning of human trafficking, particularly in relation to the distinction between trafficking and the legal offence of procuring (under section 286.3 of the Criminal Code), colloquially known as "pimping." Yet, rather than bringing anti-trafficking strategies into disrepute, this ambiguity is in some ways enabling, as it imports a definitional elasticity that effectively expands the scope of activities that fall within the definition of trafficking and therefore, who can be defined as a trafficker and a victim. This elastic definition of trafficking has been beneficial in bringing about increased numbers of trafficking arrests and prosecutions by allowing a wide range of activities to be captured by the umbrella term "human trafficking" and thus is suggestive of a successful criminal justice response to the issue.

However, Anne Gallagher and Rebecca Surtees warn that increased charges and convictions are "crude and potentially misleading success indicators" since they can be explained by a number of factors, including new or expanded trafficking laws, and the application of trafficking laws to offences previously charged under other laws, such as sexual assault and "pimping" (2012, 23). In addition to these factors, in Canada, the growth in charges can also be attributed to the development of national anti-trafficking strategies and the subsequent allocation of significant resources to this end, as well as to the relatively recent changes to sex work laws following the Supreme Court's decision in *R. v. Bedford* (2013), which have significantly increased the number of people, men especially, who can be classified as procurers.

In 2013, the Supreme Court of Canada, in the case of *R. v. Bedford* (2013), struck down key provisions of Canada's sex work laws, finding that they violated the rights of sex workers under sections 7 and 2b of the Canadian Charter of Rights and Freedoms, which protect the right to life, liberty, and security of the person and freedom of expression, respectively. The Supreme Court gave Parliament a period of one year to replace the impugned sections with provisions that complied with Charter rights. On 4 June 2014, the then Conservative government introduced Bill C-36, The Protection of Communities and Exploited Persons Act (PCEPA), which received Royal Assent on 6 November 2014. Under the new law, the criminalization focus shifted from sex workers to "pimps," "traffickers," and clients. While the status of sex workers thus shifted from criminal to victim identity, their labour continues to be stigmatized and deviantized, leaving them vulnerable to being policed and prosecuted for adjacent activities.

In addition to these legal changes, the Canadian government has invested heavily in the formulation of national strategies to combat human trafficking, with a particular focus on increasing police and prosecutorial successes in human trafficking cases. For instance, in 2012, the federal government launched the National Action Plan to Combat Human Trafficking, which promised to protect victims, prevent trafficking, prosecute offenders, and promote cooperation domestically and internationally, with a focus on organized crime networks (Public Safety Canada 2012, 9, 20). In support of the National Action Plan, the federal government allocated $25 million over a four-year period to combating trafficking, with $8 million towards anti-trafficking efforts in the 2013/14 fiscal year and $6 million annually thereafter (Public Safety Canada 2012; see also De Shalit et al. 2014). Notably, of the $8 million in funding for the fiscal year 2013/14, $5,375,000 was allocated towards law enforcement efforts (Public Safety Canada 2012, 10). Among other things, the National Action Plan emphasized the need for cooperation between various police forces and resulted in the establishment of a dedicated integrated enforcement team headed by Canada's national police service, the Royal Canadian Mounted Police (RCMP). While the National Action Plan emphasized the important role of federal policing agencies in leading anti-trafficking efforts, of particular importance to this book is the finding that the vast majority of anti-trafficking policing, as reflected in trafficking arrests and prosecutions, is carried out by newly formed specialized human trafficking teams within municipal police services.

The most recent National Strategy to Combat Human Trafficking 2019–2024 comes with an investment of $75 million over six years towards anti-trafficking activities, which includes $14.51 million to support the establishment of a Canadian Human Trafficking Hotline and $2.89 million in ongoing funding, as well as an additional $57.22 million was invested in 2019 over five years and $10.28 million in ongoing funding "to implement an enhanced suite of initiatives that will strengthen Canada's response and fill critical gaps" (Public Safety Canada 2019, 6).

Similar action plans have been enacted on the provincial level by three provinces: British Columbia, Manitoba, and Ontario. In British Columbia, the Office to Combat Trafficking in Persons (BCOCTIP) was established in 2007 to coordinate a provincial response to human trafficking and bring together partnering organizations, including federal, provincial, and municipal governments, NGOs and community organizations, law enforcement, and academics (Kaye 2017, 75; see also British Columbia (BC) Ministry of Justice 2013). The Government of Manitoba allocates $10 million every year to anti-trafficking initiatives and causes and in 2002 launched Tracia's Trust, a provincial strategy against sexual exploitation led by Manitoba Families and supported by the Winnipeg Police Sexual Exploitation Unit (Government of Manitoba 2019).

In June 2016, the province of Ontario launched its action plan entitled Ontario's Strategy to End Human Trafficking. The action plan was supported by $72 million in funding (Government of Ontario 2016) – almost three times the amount dedicated to the federal strategy. The Ontario strategy included increasing awareness around trafficking; improving community services (housing, mental health services, trauma counselling, and job skills training) for victims; enhancing justice sector initiatives, such as "effective intelligence-gathering and identification, investigation and prosecution of human trafficking," including Indigenous-led approaches; and establishing a provincial coordination and leadership, "including developing a provincial Anti-Human Trafficking Coordination Office to help improve collaboration across law enforcement, justice, social, health, education, and child welfare sectors" (Ministry of the Status of Women 2016).

In 2020, Ontario's Conservative government passed a revised version of the strategy, entitled Ontario's Anti-Human Trafficking Strategy 2020–2025. The new strategy allocates $307 million to anti-trafficking efforts in Ontario over a five-year period. As Ann De Shalit (2021) points out, while the 2016 strategy utilized the language of both labour and sex trafficking, the 2020 strategy is primarily focused on sexual exploitation, relying frequently on the language of child sexual exploitation interchangeably with the language of human trafficking (Government of Ontario 2020).

On 3 June 2021, the Ontario government passed Bill C-251, The Anti-Human Trafficking Strategy Act, 2021, which increases the surveillance powers of police, enabling them to gain access to hotel and Airbnb records without a warrant and, along with social workers, to detain youth under the age of eighteen for their own protection and force them to receive social services. The Act also enables the province to appoint inspectors with powers to enter a place without a warrant to ensure that it complies with the law. As a result of this strategy and the significant funding towards the policing of anti-trafficking, we can expect to see more specialized intervention teams across the province.

Importantly, Ontario's anti-trafficking strategy has led to the creation of a provincial human trafficking prosecution team made up of a provincial coordinator and five specialized anti-trafficking Crowns (MCSS 2018). This emphasis on trafficking prosecutions, and the introduction of specialized Crown attorneys, is likely a response to the relatively low conviction rates and high rate at which trafficking charges are withdrawn, stayed, and/or acquitted despite a rise in the number of charges following the Bedford decision in 2013. For instance, according to the US Department of State 2017 Trafficking in Persons report on Canada: "In 2016, police charged 107 individuals in 68 trafficking cases (none for labor trafficking) compared to 112 individuals in 63 cases in 2015. Prosecutions continued against 300 individuals, including 34 suspected labor traffickers, compared to 314 individuals, including 24 suspected labor traffickers, in 2015. The courts convicted 10 sex traffickers and no labor traffickers in 2016, compared to six sex traffickers in 2015" (2017, 119). The data provided to the US Department of State, therefore, shows a significant discrepancy between charges laid and convictions. As the US Department of State points out, in 2016, out of 107 individuals charged with human trafficking, only 10 were convicted (ibid.). The importance of this is further amplified by the fact that the United States, which took on the task of monitoring and evaluating the efforts of individual states to prosecute and prevent human trafficking (Gallagher 2010), uses prosecution rates of trafficking cases to rank countries on their anti-trafficking efforts (Suchland 2015, 55).

The US evaluation of global anti-trafficking efforts is based on a three-tier ranking system. Tier one is awarded to countries who have fully complied with US anti-trafficking standards, while tier-three ranking is attributed to countries that have failed to do so (Soderlund 2005). A few months before the United States adopted the UN Trafficking Protocol, it passed its own domestic anti-trafficking law, the Trafficking Victims Protection Act (TVPA)[4] (2000) (Chuang 2014, 610; Gallagher 2010; Soderlund 2005; Suchland 2015; Zheng 2010). The TVPA empowered the United States to place economic sanctions on countries that failed to abide by the anti-trafficking standards set out by them (Chuang 2014, 610). This places the United States in a powerful position to exert influence over international politics because a tier-three ranking can trigger sanctions for the rated country, including limiting access to aid from the

United States, International Monetary Fund (IMF), and the World Bank (Cameron 2008, 89).

The TVPA also had a significant impact on the definition of human trafficking used by state governments around the globe by setting out a US-developed definition of the term. The US definition removed the requirement that cross-border transportation be established to prove human trafficking, placed an emphasis on sexual exploitation over other possible forms of exploitation, and defined trafficking as being "induced to perform a commercial sex act" (Gallagher 2010, 23; Bernstein 2012). In effect, the US definition of trafficking came to replace the definition suggested by the UN's own Special Rapporteur on Violence against Women, Radhika Coomaraswamy, which focused on the distinction between trafficking and related practices (Gallagher 2010, 24). As explained by Coomaraswamy, "It is the combination of the coerced transportation and the coerced end practice that makes trafficking a distinct violation from its component parts. Without this linkage, trafficking would be legally indistinguishable from the individual activities of smuggling and forced labour or slavery-like practices" (as cited in Gallagher 2010, 25). Coomaraswamy's definition drew strict boundaries around the meaning of trafficking to distinguish it from other criminal offences. The failure to include Coomaraswamy's coupling of coerced transportation and coerced end practice in the definition of human trafficking operationalized by state governments around the world has effectively erased important distinctions between trafficking and other criminal activities. As I've noted elsewhere, "Human trafficking today is an elastic umbrella term that can be applied to a wide range of cases and situations and maintains little to no resemblance to the offence as it was understood at the time the Trafficking Protocol (2000) was drafted" (Roots 2019, 98). The US definition of trafficking then effectively undermines the goals of the UN Trafficking Protocol to focus not only on trafficking for sexual exploitation but also on other forms of trafficking, including labour trafficking, trafficking for organ harvesting, and debt bondage with a focus on migrant exploitation. The Canadian legal definition of trafficking shares the breadth of the US definition and remains in its enforcement firmly focused on sexual exploitation rather than other types of trafficking.

Influenced by religious groups, the United States is also encouraging and incentivizing countries to abolish the sex trade under the guise of fighting trafficking. The issue has brought together a diverse group of activists and policymakers, including evangelical Christians and sex work prohibitionists in the United States (Bernstein 2010, 2012; Soderlund 2005). And while these groups vary in their views on a number of issues, they are united by their advocacy for harsher penalties for traffickers, sex workers, clients, and any nation that fails to enforce these norms (Bernstein 2010). In effect, the United States has created an international alliance that "built, shaped and perpetuated an international moral and legal order of anti-trafficking movements" (Zheng 2010, 4). Accordingly, during the first two decades of global anti-trafficking efforts, the United States encouraged states to establish "aggressive, perpetrator-focused criminal justice responses to trafficking" in an effort to abolish the sex trade (Chuang 2014, 610). Canada was and continues to be among the countries feeling the pressure from the United States. In 2003, the US Department of State reduced the ranking of Canada's anti-trafficking efforts from its usual tier one to a tier two level (US Department of State 2003). Drawing a direct link between organized crime and trafficking, the 2003 US Department of State Trafficking in Persons Report criticized Canada's border-control strategies, claiming that its lenient immigration laws resulted in several Canadian cities becoming hubs for criminal organizations involved in human trafficking (Collacott 2006). Such criticisms of Canada's anti-trafficking efforts echo the accusations and actions taken by the United States during the white slavery panics at the end of the nineteenth century. At that time, the United States accused Canada of being a "veritable vice haven" for "vile practitioners" due to its lenient sex work laws (McLaren 1986, 48; see also McLaren 1986a, 1990). Furthermore, the US Department of State Trafficking in Persons Reports have continued to emphasize Canada's need to increase its efforts to investigate and prosecute human trafficking offences, increase proactive investigation techniques, and improve coordination between national, provincial, and international law enforcement (Jeffrey 2005; US Department of State 2017, 2016, 2015, 2014). The pressure placed by the US Department of State cannot be underestimated and is at least partly responsible for the increased attention to anti-trafficking efforts and strategies in Canada, which continue to maintain a particular focus on criminalization and prosecution of sex trade–related activities.

In the context of such pressures to increase trafficking arrests and prosecutions and in the absence of transnational trafficking cases (Ferguson 2012), police and legal actors have taken aim at the all-too-familiar target – the domestic sex trade industry. While anyone in the labour force can be exploited, with migrant workers being particularly vulnerable, anti-trafficking approaches focus almost exclusively on sexual exploitation.

The media, Parliamentary debates, and public concern are focused on the "girl next door," while front-line anti-trafficking police and prosecutorial efforts target marginalized girls and women involved in the sex trade under the justification that they are most vulnerable to becoming victims of trafficking. This contrasting focus reveals the class, race, and gender biases underlying Canada's anti-trafficking efforts.[5] As Jo Doezema explains, "the myth of 'trafficking in women' is one manifestation of attempts to re-establish community identity, in which race, sexuality, and women's autonomy are used as markers of crucial boundaries" (2000, 46). Indeed, Doezema's sentiments resonate in the context of Canada's concerns over domestic trafficking, particularly at a time when concerns over migration and the need to secure Canada's national boundaries is becoming increasingly heightened. Less attention has been paid to the ways these discourses have impacted individuals living in Canada. This book seeks to contribute to the conversation by focusing on the ways that class, gender, race, and nationality also shape the ways domestic trafficking is constructed as a problem for and about Canadians.

To reconstruct sex workers as vulnerable to exploitation, police and prosecutors draw on marginalizing factors, such as poverty, history of physical and sexual abuse, drug use, self-esteem issues, and their very involvement in the sex trade, to name a few. The United Nations Office of Drugs and Crime (UNODC) calls these factors "pre-existing vulnerabilities," criticizing their use by domestic criminal justice and legal actors due to their net widening effect and creating a risk of situations becoming "incorrectly or too easily prosecuted as trafficking cases" (2013, 5). Nevertheless, pre-existing vulnerabilities continue to be used not only by police but also prosecutors and defence attorneys in their efforts to shape a human trafficking case.

The significance as well as ambiguities of pre-existing vulnerabilities become evident through the trial processes. The ability of Crowns to successfully prosecute and defence counsel to successfully defend clients charged with human trafficking depends heavily on how such factors are mobilized. While police and Crown attorneys rely on these features of marginalization to construct women and girls as victims of trafficking, the same features are used by defence attorneys to discredit complainants. This legal tactic of presenting factors such as drug use, involvement in the sex trade, and criminal history to undermine the credibility of complainants has been well documented in sexual assault cases (Comack and Balfour 2004; Gotell 2008, 2012; Randall 2010; Sheehy 2012a, 2012b). This, combined with legal strategies, including controlled questions and reliance on courtroom rules, which among other things limit the complainants' ability to speak freely, often make it difficult for complainants in sexual assault cases to be heard (ibid.). These strategies have become even more important for defence attorneys due to the increased seriousness of the charge of trafficking as compared with previous "pimping" charges and the consequent need to aggressively defend their client. Yet, the aggressive approach of counsel to defend the often marginalized and racialized accused recurrently results in the hostile treatment of marginalized women and girls in court. This is particularly well demonstrated in my research, which shows defence attorneys employing a range of common legal strategies in trafficking cases to undermine complainants' testimony, character, and victimhood.

Criminalization of poverty and race in anti-trafficking efforts also extends to poor, young, and racialized, particularly Black, men. And while police targeting of Black men under "pimping" laws has significant historical precedence (Brock 1998; Jeffrey and MacDonald 2006), current anti-trafficking efforts are set apart by the recategorization of domestic "pimping" offences as human trafficking, an offence now understood through its connection to organized crime as a potential threat to national security. Although the majority of trafficking charges do not result in convictions, the charge alone can have significant impacts on accused persons. This is partly because arrests for trafficking-related offences are often covered by the news media, creating public stigma and shaming before the allegations are (dis) proven in court. The few convicted of trafficking also face increased criminal justice penalties and additional immigration penalties for non-citizens, as well as collateral consequences, fomenting what Aya Gruber calls their *civiliter mortuus* – civil death (2020, 5: see chapter one for a discussion).

A great deal of investment, financial and otherwise, has been made internationally and domestically to advance anti-trafficking objectives. In this context, one would expect focused and sustained attention to the nature and effects of these efforts. As explained by Gallagher and Surtees, "it is not difficult to sustain a strong argument that counter-trafficking interventions, including those in the criminal justice sector, should be carefully monitored and evaluated" (2012, 11). Yet, despite the proliferation of expansive anti-trafficking agendas, mandates, laws, and policies, little is known about the way they play out on the front line of policing actions and in courtrooms (Farrell et al. 2016; Gallagher and Surtees 2012). While a few studies examining these on-the-ground effects have emerged in recent years, they are primarily focused on the United States (Esser et al. 2016; Farrell et al. 2015, 2016) and Europe (Lester et al. 2017; Meshkovska et al. 2016). To date, there are three local empirical Canadian studies that examine front-line anti-trafficking policing and prosecution efforts, one of which focuses on law and migrant worker justice (Millar et al. 2015, 2020; Millar et al. 2020), another on international trafficking cases (Ferguson 2012), and a third that explores anti-trafficking efforts in Canada's settler-colonial context (Kaye 2017). This book adds to this body of scholarship by examining in finely grained empirical detail policing and prosecutorial anti-trafficking efforts between 2005 and 2016, with updates up until 2021, focusing primarily on the province of Ontario. Attending to the ways that Canadian responses to trafficking give expression to concerns over violence against women, child sexual exploitation and youth in sex work, and the intersecting issues of organized crime and national security, the focus of this book is on local front-line police and prosecutorial efforts in the jurisdiction of Ontario, where the vast majority of trafficking cases are enforced and prosecuted.

Research Methods

This study was conducted between 2005 and 2016 using multiple qualitative methods of data collection, including international and Canadian government and non-government reports, House of Commons debates on various legal bills, media publications, court documents, trial transcripts and audio recordings, sentencing decisions, interviews with criminal justice actors, and legal documents including case law and court documents. Government and non-government reports, media publications, and case law were collected Canada-wide. In contrast, the primary research, including 123 court informations/indictments where human trafficking charges (279.01–.011) were laid (between 2005 and 2016), court transcripts, and interviews with key actors, was conducted in Ontario. Given the time lapse between the research and the publication of this book, I have included updated cases and developments that have taken place since 2016, up until 2021. In addition to this, I collected recordings for eight trafficking trials from Ontario: six full trials ranging from one day to thirty-three days[6] and a case that ended in a mistrial (*R. v. Beckford 2013*). I obtained the transcript of submissions and the decision in the Ontario Court of Appeal 2015 precedent-setting case *R. v. A.A.* and the Ontario Court of Appeal transcript for the hearing and decision of *R. v. Salmon (Courtney)* (2015). Finally, I conducted a partial-participant observation of one trafficking trial (*R. v. Leung* 2015). In some cases, I was also able to get access to copies of court exhibits, which included police interviews with the accused and complainants, defence attorney summary documents, and factums. Additionally, I examined a number of court decisions in trafficking cases across Canada, which I collected from the legal search engine CanLii. Due to challenges with researching human trafficking in Canada outlined in a previous co-authored publication (Millar et al. 2017), the cases analysed in this book were ones I was able to get access to.

I also conducted interviews with various criminal justice actors, including five police officers in anti-trafficking policing units and four Crown and five defence attorneys. I also spoke to three judges, but only one of them had first-hand experience with trafficking cases, and therefore only one judicial interview is being included in this study. The recorded interviews ranged from forty-five minutes to two and a half hours in length. Although a set of questions was provided to participants ahead of time, the interviews were semi-structured to allow participants to provide information based on their own front-line experiences and to allow the emergence of unanticipated issues and questions.

Researching the issue of trafficking brought with it a number of limitations, including a low number of trafficking trials (most are resolved before trial either through withdrawn or stayed charges, plea bargains, etc.) and access issues. While the cost of trial transcripts in Ontario and other provinces across Canada is very high, I was able to access audio recordings of eight trials with the permission of the judge. Two of my requests were denied due to the sensitive nature of the issue and the need to protect complainants. The primary research materials used for this study, including interviews with criminal justice agents, court documents, and trial audio recordings, are also limited to the province of Ontario. Although Ontario has the highest number of trafficking cases in all of Canada, similar data from other provinces may have provided interesting comparisons and/or challenged the findings of this study. Nevertheless, Ontario is Canada's most populated province, with the highest number of trafficking charges and convictions. Furthermore, the vast majority of Canada's trafficking cases are domestic and do not vary in significant ways from province to province. In addition, barriers to accessing criminal justice agents, particularly Crown attorneys and judges for academic interviews, restricted the number of criminal justice actors I was able to interview, thus potentially limiting insights (Millar et al. 2017). These insights are particularly important given the central role played by legal and criminal justice actors within anti-trafficking efforts not only in Ontario but in Canada more generally. Finally, while my research maintained a focus on legal and criminal justice systems, numerous other agencies and actors play an important role in anti-trafficking efforts, including NGOs, victim-services workers, the immigration system, as well as the accused and complainants in trafficking cases. For a more detailed description of my research methods, please see Appendix F.

A Word on Terms

In taking a position critical of the anti-trafficking framework, my intention is to avoid reproducing the numerous harmful stereotypes often presented in discussions of trafficking and sex work. As such, and given the feminist, pro–sex work, and critical race perspectives of this book, I use the term "sex work/er" as opposed to "prostitution/prostitute," unless it is part of a quote or describes statements and opinions made by others. I use the terms "labelled victims," "suspected victims," or "complainants" in reference to women and girls labelled as victims of trafficking in order to avoid the totalizing narrative of the trafficking victim. Because anti-trafficking laws, policies, and criminal justice interventions focus almost exclusively on women and girls as victims of trafficking, and while acknowledging that individuals of all genders can become victimized by exploiters, the labelled victim of trafficking is treated as a gendered category. The language in this book also exposes a prevailing investment in gender binary, with the victim category being gendered as quintessentially female and the trafficker category gendered as quintessentially male in the examined discourses. This is not to suggest that gender and sex are biologically determined or that women cannot be exploiters and men cannot be victims. Indeed, a part of what this book aims to do is highlight the gender (as well as race, class, etc.) stereotyped ways in which the issue of human trafficking is presented. Throughout the book, I use quotations to disrupt the use of the racially stereotyped term "pimp" when referring to accused in trafficking and procuring cases. And finally, the word "trafficking" will refer to human trafficking, rather than drug, weapons, or any other type of trafficking.

Chapter Overviews

The book is divided into five substantive chapters. Chapter one investigates Canada's human trafficking laws and draws a comparison between the meaning of trafficking as laid out in the UN Trafficking Protocol (2000) and Canada's legal definition of the offence in the Criminal Code. This chapter demonstrates that Canada's definition of trafficking, which diverges from the UN definition in some important ways, has, through legislative amendments, expanded the definition of the term, enabling more activities to be defined as trafficking. In particular, the chapter explores how the meaning of human trafficking continues to be understood by criminal justice actors in different and sometimes contradictory ways. Yet rather than creating trepidation about what exactly is being fought and why, these varying understandings of trafficking effectively magnified the assortment of activities and offences that can be placed under the umbrella term "trafficking." Tracing the expansion of Canada's human trafficking laws alongside changes to sex work laws, this chapter details the ways in which trafficking laws have come to be applied to sex work cases and particularly ones where a third-party actor is involved.

Chapter two shows how despite the prevalence of transnational trafficking discourses, in the past few years there has been an emerging focus on domestic trafficking. In particular, this chapter demonstrates that the urgency around trafficking is created through the human trafficking matrix and fuelled by transnational discourses around organized crime, the War on Terror, and national security, and made relevant on the ground through a focus on the victim of trafficking bringing into relevance individual harms, including sexual assault, juvenile sex work, domestic violence, and child sexual exploitation. As this chapter shows, in contrast with the foreign, often Eastern European or Asian, trafficking victim emphasized by transnational trafficking discourses, Canada's trafficking victims come in three separate yet related categories: (1) "the girl next door," (2) the marginalized woman who encompasses many pre-existing vulnerabilities, and (3) the Indigenous woman or girl whose rescue reflects a larger issue of violence against Indigenous women and girls in Canada and the calls for the colonial state to do something about it.

Chapter three looks at police anti-trafficking strategies and focuses especially on the recent creation of anti-trafficking units within municipal police departments across Canada. The chapter demonstrates that despite the emphasis in Canada's National Action Plan to Combat Human Trafficking (2012) on the cooperation of police forces across municipal, provincial, federal, and international jurisdictions, the vast majority of trafficking arrests are carried out by specialized trafficking teams within municipal police forces, who compete with each other for arrest rates and funding opportunities. Drawing from interviews with members of two anti-trafficking policing units in southern Ontario, and information gleaned from reports and court transcripts, the chapter demonstrates how local, day-to-day police decision-making effectively shapes the problem of human trafficking, its victims, and perpetrators on the front line of anti-trafficking enforcement, thus becoming a part of the human trafficking matrix. The chapter also recounts how the heightened pressures for police to find and arrest traffickers have led to troubling police tactics, including the fabrication of evidence.

Chapter four examines the ways in which Canada's human trafficking laws become operationalized at trial. In particular, the chapter shows that the concept of consent, seemingly irrelevant in conversations about trafficking (since one cannot consent to trafficking), is re-centred at the trial stage since the presence of consent means that no trafficking occurred. Defence attorneys in trafficking trials often appear to be singularly focused on proving the consent of the complainant through troubling cross-examination strategies commonly employed at sexual assault trials. This chapter focuses on the way in which vulnerability factors, including poverty, substance use, and involvement in sex work, have become part of the human trafficking matrix and are used by both Crown and defence attorneys to advance, at times, very different lines of arguments. While defence attorneys use these factors to undermine the credibility of the complainant, Crown attorneys use them to demonstrate the complainant's vulnerability to exploitation.

Chapter five, "The Villain," shows how the transnational discourses of human trafficking and their intersection with issues around organized crime, the War on Terror, and national security become embedded within the trafficking matrix. These transnational discourses are juxtaposed in the chapter with the on-the-ground targeting of primarily poor, young, racialized men involved in third-party management of sex trade activities. This chapter empirically demonstrates the attempts made by police and Crown attorneys to characterize people accused of human trafficking–related offenses as dangerous, hypersexual, violent, and as posing a threat to white women and girls by drawing on racialized stereotypes of Black men. And while the accused in trafficking cases are largely involved in small-scale criminality on an individual basis, police and prosecutors go to great lengths to build links between the activities of the accused and organized crime, relying on strategies and tropes from the 1980s and 1990s panics over youth involvement in the sex trade, which targeted young, racialized men for their involvement in "pimping"-related "street gangs."

Chapter One

Legal Regimes

This chapter will begin to unpack the important role of law in Canada's anti-trafficking efforts, as relevant laws are developed by policymakers and interpreted by police and legal actors. In doing so, this chapter unravels the relationship between the international developments outlined in the introduction of this book and the flurry of anti-trafficking legal reforms and enforcement efforts that have taken place in Canada since 2002, demonstrating the way in which the human trafficking matrix is shaped through various legal amendments that have resulted in the expansion of the term "trafficking" to include mundane criminal offences, most commonly in the sex trade. These developments, can be understood using the concept of "carceral feminism," coined by Elizabeth Bernstein who explains the term as "a cultural and political formation in which previous generations' justice and liberation struggles are recast in carceral terms" (2012, 236). As Bernstein explains, the transnationalization of carceral politics has taken place through reliance on human rights discourses and has shaped policies that have folded the transnational into the domestic terrain using a feminist guise (2012, 235). When it comes to human trafficking, carceral solutions are focused on sexual violations ignoring the structural conditions that enable and even encourage exploitation (Bernstein 2012, 242). This chapter will begin to peel back the layers to reveal how transnational carceral politics has "folded back" into Canada's domestic legal frameworks through the human trafficking matrix and the essential role played by feminist efforts to protect women and girls from exploitation, which, at times, takes on a carceral focus that has significantly expanded penalties and collateral consequences associated with this offence.

Considering the Legal Definitions of Human Trafficking

Canada was among the first eighty countries to ratify the Trafficking Protocol in 2002, enacting its first law against transnational trafficking under section 118 of the IRPA the same year. The law criminalizes cross-border trafficking and applies not only to criminal organizations but also to individual traffickers. Despite the emphasis on transnational trafficking by trafficking discourses and the UN Trafficking Protocol, the law has seen limited use (Ferguson 2012, 286; Coleman 2015). Canada's first criminal law against both domestic and transnational trafficking was enacted in 2005, amending the Criminal Code to include sections 279.01–.04. According to section 279.01(1) of the Criminal Code: "Every person who recruits, transports, transfers, receives, holds, conceals or harbours a person, or exercises control, direction or influence over the movements of a person, for the purpose of exploiting them or facilitating their exploitation is guilty of an indictable offence." Since the implementation of these provisions in 2005, the law has been amended four times, each time expanding the definition and scope of the term "human trafficking" and increasing the penalties available for the offence. Tough criminalization responses to human trafficking attracted support from across the political spectrum. The increasingly punitive criminal justice reforms, which I discuss throughout this chapter, were largely spearheaded by two Members of Parliament (MPs): Joy Smith and Maria Mourani. Smith was a Conservative MP from 2004 to 2015 and made trafficking for the purpose of sexual exploitation her key priority. Smith retired from the legislature in 2015 to work at the Joy Smith Foundation, which she established to combat human trafficking. Mourani was a member of the Bloc Quebecois until 2013, then joined the New Democratic Party (NDP) but was defeated in the 2015 election. In 2017, she was appointed as the Quebec representative in Canada's permanent delegation to the United Nations Educational, Scientific and Cultural Organization (UNESCO).

The Canadian Parliament and courts take the position that Canada's anti-trafficking laws are well aligned with the UN intentions as set out in the Trafficking Protocol (House of Commons, 24 March 2011, Bill C-612; *R. v. Beckford* 2013; *R. v. D'Souza* 2016). And yet, a close examination reveals a different story. The Trafficking Protocol defines the offence as, "the recruitment, transportation, transfer, harbouring or receipt of persons, by means of the threat or use of force or other forms of coercion, of abduction, of fraud, of deception, of the abuse of power or of a position of vulnerability or of giving or receiving of payment or benefits to achieve the consent of a person having control over another person, for the purpose of exploitation" (UN 2000, 2). The key elements of trafficking, according to the UN definition, are (1) the act (recruitment, transportation, and exploitation); (2) the purpose, which centres on exploitation; and (3) the means, which negates any consent given at the outset (UN 2000). According to the UN, "all three listed elements must be present for a situation of 'trafficking in persons' to be recognized" (as cited in Gallagher 2010, 29).

In contrast, Canada's anti-trafficking law under sections 279.01–.011 of the Criminal Code differs from the Trafficking Protocol in three key ways. First, it does not require the victim to be moved, cross-border or nationally. The separation of transportation from coerced end practice contributes to the difficulties in distinguishing trafficking from other offences, while an emphasis on exploitation as the defining feature of trafficking enables the offence to incorporate activities in which exploitation has been identified. Second, in contrast with the UN Trafficking Protocol, Canada's offence of human trafficking does not require the involvement of organized crime to establish the existence of trafficking. Despite this, as I discuss in chapter three, the presumed connection between trafficking and organized crime serves to justify the expansion of trafficking laws and enforcement efforts. Third, in contrast to the UN definition, Canada's legal definition of trafficking does not require the means component (threats, coercion, force, etc.) to be established. Instead, as I discuss below, the means component is incorporated into the determination of whether exploitation has taken place. This leaves in place only the act[1] and the purpose, which is exploitation.

The extent to which the divergences between Canada's definition of trafficking and that of the UN Trafficking Protocol change the meaning of trafficking was captured by the argument of the defence in a constitutional challenge of R. v. Beckford (2013) to the new Criminal Code provisions: "there is a huge chasm between the kind of conduct that is envisioned by the UN versus the kind of conduct that is captured by the Criminal Code provisions. It misses some things which perhaps is more legitimately human trafficking and captures the stuff that lacks the moral culpability that is associated with this offence. The acts in the UN Protocol are much more narrowly prescribed. What you see in the Criminal Code is that the means have been taken out, so it's any act by whatever means provided it has a purpose or facilitates a purpose" (Application Section 7 Charter Factum Descending, 28 December 2012). The defence attorney goes on to note,

So, what you see in the UN Protocol is a definition of the offence which would eliminate a lot of defects in the legislation that I suggest exist. The entire genesis of the legislation was to put that international obligation into effect in Canada. But the legislature made a calculated decision to define it in much broader and looser terms.... It is also problematic to say that the Canadian law mirrors the UN Protocol, in fact, what I see is a wide gap between the two. The Criminal Code provision is a marked departure from what the UN or international protocol is on this issue. Canadian law is considerably broader and captures behaviour that it was never intended to capture.

(R. v. Beckford 2013, Application Section 7
Charter Factum Descending)

The disconnect between the UN and the Canadian definitions led one defence attorney interviewed for this project to exclaim, "This is all political nonsense. So as far as the *Palermo Protocol*[2] is concerned, I don't know what you're talking about. I don't think the court does either" (participant 14).

In 2016, another constitutional challenge to human trafficking laws was brought in the case of *R. v. D'Souza*. As in Beckford, the applicant (defence) in this case also rejected the Crown's contention that "international consensus" on the meaning of human trafficking exists. The applicant argued that there is "global uncertainty about the term 'human trafficking'" and that trafficking-related provisions of the Criminal Code "are void for vagueness" (2016, para. 31). The applicant further argued that "domestic human trafficking legislation has been, improperly, informed by international human trafficking protocols" noting that, "These topics are worlds apart" (*R. v. D'Souza* 2016, Applicant's Factum, para. 8). The courts disagreed. In both cases, the judges dismissed the application to deem Canada's human trafficking laws unconstitutional. Justice Conlan, in *R. v. D'Souza* (2016), noted that the language of human trafficking legislation is "fairly straightforward" and the "words used in the impugned provisions are neither novel nor complex," stating that "these statutory provisions go far beyond the minimum degree of certainty required" (*R. v. D'Souza* 2016, para. 149–51). He went on to explain that the terminology embedded in the Canadian human trafficking provision, "*is not unduly complicated. The words used have common, ordinary meanings* that are generally well known to the citizenry. In the simplest language possible, 'recruit' means to enlist or get someone involved. 'Transport' means to take from A to B. 'Transfer' means to hand over. 'Receive' means to take or accept. 'Hold' means to keep or maintain. 'Conceal' means to hide or keep secret. 'Harbour' means to shelter. To exercise 'control, direction or influence over; means to effect. To 'facilitate' something means to make it easier. 'Benefit' means an advantage or gain" (*R. v. D'Souza* 2016, para. 146; emphasis added).

Justice Conlan's position that human trafficking provisions are straight forward and easy to understand is challenged by a 2015 United Nations Office of Drugs and Crime (UNODC) study, which examined the interpretation and application of trafficking laws in domestic contexts. The study found that "important concepts contained in the [Trafficking] Protocol are not clearly understood, and therefore, are not consistently implemented and applied" by state parties (UNODC 2015, 6). This is an important finding and particularly so given the contrasting views of Canadian courts. To make sense of these diverging opinions, it is worth examining the component parts of the offence of human trafficking as they pertain to international and Canadian laws, including their interpretation and application by criminal justice and legal actors and the overall effect of these developments.

As set out above, the offence of human trafficking according to the UN has multiple stages: the act, the means, and the purpose. In contrast, Canada's legal definition of trafficking only has two stages: the act and the purpose. As another UNODC study entitled "Abuse of a Position of Vulnerability and Other 'Means' within the Definition of Trafficking in Persons" found, this shortened process and the phrasing of the terms results in Canada's trafficking laws having a wider scope than originally intended by the international agreement (2013, 47). It was precisely the interaction of the "action" and "purpose" that was at the heart of the constitutional challenge in *R. v. Beckford* (2013). According to the applicant's argument, the wide scope of *actus reus*,[3] combined with an unclear element of exploitation, casts a "net of prohibition that is so wide as to be disjunctive of its purpose and to be so difficult to ascertain its boundaries of, as to be vague" (*R. v. Beckford* 2013, audio of trial, 28 December 2012). The applicant provides an example of a driver who transports an exploited person from point A to point B to demonstrate that the law, as it is currently worded, can capture the activities of the driver, even if they have no knowledge of exploitation (ibid.).

In rejecting the argument, Justice Miller found in her decision that the specificity of the law of human trafficking is set out by the fact that "the act" (recruitment, transportation, transfer, harbouring) can only be defined as human trafficking if it is committed *for the purpose of exploitation or its facilitation* (*R. v. Beckford* 2013, Judgement, 28 January 2013, para. 35). In other words, driving a person to a destination where they will be exploited does not in itself constitute human trafficking, unless the driver had knowledge of and/or intent to exploit. While this standard appears quite straightforward, the practical application of the law raises numerous questions. For example, what does one have to have knowledge of in order to be found as having carried out the activity for the "purpose of exploitation" and thus be charged with human trafficking? If a person knowingly transports another to a location where they will be exploited but does not engage in exploitation, can that lead to a human trafficking charge? What level of knowledge of exploitation is sufficient to be charged with human trafficking? In her decision, Justice Miller emphasized that human trafficking is an offence that requires a high degree of *mens rea*,[4] therefore eliminating the possibility that innocent actions that may become a part of the trafficking process are captured by the law (2013, para. 40). And yet, without the means component, which sets other forms of exploitation apart from human trafficking, this distinction becomes fragile, capturing activities which may have been consented to. Despite these challenges, courts in both *Beckford* and *D'Souza* emphasize exploitation as the central requirement to establish the crime of human trafficking since, as both decisions point out, the wide range of conduct criminalized by trafficking laws only become so if they are carried out for the purpose of exploitation. Since these decisions, as I discuss later in this chapter, Ontario courts have acknowledged the broad nature of the offence, striking down mandatory minimum sentences due to trafficking laws capturing an extensive range of conduct, the moral blameworthiness of some of which does not warrant a mandatory minimum sentence of four years' imprisonment (five years' for the trafficking of a young person) (see *R. v. Ahmed et al.* 2019; *R. v. Finestone* 2017; *R. v. Reginald Louis Jean* 2020).

Despitet heir expansiveness, trafficking laws are rarely applied to cases outside of the sex trade, and never to point out or address broader forms of exploitation or the role of the state in creating and upholding exploitative conditions (see De Shalit 2021; Millar and O'Doherty 2020; Moore Kloss & Roots 2022). Although exploitation is not explicitly defined in the Trafficking Protocol, the UN stipulates that it includes: "exploitation of the prostitution of others, or other forms of sexual exploitation, forced labour or services, slavery or practices similar to slavery, servitude or the removal of organs" (UN 2000, article 3). Under Canadian law, the term plays a central role in the legal meaning of human trafficking. The meaning of exploitation became defined through Bill C-310, The Act to amend the Criminal Code (trafficking in persons), passed into law in 2012. Section 279.04 of the Criminal Code defines exploitation as causing another person to "provide, or offer to provide, labour or a service by engaging in conduct that, in all the circumstances, could reasonably be expected to cause the other person to believe that their safety or the safety of a person known to them would be threatened if they failed to provide, or offer to provide, the labour or service" (s. 279.04 CCC). The legislative history of Bill C-310 shows that the amended definition of exploitation was expanded to also include emotional and psychological harms in response to concerns that the previous definition focused exclusively on physical acts (*R. v. D'Souza* 2016, Respondent's Factum, para. 25). The objective of the amendment was to narrow the definition by adding the stipulation that exploitation was subject to the victim and/or their loved ones' safety. As criminal lawyer and migrant justice advocate Shane Martinez explains, it was to prevent exploitative labour conditions more generally from being captured by trafficking legislation (Moore Kloss & Roots 2022). Yet, this has not been effective for those in the sex trade industry. Indeed, the continued expansiveness of the term exploitation in trafficking provisions was acknowledged by the court in R.v. D'Souza (2016) which noted: "The Defence is quite correct that the impugned provisions are relatively broad in that they cast a fairly wide net over conduct that may fall within human trafficking and include a fairly expansive meaning of exploitation" (para 175). The term was further specified by the Ontario Court of Appeal in *R. v. A.A* (2015), where a panel of judges determined that "no exploitation need actually occur or be facilitated by the accused's conduct for an accused to be convicted of human trafficking" (2015, para. 85). The Crown needs to simply prove that the accused had the *intent* to exploit. This precedent-setting decision is noteworthy, as it expands the reach of human trafficking laws even further by effectively removing the requirement for exploitation to even take place while setting intent as the key requirement for conviction.

While the meaning of exploitation in the context of trafficking has been legally challenged several times, up until 2016, the courts maintained that the term is straightforward and commonly used (*R. v. Beckford* 2013; *R. v. D'Souza* 2016). As Justice Miller noted in her decision in *R. v. Beckford*, "the terms 'exploiting' and 'exploitation' as used in the human trafficking provisions" are not "difficult to understand or apply" (*R. v. Beckford* 2013: para. 41). As with the definition of human trafficking, here too the perspective of Canadian courts is challenged by a UNODC study entitled "Issue Paper: The Concept of 'Exploitation' in the Trafficking in Persons Protocol," which found that despite efforts to clarify the meaning of "exploitation," the term remains inconsistently understood by legal professionals (2015, 11). Such confusion and diverging perspectives were consistently captured in my interviews with lawyers and law enforcement officers who clearly held different understandings of the term "exploitation." Some Crown attorneys considered the concept to be too narrow:

> The definition of exploitation is actually harder to meet in human trafficking. I never thought of it in the terms it's set out in the Criminal Code. I didn't think about it in that way. The definition of exploitation, the person has to believe that their safety is at risk, but if I exploit a situation or an individual, I've never thought of it in terms of putting their safety at risk. It was interesting in that when I read that definition, I thought it was very narrow, much more narrow than my common sense understanding of exploitation, interestingly I've never done it, looked at the definition of exploitation in the dictionary. It's a bit harder.
>
> (participant 15)

Conversely, defence attorneys commonly saw the concept as too broad in its definition: "I mean you read the strict provisions of the Criminal Code, it really seems to suggest exploitation, coercion of a sort, what does that mean? *That seems to mean pretty much anything I want it to mean*, it almost sounds like extortion, like if you read of a case, an extortion case and you read extortion, it's really interesting, you know, it says anybody who makes somebody do something, ok, like with a threat, like through threats is guilty of extortion" (participant 8; emphasis added). Another defence attorney commented, "they [lawmakers] basically broadened this idea of exploitation … they cast the net so wide, anything could be exploitation" (participant 13).

Meanwhile, some criminal justice actors, primarily police officers, agreed that the term was broad but considered the term's broadness to be a positive factor: "the fact that the means of exploitation is very broad gives us more flexibility to look at the circumstances of each case and see how it applies to human trafficking so it's good in that sense" (participant 3).

According to the UNODC study on the concept of exploitation, this ambiguity provides legal practitioners with high levels of interpretive discretion that contributes to discrepancies in the application of law (2015, 11). The legal ambiguity and discretionary flexibility around the term have become a part of the human trafficking matrix, allowing for a diverse and increasingly broad range of activities to come under criminal justice jurisdiction. In several countries, including Canada, vulnerability factors such as age, illness, gender, and poverty are incorporated into the human trafficking matrix, becoming a part of the criminal justice professionals' understanding of exploitation, and thereby making it easier to find that exploitation has taken place (UNODC 2013, 4). These vulnerability factors, which the UN calls "pre-existing vulnerabilities (see the Introduction for a discussion) include such things as isolation, dependency, and irregular immigration status, and are seen by criminal justice actors as being on a par with trafficker-created vulnerabilities (2013, 3). This "has the effect of bringing within the potential reach of the definition, not just recruiters, brokers, and transporters but also owners and managers, supervisors and controllers of any place where exploitation can be seen to occur" (Gallagher 2010, 30). In other words, incorporating pre-existing vulnerabilities into the meaning of exploitation, and therefore into the human trafficking matrix, enables a situation to be defined as trafficking solely because the accused benefitted from the actions or services of a complainant with these vulnerabilities, regardless of whether the accused recruited, coerced, seduced, or in any way forced the complainant to engage in such activities or services.

The Consent Factor

The meaning of exploitation in the context of human trafficking is further complicated by several interrelated and equally unclear factors, one of which is the consent of the victim. The consent factor also only applies to adults when it comes to trafficking situations, since those under the age of eighteen cannot consent to exploitation. In Canadian law, trafficking of individuals under eighteen was criminalized in 2010, through section 279.011 of the Criminal Code. The offence was made punishable by a minimum penalty of five years' imprisonment. When it comes to consent to adult sex work, the UNODC explains, "the lack of consent to a situation of exploitation is considered integral to the understanding of trafficking and through the operation of the means element, has been accepted as a distinct and important part of the definition of trafficking in person" (2014, 6). And while the two preceding anti-trafficking conventions, the Trafficking Conventions of 1949 and 1933, were premised upon the assumption that all sex work is inherently exploitative and therefore a person cannot consent to it (Doezema 2007), the Trafficking Protocol distinguishes between voluntary sex work and trafficking on the very basis of consent, a development welcomed by many sex workers' rights groups. Once again, the 2015 UNODC study found that legal practitioners have difficulty distinguishing human trafficking from other crimes, particularly in relation to the principle of relevance of consent (11). Even more troubling is the finding of a 2014 UNODC study entitled "Role of Consent in the Trafficking in Persons Protocol," according to which a significant number of criminal justice practitioners that work with trafficking cases believe "consent should not be permitted to trump fundamental human and social values, such as dignity, freedom and protection of the most vulnerable within society" (9). Yet, there was no consensus on what these fundamental human and social values were (ibid.).

Sex work provides a good example of how diverging values can result in widely varying interpretations of exploitation. Those who see all sex work as exploitative equate it with trafficking regardless of whether consent is given, while sex workers' rights advocates distinguish between consensual and non-consensual (coerced) sex work based on this very concept of consent. In particular, the 2014 UNODC study found that practitioners were more likely to consider a situation as exploitative if it was in the context of the sex trade, and such cases tended to require a lower burden of proof in comparison to other forms of exploitation (11). According to the UNODC, while criminal justice practitioners recognize the importance of the concept of consent, they "appear to experience genuine difficulty internalizing a concept that in some senses appears to be counter-intuitive" (2014, 9). The extent to which consent is relevant was also found to be heavily dependent on the way the means element is understood and applied, even if the means are not directly defined but form a part of the purpose element (UNODC 2014, 10), as is the case in Canadian law.

The Means Factor

The Trafficking Protocol states that one cannot consent to being trafficked since the means, which includes "threat or use of force or other forms of coercion, abduction, fraud, deception, abuse of power or of a position of vulnerability, and the giving or receiving of payments or benefits to achieve the consent of a person having control over another person" (UNODC 2013, 16–17), negate any consent given at the outset.[5] By definition, consent can only be negated in situations where such nefarious means are used. In other words, in the absence of the means, a seemingly exploitative situation cannot be categorized as human trafficking since the person is free to work in exploitive work conditions if they are not forced into it through one or several of the activities categorized as the means (UNODC 2014, 7). Simply put, considerations of consent are heavily dependent on the presence of the means. This is applicable even when the means are not explicitly outlined in law (ibid., 10), as is the case in Canada and most other states with anti-trafficking laws. Consequently, "there is considerable scope for States to develop and apply highly restrictive, exceedingly broad or even contradictory interpretations of particular means" (UNODC 2014, 10).

In Canadian law, the means are incorporated into the definition of exploitation. According to section 279.04(2) of the Criminal Code, "In determining whether an accused exploits another person under subsection (1), the Court may consider, among other factors, whether the accused (a) used or threatened to use force or another form of coercion; (b) used deception; or (c) abused a position of trust, power or authority." However, as the UNODC position paper on consent points out, the less direct means, such as deception, fraud, or abuse of power or position of vulnerability enable a wide variety of situations ranging from working conditions to parent–child relationships being labelled as exploitative (2013, 17). For instance, the component which outlines that "giving or receiving of payments or benefits to achieve the consent of a person having control over another person," is also potentially applicable to employer–employee and parent–child dynamics (UNODC 2013, 18).

The capacious nature of the means component in Canadian law was also revealed during my interviews. The victim continuum, as one police officer calls it, refers to the range of trafficking victims from those who have been severely abused to those whose experience included more subtle means (participant 2). The extent of subtlety in some cases is captured by a comment from another interview participant who explained that the means can include something as minuscule as a threat to tell the victim's parents that they have been engaging in sex work (participant 9). Using such loosely defined concepts puts even schoolyard bullies at risk of being charged with trafficking. And yet, as the UNODC found, although the means are relevant in determining whether trafficking has taken place, according to Canadian law it is not the decisive component (2015, 99), bringing the crux of the offence back to exploitation. Finally, as the UNODC study reveals, there is a "lack of agreement among practitioners as to whether it is sufficient to just establish the use of means, or whether it is also required to prove that the means used actually vitiated consent" (2014, 10). The absence of clear means in Canadian law highlights that the offence of human trafficking hangs on the definition of exploitation, which as detailed above is another concept difficult to define with any precision.

The Fear of Safety Component

The determination of exploitation in Canadian law is established through a two-stage process. The first is to prove the accused's intent to exploit, as discussed above. The second is to demonstrate the reasonable expectation on the part of the complainant that if they did not provide the labour or service requested, their safety or the safety of their loved one(s) would

be threatened (UNODC 2013, 47). At the outset, the fear of safety requirement in Canadian law was *subjective*, necessitating that the complainant
indicate to the police and in court that they feared for their safety. While
complainants' declarations that they did not fear for their safety was
treated with suspicion by police and legal practitioners, it nonetheless
had to be respected under the law. For instance, Canada's first convicted
trafficker, Imani Nakpangi, was charged with human trafficking in 2007
after his involvement in two young women's engagement in sex work
was unveiled by an undercover police operation (*R. v. Nakpangi* 2008).
However, because the second complainant insisted that she had not
feared for her safety, Nakpangi could only be convicted of one account
of trafficking, forcing the court to acquit him of the second trafficking
charge (ibid.). The reluctance of complainants to admit to, or their failure
to feel fear and thereby testify against the accused, created a problem for
the successful prosecution of early trafficking cases in the courts (Roots
2011, 99; 2013). Consequently, Criminal Code amendments enacted in
2012 added section 279.04, which revised the wording of the law to make
the fear of safety standard an *objective* one. Based on this new standard, it
no longer matters whether complainants actually feared for their safety.
What matters is whether it can be *reasonably* expected that a person in
their situation would do so (CCC. S. 279.04). According to the Ontario
Court of Appeal in *R. v. A.A.* (2015), for there to be exploitation, "the
accused's conduct must give rise to a reasonable expectation of a particular state of mind in the victim" (para. 70). Consequently, Parliament
has placed the determination of fear of safety in the hands of the courts
since complainants, the vast majority of whom are women, are seen as
unable to determine their own risk levels. This is summed up by a Crown
attorney I interviewed:

> often times it can be like a domestic violence type situation in that sense.
> So, they might say they're not afraid even though they're getting beat up
> on a somewhat regular basis. That's what AA [referring to *R. v. A.A.* (2015)]
> was about. There was actual violence, but she wasn't afraid that he was
> going to do something bad to her if she didn't do what he wanted. But the
> reality is from an outside observer perspective, the court said it's pretty
> clear that there would have been fear there. Or that that was his intention,
> for her to be afraid. He was achieving that through actual violence.
>
> (participant 10)

This objective standard makes it far easier to charge and prosecute
suspected offenders since the Crown no longer requires the complainant's admission that they feared for their own safety or that of

their family. The UNODC found that the fear of safety component in Canada's human trafficking law has been broadly interpreted by courts and is not just limited to physical harm but, as noted earlier in this chapter, also includes mental, psychological, and emotional harm (2013, 47). This direction, as the Crown notes in her submissions in *R. v. A.A.* (2015), "to interpret the term exploitation in a broad way to include threats to, not only physical but also emotional and psychological well-being, was intended by the Parliament" (Submission made on December 2014).

In the end, Canadian laws against human trafficking have departed radically from their progenitors at the international level. They have become increasingly centred around the nebulous concept of exploitation that does not actually have to take place. It is premised on the victim's purported fear of safety that they subjectively do not have to feel (since this is an objective standard), thus creating an apparition of sorts, the existence of which can only be established through the court's evaluation of the offender's state of mind with respect to their *intent to exploit*. Chuang has labelled this approach in relation to human trafficking as "exploitation creep," arguing that it is an effort to "expand previously narrow legal categories ... in a strategic bid to subject a broader range of practices to a greater amount of public opprobrium" (2014, 611). Given the challenges with understanding the components that legally define human trafficking, it is unsurprising that police and Crown and defence attorneys, but also judges and legislators, vary in their understandings of what human trafficking means and how, if at all, it varies from procuring offences under section 286.3.

The Legal Fusion of Procuring and Human Trafficking

In addition to the complexities with the definition of human trafficking, legislative developments in the area of sex work and human trafficking have also allowed procuring offences to move rather seamlessly into the terrain of trafficking and thus, as Bernstein notes, bind transnational feminist campaigns against human trafficking with domestic sex trade. As explained above, the values and attitudes around the conduct under consideration – sexual labour – are important in determining the relevance of consent (UNODC 2014, 10). Put simply, negative perceptions about sex work may result in an automatic assumption that consent is lacking (ibid.). Because sex work is a morally condemned activity and one that, according to prohibitionists (who were strongly influential in the Canadian Parliamentary debates over the creation of new prostitution laws) can never involve genuine consent, it becomes much easier to categorize related activities as exploitative and therefore, by Canadian legal standards, fuse them into the human trafficking matrix.

In 2007, three sex workers – Terri Jean Bedford, Amy Lebovitch, and Valerie Scott – challenged the constitutionality of Canada's sex work laws. Known as the Bedford case, the women challenged key sections of the Criminal Code: section 210, which prohibited the operation of a bawdy house; section 212(I)(j), which criminalized anyone who "wholly or in part lives on the avails of prostitution of another person"; and section 213(I)(j), which forbade prostitutes, their clients, or third parties from communicating for the purpose of exchanging sex for money. The plaintiffs argued that these sex work laws violated section 7 of the Charter of Rights and Freedoms, which permits everyone the right to life, liberty, and security of the person and, section 2(b), which protects the right to freedom of expression, and therefore that the laws were not in accordance with the principles of fundamental justice. The substantive argument was premised on the fact that the laws forced sex workers to choose between their liberty and security by risking arrest and incarceration when deciding to take steps, such as taking time to assess the risk of client, working together in an indoor facility or relying on third-party managers for protection. In 2013, the Supreme Court of Canada struck down the three laws governing sex work, finding that "the impugned provisions had a negative impact on the security of prostitutes and that the state had a responsibility to protect those individuals" (Casavant and Valiquet 2014a; section 1.2). The court declined to comment on the effect of the communicating law on freedom of expression under section 2(b) of the Charter.

In response, the Conservative government introduced Bill C-36, The Protection of Communities and Exploited Persons Act [PCEPA], which was enacted on 6 December 2014. The new sex work laws (sections 286.1–.4 of the Criminal Code) follow an asymmetric model of governing sex work in which the selling of sexual services is not criminalized but the purchase of those services is, thus "making prostitution between adults a *de facto* illegal activity for the first time in Canada's history" (Casavant and Valiquet 2014a; section 1). The new law also includes section 286.4, which criminalizes the advertising of sexual services by anyone other than the individual selling the service. Those selling their own sexual services cannot be criminalized under this law; instead, they are seen as victims of exploitation (Casavant and Valiquet 2014a; section 2.17.5). This exception does not apply to those selling their service on the street who may be charged with communication-related offences (section 213.1.1) and are often the most vulnerable sex workers, indicating that the victimization/criminalization continuum in relation to sex workers persists. In effect, the legislative construction of PCEPA erases the distinction between sex work and trafficking by assuming that all sex work is exploitative.

Bill C-36, which was meant to introduce new sex work–related legislation, simultaneously introduced new changes to trafficking offences. This includes increasing the penalties for trafficking of persons to include a minimum penalty of four years' imprisonment for the trafficking of an adult, and five years for the trafficking of those under eighteen, which have recently been set aside by a number of Ontario courts. The Bill also increased the maximum penalty for procuring (s. 286.3) from ten to fourteen years, thus aligning the penalties for trafficking and procuring offences (Casavant and Valiquet 2014a; section 2.16). Furthermore, it added a minimum penalty of two years' imprisonment for the offence of receiving a material benefit from trafficking of those under the age of eighteen, increased the maximum penalty for withholding or destroying the documents of minors in the process of facilitating trafficking from five to ten years, and added a minimum of two years' imprisonment for the same (ibid.).

These laws demonstrate the ways in which feminist efforts to "save" sex workers from predators in the form of "pimps" and "traffickers" has contributed to the widening of the carceral state, an approach which received much criticism from academics and groups supporting sex workers' rights. As Dr. Chris Bruckert, a professor of criminology at the University of Ottawa who has conducted extensive research on sex work and presented on the new laws to the Parliamentary Committee, explains, "although prostitution has been removed from the definition of bawdy house,[6] as per the Supreme Court decision, individuals previously defined as keepers – owners, managers, and staff – are recriminalized through the receiving financial and material benefit provision" (House of Commons, 8 July 2014, Bill C-36; see also Bruckert 2018a; 2018b). Bruckert's research has shown that sex workers rely on the assistance of others for the "skills, assets, knowledge and labour" that they may not have (ibid.). In contrast, the framers of the new sex work legislation have proceeded on the assumption that those working to assist sex workers with their business are "parasitic" profiteers, the same assumption that fuels Canada's anti-trafficking laws and their enforcement. Consequently, the protectionist approach of the new sex work laws – which promises to focus on "pimps" and exploiters while treating sex workers as victims to be rescued – effectively enables the targeting of the sex trade through anti-trafficking legislation, as both trafficking and sex work laws now aim to protect the imagined victim and criminalize the exploiter, whoever that is defined to be. This fusion of sex work and human trafficking offences within the trafficking matrix also demonstrates Bernstein's argument that concerns over transnational trafficking are being folded into the issue of domestic sex work, the solution to which lies only in the expansion of carceral territory.

During Parliamentary debates on Bill C-36, we see further issues saturated with emotional appeal being added to the human trafficking matrix through a focus on youth and child sexual exploitation, as MPs frequently rely on the discourses of human trafficking, child sexual exploitation, and youth involvement in sex work. For instance, arguing in support of Bill C-36, the (then) Minister of Justice and Attorney General of Canada, Peter MacKay, explained that: "children, on balance when doing the calculation, can also be considered vulnerable, so the bill seeks to strike that careful balance, part of that being the provision of a tool that would allow law enforcement to ensure that children are not harmed through exposure to prostitution" (House of Commons, 11 June 2014, Bill C-36). MacKay builds on this discourse of child sexual exploitation to suggest that "prostitution, also poses risks [to children and young people] because of its link with human trafficking, as mentioned, which is another form of sexual exploitation, as well as its link to drug-related crimes and organized criminal groups" (House of Commons, 11 June 2014, Bill C-36). MacKay's submission in support of Bill C-36 is premised on a blend of emotive and urgent discourses that harness and combine concerns around child sexual exploitation with those of human trafficking and organized crime. In her pledge to support Bill C-36, MP Joy Smith relies on similar urgency and severity surrounding human trafficking to express her belief that the Bill is one of the most important ones this country has ever seen "because so many innocent victims are being lured into the sex trade under human trafficking" , and has "changed the paradigms in this country about those who are trafficked and those who are involved in prostitution" (House of Commons, 11 June 2014, Bill C-36). How someone can be lured *under* human trafficking and what this statement means is entirely unclear. Smith and MacKay's use of the trafficking discourse in this context is further troubling given that Bill C-36 was not about human trafficking but rather, sex work.

The troubling conflation of these very different issues during discussions on Bill C-36 was also captured by the comment of Dr. Bruckert:

yesterday and today, we heard youth prostitution, trafficking, and adult sex work being casually conflated. This is frankly surprising if not disingenuous, given that the law criminalizing the procuring, living on the avails of youth, and human trafficking was neither challenged nor struck down. It means that laws around adult prostitution are being framed in relation to very distinct and separate issues, those of youth and trafficking. All too often, in the absence of solid empirical evidence, stereotypes based on stigmatic assumptions and fueled by ideology persist, and third parties are cavalierly denounced as pimps, exploiters, and profiteers. The evidence tells us it is much more complicated.

(House of Commons, 8 July 2014, Bill C-36)

Despite evidence-based criticism showing the harms of such laws on sex workers and the numerous open letters opposing Bill C-36 signed by legal professionals, union groups, and citizens concerned about the impact of the PCEPA on the safety of sex workers, resistance to the Bill was not only ignored, but also ridiculed by champions such as MP Smith: "There is no reason now to do archaic thinking. There is no reason now to say, 'I'm confused'. Quite frankly, that is a very stupid comment. It doesn't matter who they are or on what side of the House, right now, in this country, Bill C-36 is a bill that parliamentarians from all sides of the House should embrace" (House of Commons, 3 October 2014, Bill C-36). In addition to labelling critics of this Bill as "very stupid" and "archaic" in their views, MP Smith's efforts to garner support for Bill C-36 even involved threatening other MPs: "They [MPs] should not do that [resist the Bill]. If they dare to do it, I promise I am going to make sure I will go to every city, every town, every constituency and I will let their constituency know. They can decide whether they want to elect them to the Parliament of Canada with that kind of attitude" (House of Commons, 3 October 2014, Bill C-36). The employment of such bullying tactics to silence dissent by Canada's lawmakers demonstrates the power of anti-trafficking discourses, whereby disagreement on the need to "do more" is seen as a sign of moral deficiency. Moreover, given that courts often look to Parliamentary debates to assess the intentions of the Parliament in setting a law, the use of emotionally charged speech, rather than evidence-based research, sets a dangerous precedent in lawmaking. Nevertheless, the tactics of MP Smith and others exemplifies Bernstein's (2012) argument that feminist activism is now bringing in the carceral arm of the state to resolve the newly discovered concerns over gendered violence and are urgently fuelled by the discursive embrace of transnationalism and organized criminality within these issues.

Since the Bedford decision and subsequent legal reforms, the vast majority of human trafficking cases in Canada have been focused on sexual exploitation – and specifically targeted third party actors in the sex trade as opposed to, for instance, those engaged in labour exploitation or organ trafficking – and are often accompanied by sex work–related charges, as demonstrated by my research as well as that of others (Ferguson 2012; Kaye and Hastie 2015; Kaye 2017; Millar et al. 2015, 2020; Millar and O'Doherty 2020). Out of the 123 individuals whose cases I studied, 106 (88 per cent) were charged with trafficking for the purpose of sexual exploitation and only 17 (14 per cent) individuals with labour trafficking (See Appendix B). All but two individuals charged with labour trafficking were part of the same case.[7] Sex work laws on "material benefit" "(s. 286.2) and procuring (s. 286.3), and human trafficking laws"outlined earlier in this chapter are effectively the same thing and reinforce one another, to the point of being not only indistinguishable but interchangeable. As the former chief of police for Toronto Police Services said in response to the Bedford decision, the police can and will "use other laws, such as those targeting human trafficking, assault and exploitation, to deal with 'pimps' and people who sell women, men and children for the sex trade" (D'Aliesio 2013).

The fusion of procuring offences ("pimping") with trafficking greatly expands the meaning of human trafficking to a fairly common domestic crime the courts have seen and dealt with for over a century (Roots 2013). And although the crime itself is unchanged, the emergence of the anti-trafficking agenda has changed the urgency around it. This is because the offence became formulated into the trafficking matrix and discursively linked with transnational organized crime and threats to national security, folding, as Bernstein argues, the transnational into the domestic under the guise of a supposed feminist agenda (see also Bumiller 2008; Gruber 2020). These developments have also impacted police and prosecutorial approaches to the offence, as evidence suggests they are now engaged in proactive targeting of the sex trade using concerns over human trafficking as the justification. For example, out of 123 accused in my dataset, 68 (55 per cent) were charged following the Bedford decision (see Appendix B). To provide context, sixty-eight individuals were charged in the two-and-a-half-year period between 2014 and the end of this research in June 2016, compared to the fifty-five individuals charged during a nine-year period preceding the Bedford decision.[8] This is also supported by the findings of Department of Justice Canada, which reported that the rate of human trafficking violations[9] almost doubled between 2013 and 2014 (2016, 3).

Because of the increasingly broad interpretations of the term "human trafficking," Parliamentary debates, interviews with criminal justice and legal actors, as well as court cases reveal existing difficulties distinguishing procuring from human trafficking. Even MPs experience this confusion. For example, during a House of Commons debate on Bill

C-452, MP Francoise Boivin (NDP) noted, "I'm finding it a bit difficult to see the difference between that [human trafficking] and prostitution as we know it.… I am trying to see, within your bill [C-452], a concrete nuance between procuring and internal human trafficking. I wonder whether it would be better to amalgamate sections 212 and 279" (House of Commons, 29 April 2013, Bill C-452). In response, MP Mourani notes, "I can tell you that in this bill, there is a slight distinction between domestic trafficking and prostitution, and that is the notion of transport … it is a slight distinction. That said, you are right in saying that domestic trafficking is mainly prostitution" (House of Commons, 29 April 2013, Bill C-452). In effect, Mourani confirms the Parliament's grouping of trafficking and sex work, while her explanation of their difference as stemming from the transportation component is curious, given that transportation is not a necessary component of trafficking under Canadian law and has been given little consideration in the meaning of trafficking.

Like Parliamentarians, criminal justice and legal actors also varied in their perspectives on whether procuring and human trafficking are the same offences. While police and defence attorneys saw trafficking and procuring as the same offence but with a new label, Crown attorneys and judges mostly considered them to be different offences. Among those criminal justice and legal actors who considered trafficking and procuring to be different, the reasons varied widely. Some relied on the concept of exploitation to draw that distinction. For example, according to the Crown in *R. v. Burton* (2016), "this element of exploitation, this element of being able to choose to engage in behaviour without being threatened or fearing for your safety or someone else's safety. And that's the distinguisher between living on the avails and exercising control and human trafficking" (Audio of trial, 18 January 2016). The defence attorney in *R. v. Byron* (2014) echoes this distinction, explaining that "there is a slight distinction between 212.1(h)[10] and 279.011[11] and that would be that the purpose of 279.011 is not gain as it is in 212.1(h), but *rather exploitation*. So, although they're somewhat similar, there is an important difference, in that 212(h) is on gain and 279.011 focuses on the *exploitation*" (Audio of trial, 17 May 2013; emphasis added). Yet, as demonstrated earlier in this chapter, the distinction between trafficking and procuring in the context of sex work is erased through the concept of exploitation, primarily due to the view that sex work itself is constituted as inherently exploitative.

Crown attorneys in particular were vocal about the distinction between trafficking and procuring, identifying a variety of differences and emphasizing the increased seriousness of trafficking. For instance, the Crown in *R. v. Byron* (2014) argued that the component that distinguishes trafficking from the "regular pimp-prostitute relationship is this: there are greater risks to victims today than there ever have been and greater motivations to the trafficker, due in large part to technology" and the ability of traffickers to recruit their victims from across distance[12] (*R. v. Byron*, audio of trial, 13 December 2013). Similarly, the Crown attorney in *R. v. Dagg* (2015) narrowed the difference between trafficking and procuring to the degree of offence severity, expressing the view that procuring is a less severe offence than human trafficking (*R. v. Dagg*, audio of trial, 13 April 2015). The increased severity of trafficking was also emphasized by a Crown attorney I interviewed, who added a focus on transportation and exploitation, explaining that human trafficking "goes beyond just being a 'pimp'; it's exploiting the person, it's threatening the person, it's moving the person from place to place.[13] The criteria to get a conviction on human trafficking are significantly harder to provide than the procuring and material benefits" (participant 15).

In contrast to Crown attorneys and lawmakers who primarily saw procuring and trafficking as different, albeit for different reasons, police officers and defence attorneys considered the two activities to be essentially the same. As one police officer contended, "pimping and trafficking? They are the same thing, just a different word. In the media, pimping is considered cool" (participant 4). Another officer expresses his disregard for the legal distinction: "to me, they ['pimping' and trafficking] are the same thing. In law, it's not the same thing" (participant 2). This disregard for the legal distinction was also seen in the reply of another member of an anti-trafficking police force who explained that, technically, "it's black and white, the law is very clear, human trafficking is one thing, prostitution is totally different," but, in practice, "I think it's the same thing" (participant 1).

In contrast to police officers who saw a legal distinction but not a practical one, defence counsel saw no difference between the two offences and believed that trafficking laws have come to replace procuring laws: "I don't think there is a difference. In my mind, they're just charging everybody with human trafficking now. Receiving a material benefit, living off the avails, so much of that conduct is captured under the umbrella term of human trafficking as well. Human trafficking is just a step up" (participant 10). According to another defence attorney, "Human trafficking and 'pimping' – same thing. Section 212 dealt with the pimps, 212 has now been repealed. Gone. Everything has shifted onto 279. The reason the human trafficking legislation was established was for 'pimps'" (participant 14). One criminal justice actor summed it up as follows: "what they do is, they're taking classic pimping cases … and they're using this section…. I've never seen a case that is the classic human trafficking situation. We all know it's going on. We all know it's happening. For whatever reason, they don't seem to be capturing the bad people and prosecuting them … so we're getting the old-fashioned pimping cases … which is just the classical cases dressed up in this new language" (participant 9).

Court decisions echo this fusion of trafficking and procuring offences. For instance, in R. v. (Gregory) Salmon (2014), the judge stated: "at the end of the day I find you not guilty of counts 1, 2 [human trafficking charges], which are the most serious of the offences, what I'm calling the *pimping counts*" (Audio of trial, 27 June 2014; emphasis added). The judge's reference to human trafficking provisions as "pimping counts" demonstrates a conflation between the two offences, revealing also the increased severity with which trafficking offences are treated. In the pre-Bedford case of R. v. McPherson (2011), Justice Baltman refused the Crown's request to introduce an expert[14] on human trafficking, finding that "prostitution, living off the avails thereof, and human trafficking … are common human experiences. The tendency of men to prey on young women who are vulnerable or needy; the use of violence by men against women in domestic relationships and the reasons why many women cannot easily extricate themselves from abusive relationships are not complicated technical issues but themes which juries and judges encounter on a daily basis in Canadian courts" (R. v. McPherson 2011, para 22). Small wonder that in R. v. D'Souza the Crown refers to the case of R. v. McPherson (2011) "as an interesting and telling illustration of the commonality to which the domestic human trafficking and prostitution themes have become commonplace and understandable within the justice system" (Respondent's Factum, para. 46).

Justice Baltman's decision demonstrates the effect of the human trafficking matrix in which the components of sex work intersect not only with trafficking but also those of domestic violence. The courts in R. v. McPherson (2011), R. v. D'Souza (2016), and R. v. Beckford (2013) all found that human trafficking is a straightforward and easily understood offence – a view that is enabled by the folding of ordinary domestic crime and legal precedents established through other offences into the human trafficking matrix.

Legal Consequences of Human Trafficking Convictions

The alignment of Canada's sex trade laws with human trafficking also brought with them increased penalties for procuring offences, bringing them in line with the tougher penalties for trafficking offences and further substantiating Bernstein's argument that the issue of trafficking is reinforcing carceralism. For instance, while the previous maximum penalty for procuring offences under section 212(1) of the Criminal Code was ten years' imprisonment, Bill C-36 increased the penalties for procuring to a maximum of fourteen years' imprisonment under the new section 286.3. These penalties aligned with ones for trafficking offences, which carry: "A maximum penalty of life imprisonment and a mandatory minimum penalty of 5 years where the offence involved kidnapping, aggravated assault, aggravated sexual assault or death, and a maximum penalty of 14 years and a mandatory minimum penalty of 4 years in all other cases" (Department of Justice Canada 2016). If the victim is under the age of eighteen the offence carries "A maximum penalty of life imprisonment and a mandatory minimum penalty of 6 years where the offence involved kidnapping, aggravated assault, aggravated sexual assault or death, and a maximum penalty of 14 years and a mandatory minimum penalty of 5 years in all other cases" (Department of Justice Canada 2016). These increases were justified by the powerful child protectionist discourses, which are mobilized as unassailable arguments and are reflected in MP Smith's comments during discussions of Bill C-268: "I just cannot understand why anybody wouldn't support mandatory minimums for traffickers of children 18 years and under" (House of Commons, 1 June 2009, Bill C-268); "the trafficking of children is not a Conservative, Liberal, Bloc or NDP issue. It is not a partisan issue. I have worked diligently to gain support from all parties for this bill" (House of Commons, 27 February 2009, Bill C-268). According to MP Smith, "Mandatory minimums will give hope to the families who have had children who were taken" (House of Commons, 27 February 2009, Bill C-268), and per Dianne L. Watts "help set standards of behaviour in keeping with our society's values of respect toward vulnerable children. And children are the future of Canada" (House of Commons, 1 June 2009, Bill C-268). What these statements substantiate is that the harsh punishments being handed out for sex work offences re-labelled as human trafficking are largely justified by the need to protect women and children from the "bad men" outside the protected space of the home. Often those feared as sexual predators are poor, racialized young men (see chapter five for discussion) who, under the new legislative framework, are subject to significant punishments.

While the focus of debates on Bill C-268, An Act to amend the Criminal Code (minimum sentence for offences involving trafficking of persons under the age of eighteen years) remained on the protection of Canada's children, the effects of the human trafficking matrix through transnational discourses continued to prevail via simultaneous, albeit less frequent, reminders that trafficking is a transnational criminal activity and one that yields significant profit for organized crime groups. As MP Smith said, "to further aggravate the problem, this type of criminal conduct is not something that just happens occasionally or on the margins of society. Rather it is widespread, as evidenced by the global revenues garnered by it, which are estimated to amount to as much as $10 billion U.S. per year. This puts human trafficking within the three top money makers for organized crime" (House of Commons, 26 November 2013, Bill C-268). The effects of such reminders of the broader national security threats posed by human trafficking through links to organized crime groups cannot be underestimated. Paired with discourses about child endangerment and the future of the very country seemingly threatened by "global" crime chains bent upon exploiting Canada's most precious resources, the seriousness of trafficking – and the need for robust and harsh penalties – was presented as something that could not be ignored. The effects of this are seen in continuous attempts to further increase penalties for trafficking offences. For instance, in 2012, MP Maria Mourani introduced Bill C-452, Act to amend the Criminal Code (exploitation and trafficking in persons), which aimed to amend the human trafficking provisions of the Criminal Code by adding subsection 2 to existing section 279.01 to make living with or being in the company of an exploited person habitually a basis for a human trafficking charge. Similar to the living on the avails provision (212[I][j]) set aside by the Supreme Court in the Bedford decision, this provision is concerning when it comes to activities of colleagues and roommates of sex workers, even if merely sharing a living or workspace, and absent any knowledge that exploitation is taking place. Although section 286.2(3), which replaced the previous living on the avails provision, comes with a number of exceptions under section 286.2(4),[15] the effectiveness of these exceptions in practice is questioned by sex workers and advocates, as noted earlier in this chapter. My concerns were echoed by Senator Mobina S.B. Jaffer who, in a Parliamentary debate on Bill C-452 noted, "all that the Crown will have to do is prove beyond a reasonable doubt that the accused lived with or was habitually in the company of an exploited person. That in itself will be enough evidence to automatically prove the remaining element, which is the intent to exploit. In other words, once it is proven that a person lives with or is habitually in the company of an exploited person, it must then be concluded that the person's intent was to exploit or facilitate exploitation of the victim" (House of Commons, 12 May 2015, Bill C-452). Section 286.2(3) and the human trafficking provisions are distinguished only by the use of the word "exploitation" in the latter And yet, as discussed above, exploitation is a widely interpreted term and encompasses a morality component that renders the application of the law highly subject to influence by personal, cultural, and religious values. Indeed Canada's lawmakers repeatedly express the view that sex work is an inherently exploitative activity, erasing this apparent distinction entirely. For instance, MP Mourani advocates targeting the sex trade through harsher human trafficking laws, noting that sex work "is never work, but rather exploitation" (House of Commons, 29 April 2013, Bill C-452).

Bill C-452 also proposed to establish a reverse burden of proof clause in human trafficking cases, forcing the accused to prove their innocence rather than being presumed innocent. When combined with the above changes, the accused who knowingly or unknowingly finds themselves in a situation of living with or habitually being in the company of an exploited person must then prove that they were not exploiting the victim. The only thing the Crown must prove is the *actus reus* element of the offence, rather than both *actus reus* and *mens rea*. This, as Senator Jaffer explains, enables the conviction of individuals in cases where reasonable doubt exists, abandoning the presumption of innocence principle central to Canada's criminal justice system (House of Commons, 12 May 2015, Bill C-452). The purpose of this proposed change, as MP Mourani admitted, is to eliminate the need for victim testimony (House of Commons, 29 April 2013, Bill C-452), which often poses the greatest hurdle for police and prosecutors in trafficking cases.

Finally, Bill C-452 introduced consecutive sentencing in human trafficking offences which "requires the imposition of consecutive sentences in a situation where an offender is sentenced at the same time for trafficking-in-persons offences and any other offence arising out of the same event(s)" (Department of Justice 2017). This is a serious revision since under the Criminal Code of Canada, all sentences imposed are to be served concurrently, unless otherwise ordered by a judge or if legislation requires that they be served consecutively for cases involving firearms, criminal organizations, terrorism (Public Safety and Emergency Preparedness Canada 2005) or serial murder (Canadian Resource Center for Victims of Crime 2012). Evidently, the crimes punished through consecutive sentencing in Canada are considered the most severe, the proposition that human trafficking be added to the list, demonstrating the perceived severity of trafficking offences.

As Parliamentary debates reveal, legislators' support for concurrent sentencing in human trafficking cases arose out of frustration over judicial discretion in sentencing. Conservative MP Kyle Seeback expresses this as follows: "Judges have the option [to pose concurrent sentences] but they haven't exercised it. If we, as Parliament, want to show our condemnation of this type of behaviour, we have to move the goalposts. The way you move the goal posts and the way you get judges out of that sentencing rut, where they continue to put forth a concurrent sentence, is to change legislation" (House of Commons, 1 May 2013, Bill C-452). When questioned about the effectiveness of concurrent sentencing, MP Seeback replied,

> My view, quite frankly is that there are two types of deterrence. One is general deterrence: you make the sentence so strong that people say, "Oh gee, maybe I don't want to do that". The other aspect of it, and this is the one that I believe in, is specific deterrence, so if a person committed this offence [trafficking] against six or eight or ten girls under the age of 18, they're going to be put away for a minimum sentence of 48 or so years. My view is that that person has been deterred because they're now in jail.
>
> (House of Commons, 1 May 2013, Bill C-452)

The view that individuals convicted of human trafficking should be locked away for over five decades at a minimum is particularly troubling when considering the broad range of conduct that can be captured under the umbrella term "trafficking" and that most people charged with trafficking offences in Ontario are poor, young Black men As noted above, this concern is increasingly also being recognized by Ontario courts who in recent years have declared mandatory minimums unconstitutional in several trafficking cases.

Bill C-452 received Royal Assent on 18 June 2015 but was not passed into law before the Parliament dissolved for an election later that year. The incoming federal Liberal government took issue with Bill C-452, pointing out that the already existing mandatory minimum sentences for human trafficking offences would bring the consecutive-sentencing portion of this law into disrepute. Specifically, it would violate section 12 of Canada's Charter of Rights and Freedoms, which protects individuals from cruel and unusual punishment. While this change seemed promising at the outset, in February 2017, the Liberal government introduced Bill C-38, An Act to amend An Act to amend the Criminal Code (exploitation and trafficking in persons), which aimed to bring into force all of the provisions in former Private Member's Bill C-452 except for the consecutive sentencing provision. In response to the omission of consecutive sentencing from the Bill, Conservative lawmakers used emotive rhetoric and discourses of child sexual exploitation (see chapter two) and slavery to argue for tougher sentences. This was captured in the response of Conservative MP Arnold Wiersen to Bill C-38: "Bill C-452 received royal assent in June 2015. Then the Liberal government came into power and has since blocked Bill C-452 from coming into force. Why? It is because the Liberals do not like the idea that sex traffickers might face consecutive sentences. *They feel it is too harsh to expect that a child trafficker should serve a long sentence for exploiting a minor in sex slavery"* (House of Commons, Dec 11, 2017, Bill C-38; emphasis added). Such a response took place despite the fact that penalties for sexual offences committed against children and youth were already amplified in 2015 through Bill C-26, An Act to amend the Criminal Code, the Canada Evidence Act and the Sex Offender Information Registration Act, to enact the High Risk Child Sex Offender Database Act and to make consequential amendments to other Acts. The law introduced a number of changes that increased punishments for those convicted of child sexual offences, including the imposition of consecutive sentences in cases where there are two or more victims (MacKay 2014).

In March 2018, the changes proposed by Bill C-38 were incorporated into a larger criminal justice reform Bill C-75, An Act to amend the Criminal Code, the Youth Criminal Justice Act and other Acts and to make consequential amendments to other Acts. The Bill re-introduced (1) consecutive sentencing for those convicted of trafficking, (2) rebuttable presumption of guilt in trafficking cases, and (3) reversal of proof onus for proceeds of crime forfeiture proceedings (House of Commons Canada. Standing Committee on Justice and Human Rights. 2018; Millar and O'Doherty 2020a). The concerns associated with this Bill were expressed by the Canadian Bar Association:

> Bill C-75 would amend section 279.01 to create a rebuttable presumption of guilt against any person who lives with or is habitually in the company of a person who is exploited, but who is not themselves exploited. The Crown would only need to prove that the alleged victim was exploited by someone, and that the person on trial lived with, or was habitually in the company of the victim. In other words, the Crown would *not* have to prove that the accused *actually* exercised control, direction or influence over the movements of the alleged victim for the purpose of exploiting them or facilitating their exploitation. The person on trial would be required to provide evidence that there was no exercise of control, direction or influence over the movements of the alleged victim, or that any exercise of control was not for the purpose of exploiting the victim or facilitating the victims' exploitation.
>
> (2018, 31)

Furthermore, the Bar Association notes that

> The proposed presumption does *not* require proof that the person on trial intended to participate in the victim's exploitation, or had any knowledge of the exploitation. Further, the presumption applies even if that person had no involvement in the actual exploitation of the victim. Given the serious nature of this offence and the penalties and stigma associated with it, the presumption would likely be found unconstitutional as an infringe-

ment of the right to be presumed innocent under section 11(d) of the *Charter*. The presumption is unlikely to be saved under section 1 of the *Charter*, as it would criminalize people other than those who exploit the vulnerable.

(2018, 32)

The proposed changes of Bill C-75 are, therefore, troubling, particularly in light of the already increased penalties for trafficking offences and the reality of the characteristics that define these cases on the ground – namely, that they are merely redefined procuring offences, the policing of which tend to capture young, poor, racialized men in the criminal justice net. The Bill received Royal Assent on 21 June 2019. However, as noted in the House of Commons Standing Committee on Justice and Human Rights report on human trafficking, "the provision requiring the courts to impose consecutive sentences for trafficking in persons offences and for any offence arising out of the same series of events will not come into force upon Royal Assent, but rather on a date fixed by order of the Governor in Council" (Housefather 2018, 10). This is because "According to the *Canadian Charter of Rights and Freedoms (Charter)* Statement on Bill C-75, this provision could be 'found to unjustifiably limit section 12 of the *Charter*.'" (ibid.).

Sentences for human trafficking have increased since the implementation of *PCEPA*. This is captured by the court's discussion of sentencing ranges in trafficking cases in *R. v. A.E* (2018): "It would appear that prior to 2014, the range was probably two or three years at the bottom end to six or seven years at the top end, depending of course on the aggravating and mitigating circumstances of the case. Since 2014, the floor has been elevated and I would say, provisionally, that the usual range appears now to be roughly four to eight years, again depending on the aggravating and mitigating circumstances present" (*R. v. A.E.* 2018 para 65). We can also see the high sentences in individual case examinations, particularly in more recently sentenced cases. For example, in *R. v. A.S.* (2017), the accused was convicted of human trafficking under section 279.01 and sentenced to twelve years' imprisonment. In addition to this, he was sentenced to five years for receiving material benefit from the commission of human trafficking to run concurrently to the twelve-year sentence; six years concurrent for conviction for aggravated assault; two and a half years concurrent for sexual assault; one year each for three assaults he was convicted of; eight years concurrent for exercising control over the victim for the purposes of prostitution, and one year consecutive for choking, for a total of thirteen years' imprisonment (*R. v. A.S.* 2017, para. 65). The global sentence exceeded the twelve years' sentence recommended by the Crown attorney.

In *R. v. A.E.* (2018), the accused was also convicted of two counts of human trafficking and a number of other offences[16] and was sentenced to a total of thirteen years imprisonment, which was reduced to a global sentence of ten years. Similarly, in *R. v. Brown* (2018), the accused was convicted of human trafficking and sentenced to thirteen years' imprisonment, a sentence which was subsequently reduced by three years due to the Gladue factors[17] relevant to the accused's circumstances, for a total of ten years' imprisonment. Significant sentences have also been handed out in the case of *R. v. Burton* (2018), where the accused was sentenced to ten and a half years for trafficking and related offences; *R. v. Deiaco* (2017), where the accused received a global sentence of eight years after pleading guilty to human trafficking; and *R. v. Antoine* (2020), where the accused was convicted of human trafficking and sentenced to nine years but the sentence was reduced to eight years after taking into account the totality principle.[18]

The most notable example of harsh sentencing in trafficking cases comes through *R. v. Moazami* (2015),[19] where the British Columbia Supreme Court sentenced the accused to twenty-three years' imprisonment. The sentence was calculated by attributing both concurrent and consecutive sentences ranging from one to three years in the case of each of the eleven complainants, totalling forty-eight years and six months in jail. The judge explained this by noting that: "Mr. Moazami's total sentence should not be calculated by imposing the sentences with respect to offences against some or all of the complainants concurrently. To do so would be the equivalent of giving Mr. Moazami a reduced sentence because he inflicted harm on many young girls rather than only one or two" (*R. v. Moazami* 2015, para. 137). In the end, the judge found that "a sentence of 23 years' incarceration is the minimum necessary to achieve the fundamental objectives of sentencing on the facts of this case. Denunciation and deterrence are the most important principles of sentencing in light of the nature of the offences against children" (*R. v. Moazami* 2015, para. 143). It is important to note that the court's reference to the protection of children, as I will discuss in chapter two, has served as a justification for the expansion of legal and on-the-ground anti-trafficking efforts.

As mentioned above the mandatory minimum penalties in human trafficking cases have received pushback from Ontario courts due to the broad definition of human trafficking and the wide range of activities that could fall under the category of trafficking whereby a mandatory minimum penalty would be disproportionate to the crime. Mandatory sentencing in trafficking cases was first challenged in the case of *R. v. Finestone* (2017), where the Ontario court found that the mandatory minimum sentence of five years for trafficking of a person under eighteen is unconstitutional under section 52 of the Constitution Act. According to the judge in this case: "When I consider the broad range of conduct captured by this section, even taking into account the heightened *mens rea*, many reasonable hypotheticals can be constructed where a 5-year sentence would be grossly disproportionate to the fit sentence. As such, in my view, section 279.011(b) violates section 12 of the Charter" (*R. v. Finestone* 2017, para. 87). And although the provincial court judge did not have the jurisdiction to declare mandatory minimums unconstitutional, she nonetheless determined that, "having found the law unconstitutional," she "need not apply the minimum sentence" (*R. v. Finestone* 2017, para. 89), instead imposing a sentence of four years, rather than the five years required by the mandatory minimum for child sex trafficking under section 279.011 of the Criminal Code. The court also rejected the Crown's request for an Order under section 161,[20] finding that based on the evidence, the accused did not pose an ongoing risk to children.

In 2019 Ontario Superior Court of Justice struck down the five-year mandatory minimum sentence for the human trafficking of a person under the age of eighteen in the case of *R. v. Ahmed et al.* In this case, the two defendants, Amina Ahmed and Nadia Ngoto, were found guilty of grooming two youths to enter the sex trade under section 279.011 of the Criminal Code. Importantly, the youths did not enter the sex trade, and no exploitation actually took place (*R. v. Ahmed et al.* 2019). The judge determined that the appropriate sentence for Ahmed and Ngoto was in the range of twelve to eighteen months and eight to fourteen months, respectively, finding further that "there is no question that a mandatory minimum sentence of 5 years is disproportionate to the sentences in the range of 8 to 14 months and 12 to 18 months that are deemed fit for these offenders" (ibid., para. 110). The judge went on to note that the circumstances of the case were such that a mandatory minimum sentence of five years' imprisonment would be cruel and unusual and therefore, in violation of section 12 of the Charter. Going beyond the circumstances of the specific case at hand, the judge concluded that the mandatory minimum sentence is "grossly disproportionate to fit sentences for offenders with less moral blameworthiness," therefore determining that "the mandatory minimum sentence imposed by section 279.011 of the Code violates s. 12 of the *Charter* and is not justified under s. 1 of the *Charter*. Section 279.011 of the Code is therefore declared of no force or effect under s, 52 of the *Constitution Act, 1982*" (*R. v. Ahmed et al.* 2019, para. 121–2).

Subsequently, the Ontario Superior Court in the case of *R. v. Reginald Louis Jean* (2020), found that the mandatory minimum sentence of four years' imprisonment that comes with a conviction under section 279.01(1), which deals with trafficking of an adult person, also violates section 12 of the Charter because it is "not proportional to the objective of the legislation and the wide range of conduct that it captures" (2020, para. 39). The court found that "the mandatory minimum sentence set out in s. 279.01(1) of the Criminal Code unconstitutional as it relates to a hypothetical offender's right not to be subject to cruel and unusual punishment under s. 12 of the *Charter*. As a result, the mandatory minimum sentence provision under s. 279.01(2) is declared to have no force or effect under section 52 of the Constitution Act" (*R. v. Reginald Louis Jean* 2020, para. 44). These decisions signal a correction and an acknowledgment by the courts that the human trafficking laws are broad capture of a wide range of conduct that may not have the moral blameworthiness to justify the harsh penalties.

Nevertheless, those convicted of trafficking often still recieve long sentences, and are also subject to other possible consequences, including a lifetime DNA order,[21] registration with the sex offender registry (if the trafficking is for the purpose of sexual exploitation), long-term and/ or dangerous offender designation and Order under section 161, which places significant restrictions on the activities of the convicted individual after their release from prison. These possible consequences leave no doubt as to the severity with which human trafficking is treated. This is further exemplified in the Crown's attempt in *R. v. Burton* (2018) to have the offence of human trafficking declared a personal injury offence. According to section 752 of the Criminal Code, a personal injury offence is defined as "conduct endangering or likely to endanger the life or safety of another person or inflicting or likely to inflict severe psychological damage on another person." The Crown's argument that human trafficking should be deemed a personal injury offence was premised on its association with sex work and the "inherent violence in prostitution" (*R. v. Burton*, audio of trial, 30 October 2015).[22] Although the court did not deem the offence of human trafficking itself a personal injury, it did find that the high threshold of a personal injury offence was met in the specific case of Tyrone Burton.

A finding that a personal injury offence has occurred opens the possibility of a Dangerous Offender Application. Under section 753(1) of the Criminal Code, a person can be deemed a dangerous offender if "the offender constitutes a threat to the life, safety or physical or mental well-being of other persons based on a pattern of repetitive behaviour." Dangerous Offender designations are rare in Canada and can be accompanied by an indeterminate sentence.[23] After the abolishment of capital punishment in Canada in 1976, indeterminate sentence has been considered the most severe penalty in Canada (Brode 2008, 107).[24] While the Crown's sweeping application in this case was unsuccessful, the attempt itself is alarming given then mundane crimes that are being prosecuted under trafficking laws.

In addition to criminal penalties, those with precarious citizenship status convicted of trafficking are subject to "double punishment" through deportation (Pratt 2012, 275; see also Pratt 2014). Human trafficking, as an offence that carries with it a maximum penalty of fourteen years' imprisonment, falls under the category of a "serious offence," enabling the deportation of those convicted of it. It is important to note that it is not necessary for one to be sentenced to the maximum or even minimum term in order to trigger deportation. Simply being convicted of an offence that carries this as a penalty automatically triggers a deportation order, regardless of the sentence imposed.

While permanent residents convicted of trafficking and sentenced to a term of six months or less retain their right to appeal the deportation order, those convicted of six months or more are subject to an un-appealable deportation order, as in a number of cases examined in this study. Changes to immigration laws have been designed to enable the faster deportation of non-citizens convicted of serious criminality, including human trafficking. The Faster Removal of Foreign Criminals Act (2013) amended the IRPA to reduce the length of the sentence that allows non-citizens convicted of serious criminality to be deported without appeal from two years' to six months' imprisonment in case of a conviction for an offence that comes with a maximum penalty of ten or more years' imprisonment.

These serious penalties, combined with on-the-ground application of trafficking laws to ordinary domestic primarily procuring offences, led one defence attorney to note:

> to me, that's what I don't like about the human trafficking provision. Most of all I just feel like it's overly broad. They captured too much different conduct. With such a nasty name attached to it, right? Like you get convicted of human trafficking, it's modern-day slavery. It's got this horrible connotation to it and the reality is even within the context of the definition, right … like it could just be the person who is, say, managing the house for the prostitute that's being trafficked by another pimp…. I don't think they should call that human trafficking. I don't think that it's fair. I think it paints it with a broad brush. I think that we're really demonizing people.
>
> (participant 10)

Similarly, another criminal justice actor argued that "the human trafficking laws are overreaching and they're not doing what they were made for" (participant 12). This sentiment was echoed by another defence attorney: "they just need to be careful that they're not casting too wide a net" (participant 11). The combination of a vague and broadly applied definition of trafficking and increasingly harsher sentences is a concerning development, particularly since, as I discuss in subsequent chapters, these laws are frequently applied to young, racialized males – a group already overcriminalized in Canada and the United States. As Elizabeth Bernstein (2012) and Kristin Bumiller (2008) have observed, the harsh criminal justice penalties focusing on sexual violence and notably, in recent years, human trafficking, target racialized and marginalized populations and are justified through an emphasis on the need to protect women's human rights (Bernstein 2012).

Conclusion

As this chapter has shown, Canada's trafficking laws, which developed out of the UN Trafficking Protocol (2000), diverge from it in some important ways and have morphed to do something else entirely – seemingly to target the sex trade and to empower the police and prosecutors in the process. This folding of the transnational into the domestic, as Elizabeth Bernstein puts it, has taken place through a number of legislative amendments which have expanded Canada's definition of trafficking and focused it on the concept of exploitation, making the application of the law easier, particularly in contrast with the combined processes of recruitment, transportation, and exploitation, set out by the UN Trafficking Protocol. These legal amendments have taken place in parallel with developments in Canada's sex work laws, which brought the two criminal offences into alignment. The result has been the application of trafficking laws to procuring offences, in many ways undermining the advances made by the Trafficking Protocol, which importantly recognized the legitimacy of sex work as work. This collapsing of transnational trafficking into domestic procuring has meant that despite opinions of Canadian courts that trafficking laws are straightforward and easy to understand, legal actors are struggling to carve out a meaningful difference. Although police and defence attorneys mainly see the two offences as being the same, Crown attorneys, for the most part, agree that human trafficking is a more serious offence than procuring. The increased seriousness, as I demonstrate in subsequent chapters, stems, at least in part from the intersection of the issue with child exploitation, transnational organized crime, and national security risks within the trafficking matrix. This increased seriousness is also shown by the fact that penalties for trafficking convictions are far more severe than they had been for procuring offences prior to PCEPA. These developments parallel those in the United States – a country that has aligned trafficking with sex work in its legal defintion of the term.

Chapter Two

The Canadian Victim

At the centre of domestic trafficking discourses is the victim. Discourses around the victim of trafficking have shifted from a focus on foreign women and girls transported across state boundaries, to more recent concerns over domestic victims (see also Durisin and van der Meulen 2020). This chapter will show how three overlapping narratives featuring different victims can be placed on a spectrum of innocence/blameworthiness: (1) the daughter of Canadian middle-class families, or the "girl next door"; (2) the marginalized victim; and (3) the Indigenous girl or woman. The last intertwines with the recent Canadian preoccupation with missing and murdered Indigenous women and girls, which is in part about displaced guilt and the continued "white man's colonial burden" to save Indigenous women from corruption and self-exploitation.

As this chapter will show, these victims are sorted based on two vulnerability factors set out by the United Nations: (1) pre-existing vulnerabilities such as poverty, gender, age, mental and physical illness, involvement in sex work, and so on (see chapter one for a discussion) and (2) trafficker-created vulnerabilities, such as the removal of passports, transportation of the victim to an unfamiliar area, language barriers, violence, luring, false promises, etc. Both vulrenablities have become part of the trafficking matrix, expanding understandings of human trafficking and its victims. The three types of victims, as the chapter reveals, exist on a continuum of blameworthiness, with the girl next door being less to blame as she is victimized through trafficker-created vulnerabilities and is "lured," "tricked," and "groomed" – all activities outside of her control. She is snatched from her respectable home by devious men and deserves a second chance by being rescued and returned to the warm bosom of the nuclear family. Yet, even the respectable Canadian daughter exists on a slippery slope, and the road from respectable to unrespectable is short and unforgiving. Thus, when young women eschew rescue and engage in drug use, have managers or boyfriends who are involved in their (sex work) business, and use the sex industry as their source of income, they fall quite easily off their pedestal and become the "at-risk" person.

Since marginalized women are made vulnerable by the presence of pre-existing factors, including poverty, history of abuse, drug and alcohol dependency, among other factors, they are seen as more to blame because they come with their own "risk factors." In other words, they are vulnerable to trafficking not because they are innocent but precisely because they are not. This position draws on disdain for sex work and lays blame against sex workers for broader structural inequalities, revealing class and race biases in the broader discourses of rescue (Pheterson 1993). Indigenous women offer additional insights. In recent years we have seen an increased focus on Indigenous victims of trafficking particularly in the wake of the Robert Pickton case[1] and the recently emerging awareness of the extent of the problem of missing and murdered Indigenous women and girls. Indigenous women and girls as victims of trafficking is a specific category of "vulnerable women" whose racial and cultural markers stand out as a uniquely Canadian preoccupation. This chapter explores the ways in which the human trafficking matrix constructs its objects in particular ways, focusing specifically on the discourses of the victim of trafficking that use sexuality, race, and class to draw transnational and domestic lines of civilization and barbarism and consequently, guilt and innocence. The observations and analysis presented in this chapter are primarily derived from examination of policy discussions, government and NGO reports, and interviews with criminal justice actors, rather than court cases. This is because information about complainants was restricted in most of the court documents obtained in order to protect the identity of the complainants.

From Migrant to Domestic Victim of Trafficking

The concept of victimization is central to the discourse of trafficking because, as Makau Mutua suggests in the context of human rights, "without the victim there can be no savage or savior" (2001, 227; see also Mutua 2002; 2007). When conversations about trafficking first began in Canada following the enactment of the UN Trafficking Protocol (2000), trafficking was depicted as a "foreign" crime, something that happens somewhere else (Durisin and van der Meulen 2020; Jeffrey 2005). The trafficking that did exist in Canada was initially imagined as transnational in nature, primarily coming from Central and Eastern Europe, Russia, and Asia and was primarily focused on the sex trade (Durisin 2017; Durisin and van der Meulen 2020; Roots 2011). As Jeffrey explains, this externalization of the issue allowed Canada to maintain an image of a "good, helpful nation" (2005, 33) – a "white knight"whose generosity and efforts to help with problems of other nations is taken advantage of by "illegal migrants" (ibid., 39).

In the past several years there has been a notable shift to a focus on domestic rather than transnational trafficking, contradicting the initial constructions of the issue as "not our problem" and beyond the civility of Canadians (Durisin 2017; Durisin and van der Meulen 2020). As Durisin and van der Meulen (2020) contend, the Canadian discourse around trafficking has also shifted from a focus on structural factors, such as poverty, to emotional and psychological ones, such as the need to be desired and loved. Yet, as this research demonstrates, both structural as well as emotional and psychological factors – the "pre-existing vulnerabilities," as the UN calls them, have become part of the human trafficking matrix and remain central in the construction of the trafficking victim. Part of that shift, as demonstrated in chapter one, has also been a redefinition of what we mean by human trafficking, moving from a transnational, organized criminal offence to a domestic "luring" and "grooming" of young and vulnerable women and girls, although both discourses remain firmly within the human trafficking matrix, to be turned to as needed. With this shift towards domestic trafficking, we see the emergence of three key domestic trafficking images: (1) the daughter of Canadian middle-class families, or the "girl-next-door," who is lured by traffickers through deceit, coercion, and "love bombing" – the practice of showering a woman or a girl with affection, attention, and love (Dorais and Corriveau 2002, 35); (2) the marginalized victim made vulnerable by pre-existing vulnerabilities; and (3) the Indigenous girl or woman whose victimhood has become central in trafficking discourse due to the Canadian state's need to respond to raising awareness around violence against Indigenous women and girls. Each of these categories will be discussed in the same order in sections below.

Canadian domestic trafficking discourses continue to insist on a framework that emphasizes vulnerable women as infantilized, and as Julietta Hua observes, embodied in "underage girls and runaways who are usually white and come from conventional middle-class backgrounds" (2010, 51). The "girl next door" literally embodies the Canadian fantasy/

imaginary about the "ideal victim" being young, helpless, and without the moral or mental resources to know what is best for her and/or who has temporarily lost her moral compass, and thus is not only in need of, but will benefit from and be grateful for rescue and a return to "normal" life. In Canada, we see the "ideal victim" of trafficking represented by the image of the daughter of a middle-class family, the "girl next door," "your daughter" who is lured and sexually exploited against her will.

The construction of white daughters of Canada's middle-class families as possible trafficking victims is exemplified in an RCMP report which warns that "females with relatively stable backgrounds are increasingly becoming victims. In recent years, there have been more victims that come from reasonably stable homes, are enrolled in educational institutions, and/or have established employment" (2013, 14). Parliamentary debates echo similar sentiments, as exemplified by MP Joy Smith's comment, "what we're finding now is that this can happen to any girl, whether they are from middle-class Canada, whether they are from another country, or whether they're aboriginal – this can happen to any vulnerable girl" (House of Commons, 1 May 2013, Bill C-452). This recognition that the dangers of trafficking even lurk in "our communities" and the shocking insight that privilege and affluence offer no protection against the trafficking of vulnerable female victims is also confirmed by a police officer I interviewed:

> this is the girl next door, your niece, your granddaughter, your neighbour.... There's girls like that, everywhere. I mean everywhere. It's not just, you know people think that it's girls that are low-income areas and yeah, there is a big part of that, the vulnerability there, yes. But we've had victims where the parents are doctors, lawyers, police officers, teachers, so this doesn't discriminate on the people that are the most vulnerable, it discriminates everywhere. It doesn't matter right, because at the end of the day if the girl is vulnerable, and her parents are doctors, so what? If someone is paying attention to her, she's going to gravitate towards that person. We've had victims that come from very affluent parents and neighbourhoods and get caught up in this.
>
> (participant 1)

The victim, then, "can be anyone" (participant 4). The perceived threat is summed up succinctly by an officer quoted in the *Toronto Sun*: "Think it couldn't happen to your daughter?" (Brown, 12 December 2016). This emphasis on the ever-present threat, as Kristin Bumiller notes, exaggerates the possibility of victimization for all women and justifies legislative change and expansion for their protection (2008, 17). Indeed, the power of the "girl next door" narrative led to the introduction of Bill-158, The Saving the Girl Next Door Act, in February 2016 in the Legislative Assembly of Ontario by Progressive Conservative MPP Laurie Scott. It was later re-introduced by the Minister of the Status of Women, Indira Naidoo-Harris, appointed by the Liberal government as Bill-96, The Anti-Human Trafficking Act (2017). The Bill received Royal Assent on 30 May 2017 to enact four changes: (1) make February 22 a human trafficking awareness day in Canada, (2) expand existing laws to allow courts to file a protection order against an accused trafficker, (3) allow victims to sue their traffickers for damages, and (4) expand the definition of "sex offence" under Christopher's Law[2] (Legislative Assembly of Ontario, Anti-Human Trafficking Act 2017, Bill 96). These panics are further fuelled by the construction of the "girl next door" as child-like, evoking powerful discourses around child protectionism within the human trafficking matrix.

As Walsh observes, we tend to "view children through the lens of innocence," virginity, and sacredness; we also expect the law to do everything in its power to protect that innocence (2010, 50). And while there are significant developmental differences between children at all ages, legally the term "child" is universalized to include anyone under the age of eighteen (UN Convention on the Rights of the Child 1989). This general categorization collapses important differences between children and young people whereby seventeen-year-olds can be treated as having the same capacity as six-year-olds (Brock 1998, 103). The result, according to Dauda, "is an essentialized concept of childhood that encompasses a variety of experiences from infancy to adolescence, or youth, and is often universalized and globalized; at the same time, it marginalizes and silences the actual experience of childhood" (2010, 228; 2010b; see also Roots and Lockhart 2021).

Nowhere is the need to protect childhood expressed more clearly than in relation to sexuality (Foucault as cited in Robinson 2012, 260; see also Bittle 2006; 2013). As Robinson notes, sexuality is seen as the terrain of adulthood, and it acts as a crucial boundary that distinguishes adulthood from childhood (2012, 261). Since the maturity required to make a free choice and provide informed consent are understood to be not fully developed in those under the age of 18, young people are seen as particularly vulnerable to exploitation (Brock 1998, 103). At the same time, however, sexuality in a child is conceptualized as always latent; should it be activated too early, it can become dangerous, making it complicated in that it is "not only endangered and needing protection against external dangers but also … dangerous and needing control as it is a threat to the broader social order" (Dauda 2010, 1168; 2010b). And the most commonly cited "danger" of "prematurely" activated sexuality is that it will lead to youth engagement in sex work.

In this framework of childhood sexuality, intervention is not only necessary and urgent but also time sensitive; failure to interfere in time can lead to the "loss" of another child. As former Minister of Justice and the Attorney General of Canada Peter MacKay warns: "many people that enter prostitution did so when they were merely children" (House of Commons, 11 June 2014, Bill C-36). This statement draws on a frequently cited but debunked claim that the average age of entry into sex work is thirteen or fourteen (Lowman 2013; see also Durisin and van der Meulen 2021) and suggests that once in, it will be impossible to leave. As Durisin and van der Meulen explain in the context of Ontario's legislative debates over anti-trafficking laws, MPPs often "expressed concern about 13- and 14-year-olds, but cited the dangers to those as young as 11 and as old as early 20," thus demonstrating not only the consistent emphasis on the youth of the victims but also the ease with which childhood can merge into adulthood (2021, 146).

Julie Kay found a similar emphasis on child trafficking in Manitoba, noting that a focus on child trafficking elicited a response and interventions unlike those afforded to adult victims, particularly if these youth victims were Indigenous (2017, 96). As JJ explains, many organizations focus on the issue of youth in the sex trade to advance their own ideological agenda, yet rather than being helpful, these efforts are oppressive to the communities they focus on (2013, 76). Instead of engaging in a "rescue mission," JJ reminds us that young people in the sex trade should be given a voice in their decision-making process and allowed to disclose their engagement with the sex trade "without fear of prosecution, or fear of being 'saved'" (2013, 76).

Contemporary focus on youth and children within the human trafficking matrix is also framed around the need to protect "our" or the "Canadian" child, carrying an undertone of Canada's nation-building and efforts to draw boundaries of belonging. As Durisin (2017) notes, trafficking discourses provide sites within which notions of Canadian civilization and moral superiority premised on national values of responsibility, caring, and compassion are reinforced. In this instance, the care, compassion, and responsibility presumed to be inherent to Canadian-ness is directed towards the rescue of Canada's own children. For instance, in lobbying support for Bill C-268, MP Smith, who is white, stressed that "These are *our Canadian* children" (House of Commons, 27 February 2009, Bill C-268; emphasis added), while MP Mourani argued, in her speech to support Bill C-452, that "*our children* are recruited at a very young age. *Our girls* are exposed to certain images" (House of Commons, 29 April 2013, Bill C-452; emphasis added). At another time, Mourani justified the need for more coercive law through her own desire to "live in a country where *our daughters* are not treated like objects to be bought and sold.... I urge all my colleagues, men and women alike, to think very seriously about the kind of society we want *our children* to grow up in" (House of Commons, 26 November 2013, Bill C-452; emphasis added).

The shocking idea of Canadian women and girls as victims of trafficking was also seen during the "white slavery" panics of the early twentieth century. Reformers in Canada argued that "Canadian girls were being procured across the border to fill the brothels of American or other foreign cities" (Valverde 2008, 93). The brothels in which Canadian daughters were being forced to work were suggested to be owned by the Chinese and Japanese men, thus revealing the panics to be embedded within racially stereotyped images of white women and girls being sexually victimized by racialized men (Valverde 2008). Concern over the safety of Canada's daughters was expressed by a Canadian social reform organization in 1911: "when we first sounded the alarm in regard to this traffic many would not believe that such a diabolical evil really existed in Canada, but we have been able to establish ... the fact that it is carried out in Canada," describing it as an "awful traffic in procuring *the daughters of our goodly homes*" (cited in Valverde 2008, 89; emphasis added). This statement from 1911 echoes that of MP Françoise Boivin over a century later: "we have to realize that this [trafficking] is happening in *our communities*. It may be happening in a street not far from *our homes*. It is scary but it does happen" (House of Commons, 29 January 2013, Bill C-452; emphasis added). Sexual violence and child sex exploitation frameworks are dependent on nationalist discourses about the significance of protecting the sexuality of "our" (read white) daughters, just as the "white slave" panic did at the start of the twentieth century as white women were then and continue to be seen as Canada's cultural, political, and moral sophistication. Childhood, as a stand in for familialism and innocence, combines with these historical fears around the sexual safety of Canada's (white) women and girls within the human trafficking matrix and works as a trope to help articulate those fears.

These concerns become even more pressing when violence is added to the matrix. The notion of "pimps" victimizing women and girls draws on an inflammatory construction of violence and brutality acted against the innocent and vulnerable. Kristin Bumiller observes that the sexual violence agenda is reinforced through the circulation of sensationalized stories by the media of "sadistic violence" carried out against women (2008, 8). These discourses merge within the human trafficking matrix, appropriating feminist discourses to suit different purposes in order to make the urgency of acting against it appear as a form of feminist intervention (into male violence) – for which, of course, one must also believe that sex work (of any kind) is itself a form of violence.

Canada's domestic trafficking discourses have developed in the context of two related but separate agendas: the feminist agenda against sexual violence arising in the 1970s, 1980s, and 1990s moralized panics over child sexual exploitation through sex work. These concerns have now become a part of the human trafficking matrix. Feminist sexual violence movement brought into the public realm issues previously hidden behind closed doors, including domestic violence, sexual assault, and more recently, human trafficking for the purpose of sexual exploitation, highlighting the harms associated with these behaviours (Bumiller 2008; Suchland 2015). The entry of the state into the sexual violence agenda, however, "had far-reaching effects for the exercise of symbolic, coercive, and administrative power over both men as perpetrators and women as victims" (Bumiller 2008, 7). First, it resulted in the dissemination of fears over "sexual terror" and "women in danger," producing broader concerns around the epidemic of sexual abuse and the threat of sex criminals (ibid., 7). And second, the merging of state and feminist efforts against sexual violence resulted in a crime-control agenda and the subsequent expansion of relevant legislation, which did not always serve feminist goals (Bumiller 2008). International, and now domestic, concerns over human trafficking draw from this Western feminists' focus on the sexual violence agenda (Bernstein 2012; Bumiller 2008, 14; Chuang 2014; Suchland 2015). As Suchland (2015) points out, the insertion of the sexual violence agenda into the anti-trafficking framework has resulted in a simplified analysis of the issue, moving away from economic and structural inequalities to a focus on the individual victim of trafficking.

Populist descriptions of the harms of human trafficking trade heavily in sensationalism bordering on pornographic voyeurism, offering narratives that graphically depict violence and female suffering. For example, Rutvica Andrijasevic discusses a human trafficking awareness poster from the Czech Republic on work in the fashion industry. The poster features a picture of an attractive dressed-up white woman – Monika – who, "tells of how she answered an advertisement in the newspaper for working as a model abroad. After a short course, the agency sent her for a photo-shooting abroad, which turned out to be a shooting for a pornographic film. The text in bold reads: 'Men took turns on me like a conveyor belt. They watched me closely, I couldn't escape'" (2007, 27). While the awareness poster was focused on migrant trafficking, Andrijasevic demonstrates the ways in which it skilfully blends migration and sex work into one. Similar narrative constructions are frequently used in Canada's anti-trafficking efforts, but in this case the focus remains on the dangers posed by trafficking to domestic women and girls. For instance in 2015, the *Toronto Star* published a sex-trafficking series which described victims as "beaten, branded with their pimp's name, and bought and sold across Ontario," with one victim having "a grisly red scar wrapping around her right ankle from an attack last year that severed her Achilles tendon and left her foot 'just hanging there.'" The same article goes on to describe other women being burned with cigarettes, having guns put against their heads or shoved inside their mouths, being "beaten black and blue [and] starved" until they service a certain number of men (Carville 13 December 2015d). Another article from the same series in the *Toronto Star* bemoaned the fact that "some of the girls are beaten by pimps, whipped with coat hangers heated up on a stove, punched, choked, burned and forced to sleep naked at the foot of the bed like dogs" (Carville, 12 December 2015c).[3] Similarly, a *Toronto Sun* "expose" of sex trafficking quoted a police officer as saying, "One pimp in a recent case decided to increase a girl's dependency on him by slashing her achilles' [*sic*] tendon. When he realized there would be repercussions, he took her downstairs and left her by a dumpster, like a pile of garbage" (Brown, 12 December 2016). Such depictions are intended to create a shock effect that draws attention away from the complexity of the issue of trafficking, presenting it in simplistic terms, the solution to which can only stand in harsh punishments for the offenders and immediate government intervention with no expense spared (see also Sibley 2020).

Emotive narratives are also often presented by provincial and federal Members of Parliament who discuss "estimates" and "stories of trafficked girls" without providing their sources for these claims (Legislative Assembly of Ontario, Private Member's Bill, 14 May 2015; House of Commons, 24 March 2011, Bill C-612; see also De Shalit et al. 2021; Durisin and van der Meulen 2021). As with media, politicians too draw out the violence involved in the offence. For instance, as federal MP Mourani describes it, "these girls are raped. They are gang-raped. They are tortured and their family is threatened.... They are so terrorized that they do not even have to be forced to do so" (House of Commons, 29 April 2013, Bill C-452). She goes on to note, "they take these girls by force and stick them in apartments. They do not even know where they are and groups of men rape them. This is what they call a gangbang" (House of Commons, 29 April 2013, Bill C-452).

A similar narrative was also advanced by Ontario MPP Laurie Scott, who described victims of trafficking as "being used and degraded over and over again. You're being raped every day for service that is provided to men. So, the long-term damage that is happening to these women is very crucial" (Legislative Assembly of Ontario, 14 May 2015, Private Member's Motion). It is also noteworthy that the argument constructs trafficking *as both violence* and *including violence*, an inconsistency that speaks to the inchoate nature of the term itself. Of course, the effects of constructing the trafficking victims as young and innocent, juxtaposed with vivid descriptions of violence and sexual exploitation, combine powerfully within the human trafficking matrix (Andrijasevic 2007; Doezema 2010; Suchland 2015).

The "girl next door" is key to the imaginary that creates the universe of human trafficking. Unlike their historical counterparts, who explicitly bemoaned the future of the "race" through the sexual degradation of "white slaves," contemporary advocates of human trafficking intervention are slightly more circumspect in their choice of language. Yet their discourses betray an adherence to a vision of the "girl next door" as probably white, just like their daughters. Given that they themselves, are often white, morally and politically conservative, "respectable" members of the public, one may safely assume that the imperilled girls they feel compelled to "save" largely resemble their own daughters. Yet, while the "girl next door" is the most innocent on the spectrum of innocence/blameworthiness compared to the other two key figures, she is no longer the virginal figure of purity that was upheld during the "white slavery" panics. Instead, she is also responsibilized to be risk adverse and even blamed for her decisions when she becomes victimized (see Roots and Lockhart 2021).

To understand this, we can turn to the work of Lise Gotell, who describes a neoliberal shift in the "ideal victim" of sexual assault, and in this case of [sex] trafficking, from a morally pure woman, to one that is a "responsible, security conscious, crime-preventing subject who acts to minimize her own sexual risk" (2012, 243; see also: Bakht 2012). This neoliberal form of responsibilization is exemplified in the RCMP (2012) "I am not for sale" campaign, an anti-trafficking campaign targeted at youth, which reads: "In recent years, there has been a noticeable emphasis on 'hypersexualization' in television ads and programs, the Internet, and particularly in music lyrics and videos. It may be easy to be attracted to a pimp and drawn into a certain lifestyle because parts of it look to be glamorous and rewarding" (2012). The contrasting rhetoric of risk and prevention sends mixed messages when combined with the positioning of the female victim as vulnerable (Hall 2004). The contradictions of the campaign are revealed through the RCMP's efforts to responsibilize women and girls to protect themselves by behaving in more modest ways. This message easily takes on an air of victim-blaming when sexual violence and, in this case, trafficking does take place, holding women and girls accountable due to expressed sexuality – an expression reframed by the RCMP as alacrity to participate in their own hypersexualization. The campaign pamphlet further notes that traffickers meet their victims through friends, boyfriends/girlfriends, family members, acquaintances, the internet, and so on and that "It can be as simple as someone messaging you on a social networking site, asking to be friends and wanting to get to know you" (RCMP 2012). Women and girls are thus portrayed as always at risk for victimization, consequently needing to be unceasingly vigilant and engage in responsible decision-making. They are directed to "be on the lookout" since "this can happen to anyone" in places where "you think you might be safe" (ibid.). Thus, the RCMP's unrelenting message is that women and girls should be afraid of traffickers, distrustful of everyone, and as a form of good citizenship take all necessary precautions to protect themselves. The assumption is that those who become victimized by traffickers failed in their efforts to be adequately responsible, careful, or vigilant – a form of victim blaming that is ready to be mined by defence counsel (see Comack and Balfour 2004; Gotell 2008; Larcombe 2002; Roots and Lockhart 2021; Sheehy 2014).

In 2017, Toronto Crime Stoppers launched a similar human trafficking awareness campaign with accompanying posters and websites intended to educate the public on the signs of human trafficking. The signs include young girls[4] with too much makeup and/or inappropriate clothing for their age; expensive clothes, jewellery, and a cell phone with no explanation for where it came from; being underweight and appearing malnourished; and companions who do all the talking for them (*Toronto Sun* 2017; see also Roots and Lockhart 2021). These age-old shaming tactics place girls' sexuality at centre stage, constructing it as "something innocent, pure, and at risk of contamination through active desire" (Ringrose et al. 2013, 307). Importantly, however, these "signs of trafficking" have wide applicability, such that owning a cell phone and experimenting with clothes and/or makeup and jewellery are commonplace teenage experiences yet in this case place many young women under suspicion of being trafficked (Roots and Lockhart 2021). Despite this overwhelming attention to protecting the "girl next door," she was not the key figure in most of the trafficking cases I analysed; instead, this position was occupied by the marginalized girl or woman.

Marginalized and Indigenous women and girls play a specific role alongside the "girl next door" in the anti-trafficking framework as established by politicians, police, and various government organizations. For instance, as (then) Minister of Justice and Attorney General of Canada Peter MacKay noted, victims of trafficking are "often the most marginalized and victimized of our citizens, vulnerable Canadians, often Aboriginal, new Canadians" (House of Commons, 11 June 2014, Bill C-36). Federal and provincial government and police reports also affirm the fact that marginalized and Indigenous women and girls are frequently the victims of trafficking. This is demonstrated by a 2007 report of the Standing Committee on the Status of Women, a key report in shifting attentions from international to domestic trafficking, which notes that "trafficking victims are often the poorest, most disadvantaged groups in society" and emphasized Indigenous women's vulnerability to becoming victims of trafficking due to poverty (2007, 9; see also Barrett 2010; the United States Department of Justice and Government of Canada 2006; Barrett 2013; RCMP 2013).

If sex is, by definition, something that becomes exploitative when it is placed within a market or is commercialized, bargained, or instrumentalized, then what should be done with women who work in the sex trade and are the most obvious targets of anti-trafficking efforts? Are they victims or villains? Do they need rescue or condemnation? This is a tricky line in the human trafficking matrix. In search of victims, women living in marginalized conditions, including working in the sex trade but also perhaps characterized by violence (street/domestic), addiction, petty criminality, and so forth, are cast as victims of their own vulnerabilities. As explained in chapter one and earlier in this chapter, there are two types of vulnerability factors: the pre-existing vulnerabilities and trafficker-created vulnerabilities. The factors characterized as pre-existing vulnerabilities are commonplace and are experienced by many individuals. Incorporating pre-existing vulnerability factors into the trafficking matrix, as done by criminal justice actors in Canada, makes the trafficking label more broadly applicable (UNODC 2013, 4). A 2013 RCMP report on trafficking confirmed their view of these factors as vulnerabilities but framed mental illness as possibly increasing risky behaviour: "Some victims have drug and, to a lesser extent, alcohol dependencies. Traffickers take advantage of addicted individuals by using drugs and alcohol to build trust with their victims, facilitate their sexual services, control them, and ensure their compliance.... A few victims have mental health disorders and other disabilities that may hinder judgment, increase risk-taking behaviour, and limit the ability to understand traffickers' intentions or exploitive situations" (2013, 15). As Kelly Hannah Moffat (2006) writes in the context of concerns over prison regimes, neoliberal strategies of governance have led to factors that should be "needs," such as abuse, need for shelter, addictions, and so on, becoming transformed into "risk factors," thus putting them on a collision course with the criminal justice system for which they, individually, are then made responsible. Consequently, in this case, while the women are seen as being "at risk," they are simultaneously constructed as creating risk by these very same vulnerability factors. This is re-affirmed by the comments of a police officer that "99% of the people we deal with are females. That's how I'm going to relate it to - but the girls that we deal with - first most of them are very young. They have mental health problems, drug addictions; they've been in the game so long that they're broken" (participant 1). These "risks," Moffat explains, are "predicated on middle class normative assumptions that are highly gendered and racialized" (2006, 253), placing anyone who stands outside societal norms to be characterized as risky.

Perhaps unsurprisingly, one of the key indicators of vulnerability is involvement in sex work. This also comes through in an RCMP report which suggests that "the two groups most vulnerable to traffickers are individuals who are underage and/or are engaged in dancing and/or prostitution" (2013, 14). The RCMP goes on to note, "Approximately 50 percent of victims were already dancing and/or prostituting before they met their traffickers. Females within this group are more easily recruited and controlled since they are already engaged in these activities" (2013, 15). Once again, we see the women being constructed as simultaneously at risk as a result of their choice in employment, and as risky since this choice makes them easier to recruit by traffickers, an approach which enables the police to decide between applying a criminal or victim label. This is noteworthy, as it justifies the increased surveillance of sex workers and contradicts the promises of Canada's new sex work laws to move away from treating sex workers as criminals. The parallel operating constructions of sex workers as risky and at risk, as Jo Doezema explains, is due to concerns over the threats posed not only by traffickers towards vulnerable women and girls, but also by the women and girls involved in the sex trade to the state itself (2010, 120). Thus, the law maintains its disdain of sex work and sex workers by criminalizing the purchasing of sexual services, which denies the workers' autonomy. However, rather than treating this as overbearing, the Canadian state congratulates itself on its civility through discourses of protecting women from what it sees as inherently violent and risky work (and thus ultimately protecting women who choose this work from themselves).

Troubled family backgrounds and low self-esteem have also become a part of the matrix and highlighted as factors that make women and girls vulnerable to being trafficked: "Victims tend to be very, very vulnerable, often addicted to either alcohol or drugs. They tend to have very low self-esteem. Self-esteem issues often because of nasty backgrounds, you know, they may have been CAS [Children's Aid Society] wards. They might have been – *they're looking for any sort of attention that will kind of appeal to them*" (participant 9; emphasis added). Importantly, the designation of low self-esteem as a vulnerability to being trafficked also suggests that it is only those with the lowest self-esteem that would enter sex work. In other words, no self-respecting woman would choose to enter into the sex trade. Vulnerability factors underlined by police officers I interviewed fall under what the UN defines as "pre-existing vulnerabilities" (see the Introduction and chapters for discussion). Inserting these pre-existing vulnerabilities into the trafficking matrix expands the number of people upon whom the trafficking victim label can be bestowed, particularly in contrast to the situation-dependent vulnerabilities created by the trafficking situation/trafficker, such as language barrier, unfamiliarity with culture or surroundings, removal of travel documents, and so on (see chapter one for a discussion). While these vulnerability factors are used to expand the net of possible victims, they can also be used to reinforce the assumption that sex work is never voluntary. Professor Chris Bruckert, who spoke at a House of Commons debate on Bill C-36, described such approaches as "part of a larger discourse that draws on stigmatic assumptions to discredit and delegitimate sex workers as youths, as mentally ill, as drug addiction, or as simply unable to make the right choices": "Then, paternalistically if somewhat illogically, [this approach] frames criminal justice intervention as a reasonable pathway to salvation…. This legal paternalism hinges on the assumption that no reasonable person would wish to engage in sex work. As such, it reifies a profoundly judgmental image of sex workers working with or for third parties as deluded, incompetent social actors and bestows upon them a disempowering identity of hyper-vulnerable victims" (House of Commons, 8 July 2014, Bill C-36). The use of these vulnerability factors as indicators of trafficking is tautological: women with low self-esteem are most likely to be recruited into sex work and exploited, while all women in the sex trade must be women with low self-esteem.

These women are then discerned as poor decision-makers, as evidenced by the comment of one police officer: "one victim that I have right now, she thought it would be really cool. She was like I was really excited to do it at first because she thought she was going to be independent" (participant 5). Here we have a young woman expressing excitement about sex work, only to be turned into a victim by a police officer who suggests she is naïve. From the perspective of the officer, whether she knows it or not, she needs him to rescue her for her misplaced idea that this is a path to independence. The use of vulnerability factors makes criminal justice actors, within their own logic, always right about this. And as Dr. Bruckert notes above, it creates the need for paternalistic crime-control strategies, to save these women not just from the villains of the sex trafficking world but from themselves.

Indigeneity is an important and specific category of "vulnerable woman" whose racial and cultural markers stand out as a uniquely Canadian preoccupation. She signals an attentiveness to the issues of race, and by her very Indigeneity makes the human trafficking story *domestic* – that is, there is a uniquely Canadian narrative being constructed about the need to act on violence against Indigenous women and girls. Many, though not all, Indigenous organizations have endorsed this perspective. Supporters of this framework include the Native Women's Association of Canada (NWAC) and Aboriginal Women's Action Network on Prostitution, among others. The Inquiry into Missing and Murdered Indigenous Women and Girls (2019) also accepted the trafficking framework, noting that Indigenous women and girls are at a greater risk of being trafficked and therefore, greater steps need to be taken to rescue and protect them. This protectionism has not always been there when it comes to Indigenous women, as they have historically been seen as sexually available and promiscuous and therefore not legitimate victims (Durisin and van der Meulen 2020; Hunt 2010, 2015; Kaye 2017). The extent to which the lives of Indigenous women are disregarded was highlighted by the fact that over the past thirty years, many Indigenous women and girls went missing across Canada. While the exact numbers are unknown (Jiwani and Young 2007), an RCMP report from 2014 was able to confirm 1,181 missing and murdered Indigenous women and girls in Canada between 1980 and 2012 (~~MMIWG Report 2019;~~ National Inquiry Into Missing and Murdered Indigenous Women and Girls 2019, 54). The Missing and Murdered Indigenous Women and Girls (MMIWG) report published in 2019 notes, however, that the statistics gathered by the RCMP underestimate the extent of the problem. Until the arrest of Robert Pickton in 2002, very little attention was paid to the issue, and police showed little interest or effort in getting to the bottom of it.[5] The publicity of the Pickton case brought attention to the widespread violence against Indigenous women and girls and criticism towards the lack of national response to it (Craig 2014; Jiwani and Young 2007). The National Inquiry into Missing and Murdered Indigenous Women and

Girls started in 2015 after Prime Minister Justin Trudeau supported calls of Indigenous organizations to address this issue.

The mandate of the National Inquiry into Missing and Murdered Indigenous Women and Girls was to investigate the systemic causes of violence against Indigenous women, girls, and 2SLGBTQQIA peoples (National Inquiry into Missing and Murdered Indigenous Women and Girls, Interim Report 2018). The inquiry received much criticism from the start, with activists, community organizations, and citizens arguing that the funds allocated to the inquiry should have been given to the Indigenous communities to address the root causes of violence against women and girls (Conty 2019). Nevertheless, the final report of the MMIWG inquiry, released in 2019, found that the issue of violence against Indigenous women is severe and systematic enough to meet the threshold of genocide. The MMIWG inquiry and growing public awareness of the issue shifted the national discourse to reposition Indigenous women and girls as victims of sexual violence, including trafficking.

The recent repositioning of Indigenous women and girls as legitimate victims within the trafficking framework is done by employing the pre-existing vulnerability factors. For instance, in the context of their study, the Inquiry into Missing and Murdered Indigenous Women and Girls heard from many witnesses about how Indigenous girls and 2SLG-BTQQIA youth are targeted by "pimps" because they are vulnerable, pointing to abusive families, early experiences of sexual exploitation, addiction, and poverty as contributing factors (2019, 660). These findings undoubtedly reflect the realities of Indigenous peoples. However, as scholars have argued, repositioning Indigenous women and girls as trafficking victims is also problematic for a number of reasons (Hunt 2015; Kaye 2017).

First, it naturalizes the violence that takes place in racialized spaces and the suffering of Indigenous women and girls (Durisin and van der Meulen 2020; Hunt 2015; Maynard 2015). Indigenous women and girls are thus seen as vulnerable to trafficking due to these pre-existing vulnerabilities, including their naïveté, lack of education, impoverished background, and the prevalence of violence in their communities and homes. This construction is different from the "girl next door," who is more likely to be a victim of situational factors. As Durisin and van der Meulen point out, policy discussions on victimization by traffickers are silent on the racial dynamics in operation here, yet "this narrative is nevertheless deeply racialized" (2020, 10) when we consider the very different framing of the victimization of the "girl next door" in white spaces, such as malls, movie theatres, and sporting events, in contrast with the framing of Indigenous women and girls' victimization in relation to violence, dysfunction, and addiction. Second, as Hunt (2015; 2017) and Kaye (2017) maintain, the placing of violence against Indigenous women and girls into the human trafficking framework diverts attention from continued absence of any real efforts to address the impacts of colonialism (see also Sayers 2017). Within this trafficking framework, Indigenous women and girls are depicted as in need of rescue by the colonial government (Jun-Rong Ting and Showden 2019).

The image of the Indigenous victim of trafficking is then well formed in domestic trafficking discourses, yet it is not grounded in empirical findings (Millar et al. 2015, 48). Millar et al. (2015) note that while the Indigeneity of the victim is a vulnerability factor that is routinely raised by the Crown in court cases where any party is Indigenous, they found no references made to the Indigeneity of the victim in any of the trafficking cases they examined. My own study supports these findings, as none of the trials examined made mention of the Indigeneity of the victim (or the accused). However, I cannot say with certainty that Indigenous women and girls are never or even rarely identified as victims of trafficking since the trial transcripts I examined represented a relatively small sample of trafficking cases and were focused in Ontario Still, the emphasis on the frequent victimization of Indigenous women and girls by traffickers prevalent in trafficking discourses does not appear to be reflected in on-the-ground practices. In other words, while trafficking discourses emphasize the frequent victimization of Indigenous women by traffickers, the police do not seem to find or categorize Indigenous women's exploitation and victimization as human trafficking. In all likelihood, this is a reflection of the fact that violence against Indigenous women continues to be largely normalized in the criminal justice system, even as it is discursively fetishized in public documents (Hunt 2015; Kaye 2017; McGillivray 1998). And although Indigenous women are overrepresented in the sex trade (Hunt 2015; 2017; National Inquiry into Missing and Murdered Indigenous Women and Girls 2019), they fail to qualify as victims of violence since "Indigenous women are seen as less than human, as unworthy of response" (Hunt 2013, 88), and any violence carried out against them is seen as normal and part of their everyday existence within Indigenous spaces. Despite the clear shifts in discourse and the placement of Indigenous women and girls into the spotlight as victims of trafficking, we then see a very different understanding of how they ended up there (as a result of pre-existing vulnerabilities, i.e., troubled background).

Conclusion

As this chapter has outlined, trafficking discourses from the first decade of the twenty-first century, which focused on the migrant trafficking victim made vulnerable by the structural conditions in her home country and her "foreignness," contrast but nevertheless co-exist within the trafficking matrix with Canada's trafficking discourses that have emerged over the last decade to now focus predominantly on the domestic victim. The three key figures of the domestic trafficking victim – the "girl next door," the marginalized woman and the Indigenous woman and girl – are constructed in classed and racialized ways through reliance on the vulnerability factors. While the "girl next door" is made vulnerable by situational factors created by the trafficker, such as being lured, groomed and tricked, therefore carrying the least guilt in her own victimization of the three key victim figures, she too is victim-blamed through responsibilization strategies that put her in charge of her own safety while poor decision-making and failure to remain risk averse, render her at least partially responsible. Marginalized women, in contrast, often experience pre-existing vulnerabilities, including poverty, drug or alcohol addiction, and/or engagement in sex work. In the past such factors have rendered them unworthy as victims but are now central to the construction of these women as victims of trafficking. Finally, the Indigenous victim of trafficking emerged out of a need for the Canadian state to acknowledge and address the widespread violence against Indigenous women and girls. She signals an attentiveness to the issue of race and by her Indigeneity makes the story of trafficking in Canada uniquely domestic. Yet, the pre-existing vulnerabilities by which both the Indigenous and marginalized woman have been made into trafficking victims turn structural needs into criminogenic risks that individualize serious social problems and for which the women are often held responsible.

Chapter Three

Policing Trafficking

The police contribute to "making" the crime of human trafficking. They do this first by deciding what human trafficking is and who the perpetrators and victims are and then "find" evidence to support this understanding of human trafficking. This chapter draws on Richard Ericson's framework of police as "makers of crime, criminals and victims" to understand their role in the making of the offence of human trafficking. As Ericson notes: "Police are at the forefront of definitional production. They are given organizational capacity to produce particular levels of crime and to produce particular types of crime to the relative exclusion of others.... Production also depends upon the collective ability of police force members to generate and use the information necessary to make crime" (Ericson 1983, 7).[1] In addition to centrally contributing to the definition of trafficking, and its victims and offenders, this chapter also shows that multi-level police collaboration and coordination of anti-trafficking efforts emphasized at the levels of domestic and international policy are not apparent on the front line of anti-trafficking policing. Instead, as this research shows, these efforts are led primarily by specialized anti-trafficking units within municipal police forces, the formation of which can be attributed, at least in part, to international pressures to show police and prosecutorial successes in Canada's anti-trafficking efforts. And while these units are primarily focused on the domestic sex trade, transnational trafficking discourses which remain centrally within the human trafficking matrix provide them with the support and urgency equal to fighting international organized crime syndicates. By gaining this elevated status, anti-trafficking police shape the on-the-ground definition of trafficking, and the characteristics and identifiers of accused and victims through knowledge produced via the human trafficking matrix, which interfuses information and knowledge from a number of sources, including pre-existing and trafficker-created vulnerabilities, race-based stereotypes, and popular culture. The police also determine the strategies of application for combating trafficking, including how investigations should be conducted, what evidence is required to lay charges, and how to best obtain it. In this way, these policing units contribute significantly to the formation of the human trafficking matrix through what is effectively established as "specialized expertise" on the topic. Yet the logics that form a part of the trafficking matrix also justify troubling investigation tactics and interrogation methods. These are guided not only by the urgency brought to it through international discourses that link trafficking with organized crime, national security, and masculine protectionism which dictates a need to protect "our women and children" at all costs, but also through mundane on-the-ground motivations of front-line police, including pressures to demonstrate effective anti-trafficking police work and competition with other police forces for arrest numbers and resources.

Multijurisdictionality and Cooperation of Policing Agencies

The re-emergence of human trafficking at the turn of the twenty-first century is often characterized as a new and pressing criminal concern that requires novel methods of policing. Responses by the UN, the United States, and now the Canadian government emphasize the need for both innovative and aggressive anti-trafficking investigative and prosecutorial efforts. Among other things, significant emphasis is placed on the need for cooperation between international and domestic police agencies to combat what is seen as a multijurisdictional offence. Evidence of this is seen in Federal Councilor and Head of the Swiss Federal Department of Justice and Police Simonetta Sommaruga's condemnation of national solutions to trafficking. Sommaruga insisted that "when crimes happen on an international level, they must also be investigated on an international level.... INTERPOL [International Criminal Police Organization] demonstrates the advantages of international cooperation" (Swiss Federal Department of Justice and Police 2016). Furthermore, INTERPOL's executive director of police, Tim Morris, suggested that "since fighting transnational crimes like human trafficking requires global solutions, it is important that all actors in the law enforcement arena work together to end this terrible crime and disrupt the criminal networks involved" (ibid.).

In Canada, the importance of international cooperation of law enforcement agencies was emphasized by Yvonne Durand from the International Centre for Criminal Law Reform and Criminal Justice Policy at the University of British Columbia, who as early as 2006 pointed out the challenges of cooperation. According to Durand,

> there are still many obstacles to international cooperation.... [G]iven that the crime frequently occurs across borders, preventing it and control-ling it and prosecuting it presupposes very good cooperation among law enforcement agencies and legal authorities in both countries, and that is still fraught with all kinds of difficulties. We have made great pro-gress not only in Canada but internationally with the *Convention Against Transnational Organized Crime*, to which Canada is a party. This certainly resolves a lot of those issues, but we're still very much at the beginning of this era of international cooperation. International cooperation comes at a risk, as I think all of us have discovered recently, so international cooperation is an area where we need to focus a little bit more of our efforts in future.
>
> (Status of Women Canada Committee
> Meeting, 3 October 2006)

Canada's two key documents on policing trafficking, the National Action Plan to Combat Human Trafficking (2012) and the National Strategy to Combat Human Trafficking: 2019–2023 (2019), also mention the importance of coordination between federal agencies and interna-tional agencies. Despite these calls for an increased emphasis on inter-national cooperation, anti-trafficking law enforcement efforts in Can-ada continue to be focused at the national level.

Law enforcement officers interviewed for this study reported that they work with various municipal police forces across Canada, but noted little contact with enforcement agencies at other levels. On the issue of the frequency of their interaction with international agencies, one officer replied, "I would say not very much, this is a human rights issue. Human trafficking is a human rights issue but we, I don't think – I don't know how to answer this question" (participant 1). Contradicting himself, the officer later suggested that the Canadian municipal police and police organizations from other states and international policing agencies frequently cooperate: "We have international partners that we deal with all of the time. We interact with INTERPOL and EUROPOL all the time. Homeland Security and the FBI all the time. I talk to them all the time, sharing information and getting best practices and what they see over there, could it come here, stuff like that" (participant 1). Nevertheless, the answers of the other officers I spoke with aligned with the officer's initial answer, that Ontario police interactions with international law enforcement agencies on human trafficking cases are rare. As one police officer explained, "International level, not to say it doesn't happen, we've actually worked with the States, we worked with Homeland Security on certain cases, it doesn't happen that frequently but it does occur" (participant 4). This sentiment is in line with a 2010 RCMP report on human trafficking, which states that "cooperation with foreign law enforcement on suspected transnational human trafficking networks yielded mixed results. Current levels of international cooperation resulted in untimely exchange of information and ineffective information sharing" (40).

One interviewed police officer attributes the lack of international cooperation to the underfunding of anti-trafficking policing efforts: "International trafficking? That's on our radar, but we just, it's going to be no different. We gotta really, really look for it and you have to have dedicated resources for that. It's going to be more difficult to investigate. Because now we have language barriers when you're talking about the international labour. You need dedicated ... that's all you're doing. We don't have that. We have a human trafficking team that falls under our mandate. Because we don't have enough resources, we can't even handle what's happening now" (participant 2). While transnational trafficking cases are more likely to fall under the jurisdiction of federal police rather than municipal forces, the officer's comment nonetheless raise serious questions about the use of the large amounts of funding allocated to law enforcement for anti-trafficking efforts (see the Introduction for a discussion).

In addition to cooperation between international and domestic police services, focus has also been placed on collaborative efforts between the federal, provincial, and municipal levels of domestic police in Canada. According to the 2012 US Department of State Trafficking in Persons Report, Canada must "strengthen coordination among national and provincial governments on law enforcement and victim services" (US Department of State 2012, 110; emphasis added). This mandate is echoed in Canada's 2012 National Action Plan, which advocates coordinated cooperation of federal, provincial, municipal, and international policing agencies in combating human trafficking. Canada's 2012 National Action Plan mandated the creation of "a dedicated integrated team, led by the RCMP, to undertake proactive human trafficking investigations. This will be the first integrated team in Canada to focus on all types of trafficking, and will be complemented and supported by the Canada Border Services Agency, and a criminal intelligence analyst. Municipal and/or provincial police forces will be invited to participate" (Public Safety Canada 2012, 18). The dedicated integrated team known as the Human Trafficking Taskforce (the Taskforce) combines the efforts of the RCMP, the Canadian Border Services Agency (CBSA), and others.[2] This emphasis on the coordination and cooperation of various levels of police across Canada and other federal organizations written into the 2012 Action Plan was also consistent with the directives in the 2016 UN Global Report on Trafficking in Persons. According to this report, international and local law enforcement cooperation are central to finding and stopping human trafficking (2016a, 1). Indeed, the 2018 House of Common's Report of the Standing Committee on Justice and Human Rights notes that "justice is a matter of shared jurisdiction and ... human trafficking needs to be tackled by all levels of government" (2018, 6).

To uphold this narrative of cooperation, notable efforts are made by police forces. One of the ways this is achieved is through raid-and-rescue operations carried out via seemingly collaborative efforts by numerous police forces and headed by provincial police forces, such as the Ontario Provincial Police (OPP) and/or federal police forces, including the RCMP and the CBSA. These raid-and-rescue efforts are widely reported on by media and in subsequent government reports on Canada's anti-trafficking efforts. For instance in 2015, the OPP the RCMP, and forty other police services across Canada carried out a raid-and-rescue operation entitled Operation Northern Spotlight (Herhalt, 22 October 2015) in forty-five cities across Canada (Public Safety Canada 2016, 15). In 2016, another raid was carried out under the same name involving the RCMP and fifty-three police services in nine provinces "in a cross-country effort to crack down on human trafficking" (*The Canadian Press*, 18 October 2016). In 2017, the RCMP reported on Operation Northern Spotlight VI, which took place between 11 and 15 October 2017 and involved fifty-seven policing agencies across Canada, while similar operations were taking place in Europe, the United States, and Asia at the same time. More recently, OPPs Anti-Human Trafficking Investigation Coordination Team, together with twelve other police forces, including Sudbury, Belleville, Durham, Halton, Hamilton, Kingston, London, Ottawa, Peterborough, Sarnia, Waterloo, and York Regional Police, carried out a raid entitled Project Crediton (Zangouei 2020). These raids are an effort to demonstrate police actions as a part of a sophisticated anti-trafficking policing network akin to a highly organized military operation.

Yet the raid and rescue operations carried out for grand demonstration of police cooperation have significant negative consequences for sex workers, migrants, and racialized communities (Canadian Alliance for Sex Work Law Reform 2018; Lam and Lepp 2019; Moore Kloss & Roots, 2022; SWAN Vancouver Brief to the Standing Committee on Justice and Human Rights on Human Trafficking March 19, 2018). For one, the raids conflate sex work and human trafficking and result in the harassment, surveillance, and criminalization of actors in the sex trade industry. And while the raids are conducted under the guise of finding victims of trafficking, they often end up criminalizing the very same people the police claim to be helping. As O'Doherty et al. (2018) explain, "rescue" operations have significant negative impacts on sex workers, including closure of licensed establishments forcing workers to move their services to unlicenced establishments that are less safe and more difficult to access. The raids also have health and safety consequences, as sex workers are hesitant to have large quantities of condoms with them in case of a raid (O'Doherty et al. 2018). These are only some of the harms that are suffered by sex worker, migrant, and racialized communities as a result of these raid-and-rescue operations.

In the course of carrying out anti-trafficking raids, police forces also engage with the Canadian Border Services Agency (CBSA), informing them of migrant (mostly) women who work in the sex trade and subsequently causing their deportation and/or criminalization. For instance, in 2015 Ottawa police carried out a "human trafficking investigation," raiding commercial massage parlours and body-rub facilities. While the raid was carried out with the intention of finding human trafficking victims, none were found. However, the CBSA did detain and deport eleven migrant women working in the sex trade (MacKenzie and Clancey 2020; Roots and De Shalit 2015). According to a report by Butterfly: Asian and Migrant Sex Workers Support Network: "Asian migrant sex workers are perceived to be at risk of abuse from their 'traffickers,' who are often in fact their colleagues, partners, or friends. In fact, Asian migrant sex workers who are being targeted through these policies are rarely (and based on current data, never) trafficking victims, and become at risk through these anti-trafficking policies which allow them to be exploited, locked up, abused, and violated by law enforcement officers" (Lam 2018, 3). Migrant sex workers are often deported for "their own safety" and/or criminalized for violating the law since they are not permitted to sell sex (Lam and Gallant 2018). Those who collaborate with, assist, or support migrant sex workers in any capacity are criminalized as human traffickers (Lam and Lepp 2019). As such, the raid-and-rescue operations carried out by police services across the country under the guise of combating human trafficking have significant harmful consequences for marginalized and particularly sex-working communities.

Despite these harms, the raid-and-rescue operations demonstrate that there is "cooperation" among police services, which local forces appreciate. Yet on the ground, this cooperation does not materialize into anything significant. For instance, federal police agencies seem to play a rather peripheral role in anti-trafficking efforts on the ground. As explained by one municipal police officer:

> Federally, the RCMP don't have a human trafficking team per se. They have a team out in Quebec that is somewhat like a major crime squad that deal with human trafficking but I don't know how much work they've really done. We have a coordination centre, the RCMP has a coordination centre, we talk to them every day. They have one officer and they have one analyst. They're the best. They deal with all of the cyber tips. There are cyber tips that come from across Canada and the States, and they coordinate that information and then disseminate that information to where the crime is being committed. We get them all the time.
>
> (participant 1)

An ideological emphasis on international, national, and regional cooperation thus translates differently in practice. While grand demonstrations of police anti-trafficking efforts tend to capture the attention of the media and serve well in reports on Canada's anti-trafficking efforts, the majority of anti-trafficking efforts are carried out by specialized human trafficking teams operating relatively independently within municipal police forces.

Specialized Units

Human trafficking is a crime that is treated proactively by the police. "Proactive" policing means that dedicated officers do not just wait for "cybertips" from an international coordinating body to guide their activities; instead, they go looking for evidence of trafficking. This is captured by the comment of a police officer from an anti-trafficking police unit: "the reality is this problem has been here for a long time. You talk to individuals who have been in this line of investigation for years and years and this problem hasn't escalated. The frequency hasn't changed…. [T]he only difference was, whenever you deploy resources and money at a problem, you will find results" (participant 3). Another police officer explained that the problem of trafficking requires proactive efforts: "If you want to tackle this, you can't do it with four people. I was trained that you have to be more proactive so you have to do surveillance on people. More search warrants. You have to have boots on the ground. We've got to talk to these girls. We've got to know how to interview these girls. It encompasses everything, that of all my experience. We have to throw everything at it to see if we can do a better job" (participant 1). The same officer suggested that previously existing policing units that dealt with human trafficking were inadequate because in the old system: "you can only react, you can't be proactive." In the new organizational structure, officers can be more proactive by conducting mobile surveillance, checking social media sites, among other things (participant 1). The importance of proactive policing is summed up by the comments of another police officer: "you can't wait for a girl to come and report it. It's not a crime where somebody breaks into your house and you call the police to come and investigate. It's a crime that's happening and if you don't look for it, you're not going to get it" (participant 2). The formation of these specialized human trafficking units is in some sense, then, a solution looking for a problem.

Specialized anti–human trafficking police units have been formed in municipal police forces across Canada, and it is these localized units that have been responsible for the majority of domestic trafficking charges to date. At the time of writing in 2021, specialized anti-trafficking policing units exist in Toronto, Peel Region, York Region, Durham Region, Ottawa, Winnipeg, Calgary, and London, while other municipal police forces, such as Vancouver and Edmonton, house them in their vice units (see also Roots 2019). As noted in the Introduction, more specialized units are expected following the significant investment of the Ontario government into anti-trafficking. The specialized units are largely responsible for the increase in domestic human trafficking charges and arrests in recent years. This is in part because, according to the National Action Plan, the local police, along with the RCMP and the CBSA, have a "mandate to conduct proactive human trafficking investigations" (Public Safety Canada 2012, 18; see also US Department of State 2010). The need for proactivity was reflected as early as 2005 in a combined report by University College of Fraser Valley, the Royal Canadian Mounted Police, the UN Office of Drugs and Crime, and the International Centre for Criminal Law Reform & Criminal Justice Policy entitled "Human Trafficking: Reference Guide to Canadian Law Enforcement" (2005), which noted that when it comes to human trafficking investigations, "a proactive approach is often required" (University of Fraser Valley 2005, 23). Indeed, proactivity in identifying victims of trafficking is deemed by the US Department of State (2010) as one of the qualifying factors for countries to obtain a Tier One ranking. Failure to do so may have significant consequences.

To demonstrate proactivity, municipal anti-trafficking policing units at times carry out investigative operations independent of other policing agencies. For instance, in a 2015 operation entitled Project Guardian, Toronto police carried out thirteen raids (680 News 2015). And in April 2017, *Global News* reported that York Regional Police "arrested

104 men for attempting to have sex with children forced into prostitution, following a four-year undercover human trafficking investigation in which 85 underage victims were found and 49 pimps charged in York Region since 2012" (Miller and Shum 2017). And if you look, you will find. As a defence attorney I interviewed explains, "now that they have specialized police departments or teams for police forces who are only investigating human trafficking so you're going to see more human trafficking charges. That's the biggest reason that you weren't seeing it before. It's cause the police weren't looking for it" (participant 10).[3] Similarly, an interviewed Crown attorney explains the recent increase in human trafficking arrests as a product of "the establishment of a squad, not only in Toronto and the GTA [the Greater Toronto Area], like they're in York Region and other regions.... [T]he advent of that is helpful" (participant 15),[4] while a police officer confirms that the increase in trafficking charges is "because [the specialized team was] formed two years ago" (participant 4).

Reactive investigations, according to an RCMP report on trafficking from 2010, are limiting since they are dependent on the cooperation of suspected victims and fail to "examine the criminal operations of facilitators involved in the exploitation of the victim" (40). Presumably the solution to the problem of police dependence on victim cooperation and the difficulties of finding large-scale trafficking operations, then, is police proactiveness. Proactive policing has become a part of the trafficking matrix as an anti-trafficking policing strategy and has led to the production of a new crime category which justifies the very existence of the specialized units tasked with proactively policing it in the first place.

As noted in the Introduction, significant resources have been allocated to anti-trafficking policing efforts from various levels of government. Increasing the federal funding for anti-trafficking policing efforts was one of the recommendations of the Standing Committee on the Status of Women Canada's report on human trafficking in 2007. The justification for more resources provided by police officers to the committee was the complexity of (presumably transnational) human trafficking cases. As the officers explained, trafficking investigations involve aspects such as the potential need of investigators to travel to the victim's country of origin and cooperation between various levels of government due to the movement component of trafficking, among other similarly costly factors (2007, 43). Yet, despite these arguments about costly international engagements, the funding recipients tend to target domestic small-scale "pimping" offences, which are not nearly as complex or geographically expansive as the committee was led to believe, nor are they transnational in nature.

The generous funding allocated to anti-trafficking efforts has also created a competition for resources, resulting in more divisive, non-collaborative, and self-interested police departments. Competition for funding means that, despite the calls for multijurisdictional cooperation, police forces watch each other carefully for key performance indicators, such as raids and arrests, and view the statistics produced by different local units as suspicious. As one police officer explains: "a question that was posed to me in 2008, *how come [name of police force] are arresting all these guys, is it not happening in our region?*" (participant 2; emphasis added). Another officer recalls a conversation he had with the chief of his police force, who expressed a desire for his force to be "leaders in this [human trafficking] field" (participant 1). A third officer notes, "There's a lot of grants that float around. As to who gets the grants and what it's going to be used for, sometimes there's competing forces who are trying to get those grants and who's going to manage money.... I guess it would be dishonest to think that [municipality] would not have a stake into that provincial strategy and how much we would get out of that. So, I could see a lot of services that didn't have human trafficking investigators come up with them so they would get some money" (participant 3). The questions raised by the officer regarding who gets the grants and whether police services indeed introduce human trafficking investigators with the motivation of obtaining more funding cannot be confirmed since reasons for funding decisions are not made public. However, based on the Ontario government's emphasis on the need for more specialized anti-trafficking policing units, we can infer that there is some truth to this suggestion (Government of Ontario 2020). And despite the emphasis on cooperation in official rhetoric of the UN, Canadian and provincial governments, and the collaborative raid-and-rescue operations well covered by media outlets, interviews with anti-trafficking police reveal a certain competitiveness between police forces for funding and the desire for each to be the leader in anti-trafficking operations.

Trafficking arrest rates are a key variable in the competition between police forces for funding. The more arrests a police service has, the more likely they are to receive funding. To demonstrate the prevalence of human trafficking in their jurisdiction, one police service in Ontario began collecting statistics, explaining that "one of the biggest assets I had was I started collecting stats. I needed to show the chief and my boss that this [human trafficking] was an actual problem here in [location x]" (participant 1). Other officers identified more direct pressure to arrest and charge accused with trafficking offences, explaining "*my boss essentially said, I don't care what you do, bring us some pimps and trafficking arrests*" (participant 2; emphasis added). The relevance of this pressure in motivating anti-trafficking policing is confirmed by another officer, who commented that "obviously, there's the measurement tool of how many people you arrest or how many people have you helped successfully get out of the sex trade" (participant 3). Thus, capturing the trafficker and "saving" the victim justifies the very existence of the anti-trafficking units. As Foucault notes, "fabricating delinquency" gave the criminal justice system an object to focus on, bringing it legitimacy and enabling it to "function on a general horizon of truth" (as cited in Rabinow 1984, 224).

The pressures to "find" trafficking cases and make arrests was felt by police as early as 2006 (shortly after the enactment of Canada's first federal anti-trafficking laws) and may be attributable to a number of factors, including the political context within which pressure from the international community, and most notably the United States, trickles down to the municipal police but also a need to justify increased funding for trafficking units, particularly at a time when police budgets are under scrutiny and/or in competition for further funding. This kind of "proactive" policing, however, often looks a lot like rounding up the usual suspects: the young, poor, and racialized men often involved in the sex trade in some way (see chapter five for a discussion).

Despite the pressure on anti-trafficking police to find trafficking cases, these specialized units nonetheless see themselves as elite squads whose expertise and know-how are in demand, and at times overwhelming. This is reflected in one officer's comments that the human trafficking unit, "is the busiest place I've ever worked. And I used to work at guns and gangs where we would break down a door every other day looking for guns. This is by far the busiest place" (participant 3). The demand on the time of these anti-trafficking officers comes, at least in part, from the expertise they are perceived to have on the issue of human trafficking, creating an impression of these units as an elite force with special status, whose knowledge and expertise are irreplaceable. As Reyhan Atasü-Topcuoglu contends, actors working within the anti-trafficking field compete for dominance, which allows them "more acceptance and more recognition" (2015, 23). The effort by these anti-trafficking police squads to earn a place as "experts" on human trafficking is clearly evident. As one police officer explains the process: "the division will respond to a radio call and a victim would present themselves. During that preliminary investigation they disclose being a victim of human trafficking. They [the attending officers] call us whether we're working or not. If we're not working, we go out, we have guys who are on call. What they'll do is they'll go from their home into the division and take over the investigation" (participant 3). Front-line patrol officers are, therefore, seen as unqualified to deal with a human trafficking situation, requiring a call-out for an expert in the field. This "expertise" comes with a sense of importance, whereby the suggestion is that those selected for human trafficking units must meet a higher standard. As one officer explains it, "you can't have crusty people doing human trafficking investigations looking at these girls saying derogative things" (participant 2). The seeming specialness of these officers is further captured by another comment of the same officer: "you have to have a dedicated human trafficking team. I can grab another organized crime enforcement team to supplement and to assist but I need my specialists, the expert guys there" (participant 2). The superiority of the human trafficking team thus largely stems from the expertise of the elite and carefully selected officers.

Technological knowledge required to investigate and uncover trafficking cases contributes to the perception of expertise among specialized trafficking squads. Technology, which is used by sex workers to advertise services, screen clients, share information with others in their profession, and conduct online banking (Blunt and Wolf 2020; Musto 2016; Musto et al. 2020; Tichenor 2020), is unsurprisingly seen as playing a big part in facilitating human trafficking. According to the UNGift report entitled "Technology and Human Trafficking," "Trafficking in persons requires extensive coordination throughout the process of planning, recruiting victims, transporting them, meeting and transferring people at various times and locations; it is, therefore, likely that criminals are using new technologies or old technologies in more complex ways to facilitate their communications and avoid detection. It is not known whether the use of new technologies has increased trafficking in persons, but it is believed that increased use of technologies has made trafficking activities easier to perform" (2008a, 3). The centrality of technology in trafficking investigations was also confirmed by this research. As one anti-trafficking officer explained, technology is "extremely important, 'cause we're dealing with cell phones, we're dealing with the different [web]sites these girls are on, we're dealing with technology pretty much with every case we deal with so it's extremely important" (participant 4). Another officer confirms that "technology is everything because all of this is done over the internet. It's all technology based. All of the texting is done phone to phone, computer to phone, computer to computer … The advertisements that are posted on Backpages[5] or other internet sites" (participant 1). This finding was also made by Mitall Thakor and danah boyd (2013) in the context of the United States. Many anti-trafficking experts they spoke with "were overwhelmed with anxieties over a seemingly technologically enhanced network of traffickers," which would "foster connectivity and speed of connection among potential exploiters that gives the network of traffickers heightened confluence" (2013, 287).

Police ability to detect and intervene in these technology-enhanced operations is considered of utmost importance, as explained by one officer: "some of these guys, when they are on the phone, like if we seize it, they have the technology sometimes to delete everything so that's why we have to grab the phone quickly and turn it off" (participant 4). In the case of *R. v. Byron* (2014), we also see a heavy reliance by the Crown on evidence produced through technology, including text messages between the accused and the complainant, hotel records, Facebook conversations, and advertisements of the services offered by the complainant on Backpages.com. As the Crown in this case notes, "the police assembled the escort ads, the cell phone records and the hotel records to demonstrate where they [the accused and complainant] went and when" (*R. v. Byron*, audio of trial, 6 May 2013). Technology was thus central in police ability to build a case against Byron.

Given that technology-based evidence presents such a significant component of trafficking investigations and in order to adequately deal with what the police suggest are sophisticated technological aspects of the crime, anti-trafficking police receive specialized training: "This is the stuff that all my team members are trained on. They have to be trained on. Cause that technology evolves every month. It's incredible how technology [snaps fingers] you know one day it's here the next day it's something totally different … so, it's very important for us to have the tools to assist us in investigating these types of crimes" (participant 1). In addition to training, the police in anti-trafficking units also "talk to computer companies all the time for tools" (participant 1). The specialized expertise and technological know-how embedded into the human trafficking matrix and seen as required in order for police to combat human trafficking contributes to the notion of these anti-trafficking units as specialized teams with expert knowledge on the issue.

The officers' knowledge of human trafficking is deemed as expert not only by the officers themselves but also by courts. As one Crown attorney adds, "I find that the specialized squad has a very good knowledge base about what constitutes human trafficking. They read the case law. Like, you know, these officers are very focused on human trafficking, so I find that they are very knowledgeable about the area" (participant 15). In the context of police expertise in courts, one police officer explains that: "we weren't experts in this at the beginning, you know, but I can tell you that they're [specialized human trafficking officers] trained now as experts and they actually testify in court as experts. They've been deemed experts by certain courts in the province of Ontario, which is great. That's what we need…. [W]e need human trafficking experts" (participant 1). This expert knowledge and police status as the expert knowers gives officers the authority to transform sex workers into human trafficking victims, as captured by the comment of one officer: "at the end of the day, people still think a hooker is a hooker. They do! … and that's why we need experts to tell them…. [W]e need investigators to be experts, so they can explain the whole area to them. So, we've become a lot better at that in court now" (participant 1).[6] Thus, the officers' ability to redeem "hookers" as victims of trafficking is understood as requiring specialized knowledge only possessed by a few experts.

The *R. v. Brighton* (2016) case supports this perspective. In this case, the judge accepts and sees value in the expertise of Detective Thai Truong from the York Regional Police anti-trafficking unit on the topic:

> Truong's evidence provides context, background and terminology used by the different players in the prostitution milieu. Truong is able to assist the jury in understanding methods of advertising, and how 'Backpage', the pornographic website on which ads involving the complainant were placed, works. Truong's evidence explains methods employed by pimps in grooming and recruiting women into prostitution. It provides information regarding the types of women whom exploiters seek to recruit. It explains the dynamics between exploiters and prostitutes within the prostitution subculture, especially with respect to control issues, business issues and the money relationship. It also offers significant insight into the conduct of prostitutes in their dealings with exploiters and the police.
>
> (para. 33–4)

In particular, the judge draws a distinction between lay knowledge of sex work and the "expert" knowledge of police in the field: "While lay people may have some popular and uninformed knowledge and opinions about pimps and their relationship to prostitutes, the task of the jury in this case will require the informed understanding that they can only gain through the assistance of the detail and comprehensiveness of the expert evidence. In addition, the complainant in this case is, or was, a prostitute, a figure that may not command much compassion or understanding from a lay person. Truong's opinion in the delineated area is absolutely essential for the jury to do its job properly" (*R. v. Brighton* 2016, para. 37). In this instance, the court upheld the view that police not only understood the intricacies of the (exploitative) sex trade better than a lay person but also had greater compassion and caring for the ostensibly trafficked individual, whose victimization may not be recognized by an ordinary person. This raises questions about how police know what they know about human trafficking.

The participants in my study admitted that they began their specialized work with little knowledge of human trafficking. As one officer explained, when he initially joined the human trafficking unit, "there was nothing [in terms of knowledge on the offence]. I was like, this is fucking terrible, no one knows what's going on here. We've come a long way." There was also "no formal training on human trafficking. There was none"[7] (participant 2; see also Farrell et al. 2015). To round out the little information they were given through official circuits, they turned to other sources of information, and in particular to popular culture, which some officers used as "historical" knowledge. For example, participant 2 explained his own "homework" trajectory: "*I didn't know nothing about it [human trafficking]. So I read a book ... "Somebody's Daughter"....* [T]hat book takes place in the early 90s, late 80s. It's basically about the Toronto, Halifax pimping ring back then ... I read that book that he read [his boss], and thought, holy, this stuff is happening from back then and we're not doing anything about it? So, I went almost immediately and we started changing the way we did things" (participant 2; emphasis added).[8] The book, described by the officer in the above quote as a source of knowledge about human trafficking, is called *Somebody's Daughter: Inside the Toronto/Halifax Pimping Ring* (1996), written by journalist Phonse Jessome. The book has been criticized by scholars like Leslie Ann Jeffrey and Gayle MacDonald for "fictionalizing parts of the story and creating some characters to make the storyline more readable (and dramatic). Fact blends with fiction throughout to create a melodramatic story of innocent victims and evil predators" (2006, 160). As one sex worker interviewed by Jeffrey and MacDonald explained, the book "presented a lopsided view of prostitution and, in the end, such an approach fails to address the real issues" (2006, 160). That the convenience of the melodramatic arc blending fact and fiction serve as the source of knowledge for official responses and have become a part of the trafficking matrix is worrying to say the least, but it is not the first time in history that this has happened around the issue of trafficking. To fuel the white slavery panics during the nineteenth century, William Stead, an investigative journalist much like Phonse Jessome, wrote a series of particularly sensationalized accounts of the prevalence of white slavery in Europe, including an article entitled "Maiden's Tribute to Modern Babylon." The articles described in sensationalized terms the ways in which hundreds of young and innocent British girls were being forced into the sex trade across Europe. While Stead was indifferent about the factual validity of the articles he wrote, focusing instead on the construction of melodramatic narratives, his work had a substantial impact on pushing the white slavery campaigns forward and was soon followed by white slavery legislation in Britain (Doezema 2010).

To learn more about the issue of trafficking, the above participant read "reports, studies, blogs, internet stuff … [p]imping books, breaking down hip-hop culture, listening to lyrics, understanding what they're saying. Realizing that it's [knowledge on human trafficking] embedded in popular culture today"[9] (participant 2). So, why would the officers turn to hip-hop music to understand the issue of human trafficking, and what does this tell us? While the racialized effects of this knowledge production are deconstructed in chapter five, here it is worth briefly exploring about how those assumptions have seeped into the ways human trafficking is constructed in the first place.

In the public imaginary, hip-hop music and culture are often seen as outward manifestations of what bell hooks calls "outlaw culture" that is linked with the perceived dangerousness of Black people (Fatsis 2019, 447). Policing Black music, then, has been a way to police Black people, which reveals deep-seated cultural stereotypes of Black people as "'different separate and incomprehensible' to the police and threats to the White community" (ibid., 450). The merging of Black culture and criminality within the human trafficking matrix, revealed by the officer's quote above (and as detailed in chapter five) shows not only the policing of Black communities through linking of their cultural symbols with criminality but also reminds us of the cultural process through which some acts are made into "crime" and some people into "criminals." This linking of Black culture with criminality, and in this case specifically human trafficking, demonstrates the ways in which police produce racialized knowledge about who or what is a criminal, bringing Black culture into the human trafficking matrix and making listening to hip-hop music or engaging in expressions of Black culture suspect activities in the eyes of the police and the public (Nielson 2019).

The meaning of human trafficking produced by police is disseminated through public education, a mandate also prioritized by the 2012 as well as 2019–24 National Action Plan to Combat Human Trafficking. As one officer contends, "education is our biggest tool. Knowledge. The more people know about this the better off we are. That's one of the key components with us, we do a lot of presentations to a lot of groups, we are now approaching colleges to see if we can teach in their hospitality industry courses so they know. Knowledge is a great tool to have" (participant 1). Media is an important avenue through which this knowledge is disseminated, as explained by an anti-trafficking officer: "we need the media. The media is a great tool for us. They assist us in our investigations immensely. We get further victims, we get things like the guns, it assists us in our investigations. So, they're great, they call us all the time. We have a great relationship with them" (participant 1). The relationship between the police and the media is reciprocal, as the media appears to favour reporting on human trafficking cases, which, in turn, feeds the populist narrative about what human trafficking is. As Chermak and Weiss explain, police organizations are in a constant struggle to maintain their legitimacy. The media helps the police maintain this legitimacy by enabling police organizations to "manipulate and manage their external environment," including importantly public emotions (2005, 502). As such, police rely on powerful actors that work within their environment to disseminate some and block other information (ibid.). In the context of trafficking, we see this through the stories reported by the media, which are driven by stereotyped narratives of young victims duped into exploitation through persuasion/ their craving for either love or material goods, coercion, addiction to drugs, among other things. These young and innocent victims – Canada's daughters – are depicted as unable to escape the nightmare of their existence and in need of heroes to rescue them. The stories often end with a happy return of the victims to their families, with nothing but gratitude and remorse in the end. The support for such media stories is shown by one interviewed officer: "I personally have not seen anything negative come from the media when we, for example, do press releases because it's pretty heart wrenching, this crime. Especially when they see the victims, how old the victims are, what they are made to do, what they are forced to do, what they endured" (participant 5). The narratives are contrasted with racial stereotypes of white victims – the daughters of Canadian families, the "girl next door" being victimized by Black "pimps" – and are firmly present in several investigative pieces which create an urgent and emotionally driven story of the horrors of trafficking while simultaneously constructing police officers as heroes who rescue victims (see Carville 2015a; 2015b; 2015c; Quinn and Crib 2013).

In addition to the media, police also disseminate information to other criminal justice actors. It is the officers in these specialized human trafficking squads that educate others on trafficking. As one police officer proudly announced, two of the officers in his unit "actually run the [human trafficking] course at the Canadian Police College," and "that's what I've been doing for the last two to three years, is education" (participant 1). The training, however, is not only given to those in the criminal justice system and/or working with the issue directly; it is extended widely to include the hospitality industry, the education system, health care, social services, and NGOs (non-governmental organization) (De Shalit 2021) responsibilizing these actors to be on the lookout for signs of trafficking and to report back to the police. According to David Garland, "the attempt to extend the reach of state agencies by linking them up with the practices of actors in the 'private sector' and 'the community' might be described as a responsibilization strategy…. The intended result is an enhanced network of more or less directed, more or less informal crime control, complementing and extending the formal controls of the criminal justice state" (2001, 124). In this way, while local anti-trafficking policing units do not appear to be collaborating as effectively with other policing units as mandates and policies would have us believe, they do form partnerships and collaborative relationships with organizations in other industries. The information being disseminated by police through these avenues is crucial as it becomes an important part of the human trafficking matrix, shaping the definitions, indicators, and characteristics of trafficking that are used by the public to determine the situations that warrant police attention.

The dissemination of information on human trafficking through media and other avenues expands state surveillance and police reach and is, as David Garland (2001) explains, the simplest and fastest way to engage the public in crime prevention by raising public consciousness. The motivation to do just that is captured in a Report of the Standing Committee on Justice and Human Rights on Canada's anti-trafficking efforts: "raising awareness [on human trafficking] allows more people to be 'the eyes and ears' required to prevent human trafficking from occurring" (2018, 29). These efforts appear to be effective since police describe public eagerness to report suspected cases of human trafficking. Interviewed officers reveal that many of their calls on potential trafficking cases come from the public "because of the news. Because we're putting out a press release every day, so people become more aware of it. We're educating officers, we're educating Crowns and so forth, and judges, and educating the public. Because they know this now, they call the police, and in turn we investigate" (participant 4). By this account, press releases on police raid-and-rescue operations, as well as news articles on human trafficking arrests have a notable impact on public perceptions around the prevalence of trafficking and create vigilance around the issue. Public awareness is also increased by numerous awareness campaigns that have emerged in recent years. One such example is a campaigned launched in 2020 by Covenant House Toronto and Toronto Police Service called #Shoppable Girls. The campaign depicts images of young women as products to be purchased, with captions such as "shop this season's most unsettling collection today" and "some things shouldn't be for sale" (Covenant House Toronto 2020). The physical manifestation of this campaign includes images of young women as items displayed on storefronts at a popular shopping destination on Queen Street in downtown Toronto. Posters depicting the same were also displayed in Toronto's subway system. The goal here is to train the public to hold expertise in signs of trafficking and to report or avoid them (De Shalit 2021, 11; see also Roots and Lockhart 2021). Seemingly these strategies work, as interviews with police reveal that most trafficking cases are brought to the police by concerned citizens, including parents of young people who have gone missing, anonymous tips, and sometimes complainants who come in contact with the police for other reasons, but also hotel staff, social service workers, and NGOs, among others.

To encourage even more public cooperation and victims to come forward, the federal government provided Public Safety Canada with $14.51 million over five years and an additional $2.89 million annually after that to fund a human trafficking hotline that began operations in 2019 (House of Commons 2018, 13). This hotline enables the public to report their suspicions of human trafficking over the phone 24/7 or through a website. Tips received from the hotline are then forwarded to the police for vetting and investigation. The related website encourages the public, service providers, and victims of trafficking to get in touch to share information and get help, if needed. The Human Trafficking Hotline, then, acts as a significant source of information and tips for the police. To this end, as Ann De Shalit concludes, "the public performs security and crime fighting functions through which it can become a productive gatekeeper" (2021, 214).

These "public education" campaigns, however, may be leading to hyper-vigilance, with people too often assuming that human trafficking is taking place. In response to a question on how frequently a reported case turns out not to be human trafficking, one police officer replied, "often it is, especially a lot of the girls that go missing. A lot of the parents automatically think it's trafficking, but we'll do some research. Some of the girls may be on Backpage. It all depends on their age as well, cause we'll get some people, they wanna do it, therefore it's not trafficking" (participant 4). Such hypervigilance increases the caseload for human trafficking units and contributes to the perception that trafficking is prevalent, as reflected in an officer's statement:

Since we did that [educate the public], oh my goodness. We're getting calls all the time. Which is great, cause that's what we wanted. We've had a couple of cases now where it's worked out. But it's a lot of work. Like I said, there's hundreds of hotels and motels in the city of [name]. We get calls all the time now. But it's a good thing because you know, it might be that one time you call, will be the only time we can intervene with that girl. So, call us, that's why we're here. It's not us that will go, we'll get uniformed officers to go first and see what's going on and if something pans out we go in and investigate. But that's what we're doing. It's education.

(participant 1)

Police efforts to educate other criminal justice actors, relevant industries and organizations, and the public through media reports and awareness campaigns to identify and report signs of trafficking should give us pause in light of what this research shows about the source of police knowledge on human trafficking. Police labelling of highly racialized factors, such as hip-hop culture as indicators of trafficking, among other things racializes the crime of trafficking and directs the public and relevant industry workers to be on the lookout for "suspicious" Black men.

In addition to partnerships with businesses and news media, police information also comes from community agencies. These community agencies (e.g., NGOs, shelters) play a significant role in anti-trafficking efforts by taking over witness care but also convincing women and girls to report the offence to the police as well as helping to prepare them for court (De Shalit 2021; Kaye 2017; Lester at al. 2017; Musto 2010; 2016). This multilayered role is reflected by police officer responses: "we do have a really close connection with [name of shelter] because they deal with human trafficking, they have beds for human trafficking. [Name of person] helps us. She's in charge of the program because we remove our girls, they don't have a place to go so she's the first person we contact. We also have [name of shelter] and Victim Services" (participant 4). The importance of community agencies in assisting women and girls suspected of being victims of trafficking is also reflected in the response of another officer: "Something else we also utilize which I think is great: some of our girls especially if they used drugs, we send them to different places in the country. For example, some of them can go to B.C. We can't necessarily let you know what the program is called because it's a safe house. Some of them go to detox out there, and they enter in this human trafficking recovery center where they can deal with the physical and psychological impacts" (participant 5). In addition to the care work, community agencies also encourage those who come to them to go to the police. As one officer explains it: "we also get them [complainants] from our non-government organization agencies if there's some victims that aren't prepared to go to the police right away and they'll go to the [name of shelter] or some other support network group. Once they get the strength and confidence and the willingness to come forward, they'll call us and we'll meet with them and go from there" (participant 3). After the complainants agree to testify, community agencies help ensure they do not back out of testifying: "I think a big portion of our success is that we've been able to partner up with some great community partners like [name of shelter], [name of shelter #2], [name of shelter #3] victim services. And, we've been able to now get all the assistance for our victims. Because we've now been able to get those services right from the start, right from when we speak with the girl, it's helped us immensely in court" (participant 1). These responses demonstrate the important role played by community agencies in the care of complainants but also in assisting the police to find, investigate, arrest, and successfully prosecute traffickers. In the context of anti-trafficking efforts in Vancouver, Julie Kaye (2017) found similar collaboration and indeed reliance of police on the support of community agencies (see also De Shalit 2021).

Victim protection is the second of five pillars set out by Canada's National Action Plan to Combat Human Trafficking (2012; 2019–24). As my interviews reveal, police take this goal seriously and have a passion for what they do. For instance, in response to a question on the most rewarding aspect of his job, one officer replied, "Dealing with the victims. Cause when they write you a letter, a heartfelt letter saying 'thank you, you saved my life', it sits with you" (participant 3). The same officer further suggests he would measure his own job performance through the interactions he has with complainants: "I would measure my successes on my interactions with my victims and my complainants. So, are they satisfied with the services they are receiving? Do they feel comfortable with proceeding to the next stages of the prosecution? Do they feel comfortable making further disclosures? So, I think that's how I'd measure it, in terms of how they feel on the other side of the table, as to the service we've provided them" (participant 3). Another interview participant stated,

In this work, you're here because you have a passion for it. So, you're not going to fail in any regard really. At the end of the day, I have a fourteen-year-old daughter and one of my biggest motivations for me is that this could happen to my daughter.... So that's a big motivational factor for me, is that I need to protect my daughter. I see these girls at their ages and I think, wow they could be my daughter and thank God me and my wife have a good relationship with my daughter and with my son. We talk and we have – it is a good relationship. But there are girls out there who don't have that with their parents, which is sad.... So, I see these girls and

I equate it to my daughter and I'm thinking, they need help. If I can just help one of them, I've done my job.

(participant 1)

Interestingly, while all male police officers interviewed discussed their job-related motivation in the context of "protecting their families," this was not evident with female officers, who made no mention of their families. The male officers' need to protect their families is a part of "the logic of masculinist protection," which "constitutes the 'good men' as those who protect their women and children in relation to other 'bad' men" (Young 2003, 227; see also Glasbeek 2006). Such protectionism extends further than individual law enforcement officers' desire to protect their own, private, families and takes on the sentiments of Canadian nationalism and the need to protect Canada itself through protection of its women and children. As Elya Durisin explains: "Expressions of Canadian nationalism are interconnected with the politics of sex trafficking: the linking of subaltern masculinities with violence against women in the figure of the trafficker and sex purchaser, and the articulation of a Canadian masculinity embodied in the figure of the gender egalitarian national subject who protects women" (2017, 39). The logic of masculine protectionism serves as a powerful motivator for individual officers within these anti-trafficking units and is central to the white saviour role assumed by police.

The term "white saviour" was developed to critique the short-term humanitarian efforts of Westerners that serve to fulfil the emotional needs and guilt of white people (Cole 2012; Jefferess 2021). The naïve and harmful efforts of these white saviours result in dichotomizing expressions of humanitarian care that construct racialized people as unable to care for themselves and, as Kamala Kempadoo (2015) explains, placing the burden of saving them on the white man. The historic and geopolitical context of what Teju Cole called the "white saviour industrial complex" includes not only the "spectacle of the sufferer" but also the complex structures that produce these conditions in the first place, including the programs imposed by the International Monetary Fund that economically devastated many African countries and the purposely harmful US foreign policy (Jefferess 2021). The white saviour industrial complex, then, is a way to release the built-up pressure from these harms through occasional contributions by do-gooders (ibid.). In the context of human trafficking, the white saviour role was taken on by state and non-state agents in the past in an effort to save the racialized victim of the Global South from traffickers (Hua 2011; Hua and Nigorizawa 2010; Kempadoo 2015; Soderlund 2005). In more recent years, as discussed in chapter two, the object of saving has shifted to the domestic victim – both racialized and white (see also Baker 2018). In this context, anti-trafficking police take the lead as the white saviours and are supported and accompanied by NGOs, activists, politicians, industry workers, and vigilant citizens.

The well-intentioned activities of white humanitarianist do-gooders, as Cole (2012) explains, are meant to fulfil an emotional need that prioritizes enthusiasm over utility and efficacy. As with humanitarian volunteers hoping to "Save Africa" (Jefferess 2021), I found the police also to be emotionally invested in the cases they dealt with (and see, too, Lester et al. 2017). However, officers in my study tried to offload some of the emotional work to what one officer called "the huggers," who most commonly take the form of (predominantly female-staffed) community agency workers. My interviews with police officers suggest they see their time as better spent elsewhere and believe that care work should be delegated to those who specialize in it. This is captured by the comments of one officer:

> The reality is when we show up and talk to the victim on day one, we need to have another team of people who aren't police officers, who are social agencies. The guy who gives them housing, the one who's going to get you your ID back in a week, some of these girls, the pimp's taken their driver's license, their passport, they've got no ID. They're Aboriginal card, which is a big deal, it's how they identify themselves. So, we have those people that come with us and once we finish taking the statement and have given the evidence are introduced to this team of people who are the huggers and the loving kind, and they'll take them.
>
> (participant 3)

He further notes,

> Like I've taken girls to get an ultrasound. Not that I mind doing it but I'd rather use that time to put somebody else in jail. There's people out there who go to school for these things, who love that. You know what, let's employ these people who know what to do. Cause I love putting people in jail. I want some other people who love, to do what they love to do. So, you get people who are good at what they do. We're picking up girls who are all over the place and driving them to court things of that nature, that's resources that I can't afford to lose.
>
> (participant 3)

As the above quotes show, and in line with the discourse of masculine protectionism, specialized (male) anti-trafficking police see their role as

first and foremost protecting society from "bad guys" and rescuing victims, demonstrating the link between protectionism and carceral logics
that emphasize the need to imprison in order to protect. To protect the
vulnerable, specialized human trafficking police expressed a need to
catch, arrest, and prosecute perpetrators, as noted by another officer:
"I used to monitor sex offenders, what I do now is actually put them in
jail" (participant 4). Putting bad guys in jail therefore forms a part of the
masculine rescue script.

Investigating Trafficking Cases

Human trafficking charges laid by the police are often withdrawn or
stayed. According to the findings of this study, in fifty-five[10] out of
eighty-four (65 per cent) cases for which a disposition was available by
the conclusion of research time, trafficking charges were withdrawn,
stayed, or acquitted by a judge. These numbers suggest that police may
be over-eager when laying trafficking charges. The liberties taken by
the police with their broad discretion and eagerness to charge is conveyed by one officer's response, in which he attributes the high number
of withdrawn and stayed human trafficking charges to "a number of
reasons, like the complications with the victim's case, the quality of the
police investigation. I'm critical of ours, *a lot of police services just want to
lay a human trafficking charges but they don't go nowhere because they probably inappropriately did the investigation just to lay the charge*" (participant
2; emphasis added). This is also confirmed by a defence attorney who
noted that the police lay charges before they investigate human trafficking cases: "it's not supposed to be like that at all. You're supposed to
arrest only after you investigate" (participant 13).

In addition to overzealous charging practices, my case studies also
suggest that police engage in questionable investigation tactics and
intimidation of complainants and accused, likely attributable to the
pressure they feel to bring forth trafficking cases. In some cases,
police lied to the accused to try to cover up their lack of evidence and
in hope of gaining a confession. This occurred in *R. v. Dagg* (2015),
where the police asked the accused to take a lie detector test but then
disallowed him to take it after he agreed to it, telling him instead that
they had corroborating evidence. As the submission of the defence
counsel suggests, by challenging the accused with a polygraph test
which they were unwilling to administer and promising him that
the video [of the police interrogation] was off when it was not in
an effort to obtain information, the police engaged in what Ericson
calls trickery and deceit: "detectives can be compelling in their tactics

for gaining cooperation" and "many of the tactics they use are tacitly supported by the law of confession" in Canada (1983, 157). Dagg was acquitted of trafficking charges.

In other cases, the accused reported police harassment and efforts to frighten leading them to provide information they later denied. For example, in *R. v. Byron* (2014), the accused was pressured by the police to continue to answer questions despite his insistence that he did not want to talk. As the defence attorney argued in court, the accused made certain statements to the police "because of the fact that he is under pressure by the detective" (*R. v. Byron*, audio of trial, 17 May 2013). The Crown challenged this position, suggesting that "He [the accused] could not comment when the detective was pressuring him. But that's just what the police do. They are trying to investigate. And if he didn't want to talk to the police, [the accused] didn't have to lie" (*R. v. Byron*, audio of trial, 17 May 2013). Similar police pressure tactics were also seen in *R. v. Leung* (2015). Like in the Byron case, the Crown in Leung also highlighted the lies told by the accused during police questioning. The accused explained that he didn't want to just sit there 'cause he [the police officer] could have gotten angry. That's what usually happens with cops' (*R. v. Leung*, 2015, participant observation). It is important to note that all three of the accused mentioned above are racialized young men whose expressions of discomfort and fear around police must be understood in the context of broader concerns around police violence and brutality towards racialized communities, particularly racialized young men (Cole 2020; Maynard 2017; Tanovich 2006; Walker 2010; Wortley 1996).

When these more common-place tactics fail, police have sometimes even turned to falsified evidence. In *R. v. Salmon* (2011), this was cause for the conviction to be overturned on appeal.[11] In this case, the investigating officers testified in court that they had seized the complainant's fake ID from the accused's wallet – a fact which would be significant in demonstrating his control over the complainant. Yet, evidence later revealed that the ID was in the complainant's possession at the time of her contact with the police. In his written decision, the judge pointed out that the officer's erroneous testimony, that the complainant's ID had been in possession of the accused, resulted in four additional charges related to being in possession of a false identification (*R. v. [Courtney] Salmon* 2011, para. 139). The judge went on to say that: "The fact that the documents were apparently found in his possession added considerably to the Crown's case on the other counts. If the documents were in Mr. Salmon's possession, it would go some way to showing a connection between Mr. Salmon and the complainant. It would also go some way to showing that Mr. Salmon had a degree of control over the complainant" (*R. v. [Courtney] Salmon* 2011, para. 141). As the judge indicated, there was significant gain to be made on the case if the complainant's ID had been in the accused's possession. While this is not the first time the police have been found to have fabricated evidence, police motivation to do so in this case must be seen in the context of anti-trafficking regimes and the significant pressures placed on police to produce trafficking cases. While in the above outlined cases courts have fulfilled their role in maintaining checks and balances by dismissing charges brought through troubling police investigations, questions around prosecutions' decision to proceed with the charges despite problems with investigations and evidence remain. And, as I detail below, the very act of laying charges for a high-profile crime such as human trafficking, which is often accompanied by media coverage, has significant implications for the lives of the accused and those around them.

Police are at the forefront of defining crime. They identify the suspect and the victim and work to make that narrative stick. In a sense then, police "make" crime. As a part of "making crime," Ericson notes that police "coerce, manipulate and/or negotiate with victim-complainants and informants to achieve dispositions that meet police organizational criterial" (1983, 94). Once there is a possibility of apprehending a suspect, the task of the detective is then "one of convincing the victim-complainant that the outcome the detective decided upon was the appropriate one" (1983, 109). In the context of trafficking, criminal justice actors go to great lengths to convince (mostly) women and girls that they are indeed victims of trafficking. Interviews with criminal justice actors and analyses of trafficking trial proceedings reveal that the girls and women who are identified by the criminal justice system as victims are pressured and scripted by police so that they will stand up in court and perform as a victim. In many cases, this means they must first be convinced that they *are* a victim. As summed up by one interviewed officer, "if you have a victim who says she is consenting, you're not going to get a conviction. You need him or her to say they were taken against their will" (participant 9).

The police's need to convince women that they are victims is shaped by a number of factors, including police need to justify the existence of the specialized units, competition for funding and the fact that Canada's anti-trafficking efforts are largely measured by the number of trafficking convictions. As summed up succinctly by one police officer, "these girls are the crux of our investigation. Without that girl testifying, we're screwed. If they don't come and testify, we're never going to get a conviction" (participant 1). Yet getting cooperation from those labelled as victims is difficult. According to one criminal justice actor, "We know this is going on, it seems to be awfully difficult for the police to somehow investigate, get the witnesses, and get a prosecution. Cause the witnesses are so often damaged goods, damaged people, damaged young women" (participant 9). Police officers also understand the difficulty with obtaining trafficking convictions as stemming from unreliable witnesses: "with this [trafficking], the victims we have ... they're [victims] so broken that ... from the time we get a hold of them, from the time we take that statement to a court process that takes two and a half to three years – is very very hard" (participant 1). Given these circumstances, police go to great lengths to ensure the cooperation and eventual testimony of the labelled victim. The pressure placed on the complainants by police was captured by the comment of one defence attorney in reference to a case he dealt with: "I know things were said to those girls [complainants], I know because the girls would say to my client what they had been told [by the police]" (participant 14). Another defence attorney describes the scripting of the suspected victim's narrative that took place in one of her cases: "Right in the interview with the police, it's him scripting her towards this: 'Do you feel exploited? Did he take your money?'.... I would call that scripting" (participant 12).

Police insistence that the girls and women are in fact victims of trafficking despite their frequent rejection of the victim label is also evident in legal cases. For instance, an exchange between the defence attorney and the police officer in charge of the *R. v. Burton* (2016) case reveals that the situation came to the attention of the police when one of the complainants contacted the police to discuss a sexual assault committed against her by another man, with no intention of making a statement against the accused (her "pimp"/boyfriend):

DEFENCE: Let's talk about [the complainant]. You'd agree with me that from the very beginning December 2012, when you first interviewed [the complainant], it was clear that she did not want to be there speaking to the police, correct?

OFFICER: Correct.

DEFENCE: And, as you've indicated in the examination-in-chief, it was clear that she was more anxious to speak about a sexual assault that had occurred against her over a three-day period at the hands of a customer, correct?

OFFICER: Yes.

DEFENCE: She did not want to speak about Mr. Burton in any way shape or form?

OFFICER: Correct.

(Audio of trial, 16 December 2013)

Later in the same cross-examination, it also became evident that the complainant saw her statement to the police as an exaggeration of the truth.

DEFENCE: One of the things she [the complainant] also said on June 18 was that she exaggerated her statement, right?

OFFICER: Correct.

DEFENCE: One of the things she also said during these conversations was, she felt that she was being threatened by both police and the Crown, correct?

OFFICER: Correct, but then *we stopped her*. The Crown told her, no one is threatening her. She apologized and said she didn't mean the word threaten. *She felt like, when she came in to give the statement to myself and my partner that day, that all she wanted to do was talk about the client who sexually assaulted her but yet, somehow, we got on questions about her pimp and now she is here and that's what she said that day.*

(R. v. Burton, audio of trial,
16 December 2013; emphasis added)

The complainant's testimony led to the client being charged with sexual assault, forceable confinement, and threatening death – a case that was still ongoing at the time of the trial. Yet, trial transcripts demonstrate that the police were more interested in the role of Burton in the complainants' lives than in the sexual assault that had taken place, in effect revealing police interest in directing the stories of sex workers to convey control and exploitation. The complainant attempted to communicate to the court that she had exaggerated the story about her "pimp" in response to police and Crown pressure (although it was not clear from the trial transcripts what type of pressure) – her efforts were silenced by the Crown and the investigating officer, who denied any wrongdoing and insisted that she was not being threatened. The silencing of the complainant and her retraction of the word "threatened" must be read in the context of significant power differential between the complainant and the criminal justice actors, whereby the complainant's refusal to recant her statement may have resulted in criminal consequences for her.

Police scripting of complainants' stories and the application of pressure to accept the victim label under threats of criminalization is almost too clearly demonstrated in the case of *R. v. Johnson* (2011). In this case, the complainant had been charged with using a fake ID to work at an exotic dance club. The police, however, were seemingly interested in bigger fish, dangling the charges over her head as a fear tactic and willing her to testify against her "pimp." The complainant did not believe she had a "pimp" but found herself in a difficult situation becuase "the interviewer, Constable Watson, told her from the outset and persistently, that he believed she was being pimped and victimized. She knew from the officer that he was still deciding what to do about the charges on which she had been arrested.[12] [The complainant] agreed in her testimony that she relayed to the officer that there were no pimps involved and that she was in no danger" (*R. v. Johnson* 2011, para. 28). The complainant further noted in her sworn statement, "I've never had a pimp or whatever" and "I've never had to give anybody my money, that's all I know. I've never been pimped" (ibid., para. 29). The pressure placed on the complainant through threats of criminalization was also noted by the judge in this case: "[the complainant] agreed that at the time of her December 2008 interview she feared getting more time in custody – jail gave her nightmares" (ibid., para. 32). Agreeing with the defence attorney, the judge observed that "a real prospect of witness contamination exists given the nature of the police interviewing" (ibid., para. 97), consequently finding the accused "not guilty on all accounts" (ibid., para. 174). The significant efforts put forth by the police in this case demonstrates Ericson's argument that police conduct backwards investigations by first drawing a conclusion and then "finding" evidence to support it, in this case seemingly out of thin air.[13]

It is also noteworthy that in the majority of the cases analysed, the complainants were in a position of vulnerability with the police, having either outstanding arrest warrants, previous and extensive criminal records, or admission of activities that could result in arrest and incarceration. As one interviewed defence attorney describes police tactics: "The cops were pretending to be clients, then going in [to the hotel room] and then suddenly like saying, I'm a cop, are you ok, and what not. And of course, here's a complainant who's seventeen or eighteen years old, who has this cop there, potentially thinks she's about to get busted, will pretty much say anything she needs to say to save her own skin" (participant 13). As such, complainants may agree to go along with the police's proposed version of events due to fear of being charged. Similar reliance on the complainant's vulnerability was also evident in the case of *R. v. Dagg* (2015). In this case, the complainant said she was victimized only after she was caught stealing and threatened with jail time. According to the defence, "[The complainant] had a great motive to exaggerate – and even lie about – the events that may or may not have happened as she testified that she only opened up to the officer when she was caught red-handed stealing at the LCBO [Liquor Control Board of Ontario]. According to [the complainant's] testimony, she was 'jonesing'[14] and didn't want to go to jail – because she 'didn't want to go into DT (tremors)', and it is only when the officer told her 'give me one reason why I shouldn't arrest you' that she decided to open up" (Trial Exhibit). Although the police were successful in getting the complainant to accept the victim label, in this case the label was removed by the judge based on her drug addiction. This is interesting since in trafficking cases addictions can be viewed as factors that make someone vulnerable to exploitation or as reasons to explain work in the sex trade. The label of victim was also removed due to the complainant being thirty-six years of age at the time and therefore not fitting into the "ideal victim" narrative of being young, naïve, and therefore in need of rescue.

Pressure to accept the trafficking victim label can also come from other sources, including parents or the involvement of the Children's Aid Society (CAS) for those who have children. This is summed up by a comment of one defence attorney: "Well often, you know, you see things like the mothers or their fathers being there, you know, and you get a feeling that these people [complainants] are having to testify to make their parents happy, or they're going to get kicked out, or they might lose their child. For example, I've seen many cases where you think that they're testifying and they have to say these things otherwise the CAS is going to get involved or the CAS is going to do something. So, for sure, it's definitely, you never know what the entire truth is" (participant 11). In the face of the many pressures on police to arrest and prosecute traffickers discussed earlier in this chapter, the "ideal victim" as represented by youth, innocence, and naiveté is replaced at the front lines of anti-trafficking efforts by anyone who is willing to admit to or can be convinced to claim victimization. While the targeting and criminalization of sex work through anti-trafficking efforts has been well documented by now (Anderson 2012; Anderson and Andrijasevic 2008; Bernstein 2010; 2012a; 2012b; Bruckert 2018; Bruckert and Law 2013; Hua 2011; Millar and O'Doherty 2020; Roots 2013; Roots and De Shalit 2015), far less attention has been paid to the girls and women who are charged with trafficking offences as a part of this protectionist undertaking.

When police scripting and application of the victim label fails, we see front-line police efforts directed towards "bottom bitches," a street term for "recruiter" that the police have adopted and are reproducing. As the police explain, these are women and girls involved in the sex trade who have earned the trust of the "pimp"/trafficker and are relieved of their duties of servicing clients. Instead, they take on more leading roles, recruiting girls and women for the "pimp"/trafficker and directing operations in their absence. As one police officer explains: "It's so often where you see the girl in the industry, they call them 'bottom bitches'. It's not a very favourable term, but she's kind of like the extension. She'll find the girls for him, maybe self-serving cause she doesn't want to work anymore, so maybe if I find him, three girls, I don't have to work and then I can be a manager and she kind of goes up the pyramid" (participant 3). The bottom bitch is a narrative that rarely makes it to the public forum. The criminalization of the sex worker and/or the bottom bitch was previously carried out under the procuring legislation (s. 212[1] a,b,d,e,h) (van der Meulen 2010, 230). Now it is also done through trafficking laws, a shift which has far-greater consequences due to the operation of the human trafficking matrix.

As this section has shown, the police use their wide discretionary powers to compel women who might otherwise not self-identify as victims or as trafficked to take on the label of the trafficking victim. Obviously, women who are at risk of arrest or prosecution themselves are highly vulnerable to being successfully convinced, including sex workers who get caught breaking the law, mothers trying to fight off CAS, and "bottom bitches" who walk a fine line between victim and criminal. This is all done in an effort to fulfil the pre-determined conclusion of the police that trafficking is indeed taking place, fuelled by the need to fill arrest quotas and demonstrate the real need for specialized anti-trafficking units and more resources to support their work.

While these dynamics of protection and coercion have a long history in Canada, the intersection of procuring offences with transnational harms associated through the human trafficking matrix have resulted in far-greater repercussions for those criminalized and labelled as human traffickers even if not convicted. For example, Vanessa Cachia was charged with human trafficking in the midst of a widely publicized raid by York Regional Police. Human trafficking charges were withdrawn by the Crown immediately after the preliminary hearing, and later so were the rest of the charges, as the judge noted that "there was simply no evidence to go to trial" (as cited in Mandel, 17 September 2013). Despite this, as a *Toronto Sun* article explains, being charged with such high-profile crimes in the public eye had a profoundly negative impact on Cachia's life: "Her mug shot is all over the internet. She has been the subject of two arrests and two press releases put out by the Drugs and Vice unit of York Regional Police [YRP]. CTV's W5 was invited to film her takedown as a part of YRP's efforts to showcase their heroic efforts against the sex trade…. [S]he spent 10 days in jail, five of them in solitary confinement when the police and the Crown opposed her bail" (ibid.). According to Cachia's lawyer, "this was supposed to be their [York Regional Police] first big bust and it was all smoke and mirrors…. [T]hey really did ruin this girl's name" (as cited in Mandel, 17 September 2013). She went on to note that the police would not drop her charges since "she wouldn't 'roll' on" her boyfriend (ibid.). This case shows the ease with which the serious charges of human trafficking are laid and the damaging repercussion this can have on the lives of those caught up in it, even if not convicted. The protectionist discourses embedded in the UN Trafficking Protocol (2000) and Canada's National Action Plan to Combat Human Trafficking (2012; 2019–24), which form the foundation of these actions by authorities, are seemingly having a very different effect on the ground, as the burden to save victims and prosecute offenders leads police to pressure women and girls into claiming victimization and to charge those who are unwilling to cooperate. This finding is not exclusive to Canada. As Farrell et al. found in the context of the United States, "securing or, even more problematically, coercing a victim's cooperation through arrest or threat of an arrest is a primary driver of state-level human trafficking prosecution" (2016, 63), thus raising questions about the harms, rather than utility, of anti-trafficking policing.

Conclusion

Despite the ideological push for multilevel collaboration and coordination of anti-trafficking efforts by police on the ground, the evidence presented in this chapter suggest that these efforts are in actuality led primarily by specialized anti-trafficking units within municipal police forces. Rather than cooperating with each other, the specialized teams are often in competition for funding and for the reputation of the leader in anti-trafficking policing. To achieve this, anti-trafficking units are proactive in their approach, taking steps to seek out trafficking activity. In doing so, they produce human trafficking as a new crime category. This process also includes the establishment of the category of the trafficker, which, as discussed briefly in this chapter, involves the use and reproduction of racialized knowledge, and the category of the victim, which enables the police to transform the sex worker into a trafficking victim. In this way, these policing units contribute significantly to the formation of the human trafficking matrix through what is effectively being established as specialized expertise on the topic. By leading the education campaign on trafficking, the police then disseminate the very information they produce to relevant industries, such as tourism, hospitality, education, community organizations, and to other police services but also to the general public through highly emotive stories published by the media. In taking these steps, the police see themselves in a masculine protectionist role leading the fight against human trafficking by targeting the traffickers and rescuing the girls and women from them. In this important primary role of "crime fighters," they prefer to leave the care work to community agencies and what one officer called "the hugging types," occupations primarily fulfilled by women. In their efforts to "save" the women and girls and arrest the traffickers, however, the police engage in some troubling investigation tactics, presumably fuelled by the pressure to demonstrate their effectiveness as fighters of human trafficking. In other words, the police play a vital role in producing and disseminating the knowledge on human trafficking in Canada.

Chapter Four

Trafficking on Trial

As we have seen thus far, human trafficking is a contested and unstable criminal offence that incorporates a wide variety of tools, strategies, discourses, and knowledges that merge within the human trafficking matrix. This chapter will focus on the ways in which legal actors navigate arguments and build their case for this relatively new criminal offence. In particular, the chapter examines the challenges posed by the concept of consent in legal cases. Although consent is thought to be irrelevant in trafficking cases since one cannot consent to being trafficked, the distinction between sex work and trafficking established by the Trafficking Protocol (2000) revived its relevance. Thus, to establish consent and therefore prove their clients' innocence, and in the absence of trial strategies for the relatively new offence of human trafficking, defence lawyers, for instance, default to familiar legal frameworks, such as those used in sexual assault and domestic violence trials. As this chapter will demonstrate, strategies used by both Crown and defence attorneys borrow from a wide range of new and existing knowledges, logics, and tools to demonstrate either the lack of consent and the presence of exploitation, as in the case for Crowns, or the presence of consent and, therefore, absence of trafficking as argued by the defence. What is particularly interesting about these trial strategies, and will be detailed in this chapter, is that Crown and defence attorneys sometimes use the same factors to support different, and sometimes completely opposing, arguments. In the process of deciding which legal frameworks to apply, which factors to lean on, and which arguments/narratives to advance, legal actors are actively borrowing from and contributing to the human trafficking matrix, and in turn shaping the legal definition of the crime of human trafficking.

Lawyering and Trafficking Trials

Crown attorneys exercise an enormous amount of discretionary power on how to proceed with charges laid by police. They may prosecute, proceed with lesser charges, negotiate a plea bargain, or stay or withdraw the charges (Comack and Balfour 2004; Davis 2017; Farrell et al. 2016). The Crown's role is not to convict but to lay out all the relevant evidence to a crime and only proceed with charges if there is enough evidence for a conviction (Comack and Balfour 2004, 24). In their study of human trafficking in the United States, Farrell et al. (2016) found that prosecutors[1] were less likely to proceed with human trafficking charges, compared with other charges, since it's an untested legal territory, making it difficult to explain and prove facts of the relatively new offence (Farrell et al. 2016, 60). In the early days of the new trafficking laws, prosecutors lamented the fact that they were "operating on their own with little to no source of legal guidance" on the issue. When prosecutors decided to move forward with prosecuting trafficking cases, they had to "create" their own rules and standards on jury instructions on the issue (ibid., 61).

Crown attorneys in Ontario seem to also be reticent to prosecute human trafficking charges for similar reasons, namely, their sense that they have limited training in the area.[2] As one Crown attorney told me, Crowns must seek out their own training on human trafficking, in the form of conferences and so on, since it is considered a specialty area (participant 8). Another interviewed Crown, who was designated a lead in all human trafficking cases in her courthouse, similarly bemoaned that she had not "received any specific training. The topic has been discussed at various conferences that I've attended so I guess that's training" (participant 15). It may not be surprising, therefore, that police officers attribute the low conviction rates for trafficking offences to Crown attorneys' lack of knowledge on human trafficking. As one officer told me, "human trafficking is a very complex investigation and Crown attorneys and judges don't understand it. They don't understand the complexity" (participant 1). In expressing his frustration with plea deals, the same officer explains, "we see this more now because Crowns aren't educated as much and they don't want to deal with these complex cases. So, we charge a person with trafficking, sexual assault, aggravated assault, use of a firearm, whatever it is, and they will take pleas to lower offences.... [N]ow I think we're finally starting to get through to Crowns that you can't do that. You're hurting us because we need these guys ... these guys are going to go back to it" (participant 1). As the police perceive it, Crowns' lack of familiarity with the components of the offence, combined with their high work-load, produces an inefficient and uncoordinated response that fails to take trafficking as seriously as it should be: "at the end of the day, it comes down to, they [Crown attorneys] just don't want to do the work, cause they're so bogged down with other cases. And I don't blame them, right, because they're as overworked as we are" (participant 1).

In recent years, specialized human trafficking Crowns have emerged in some jurisdictions, including in Ontario, Manitoba, and Nova Scotia. This makes it more likely that cases will go to trial and that the Crowns will feel motivated to put their best foot forward to achieve convictions. As one Crown attorney explains, "human trafficking has been an impor-tant issue, and I think there was an initiative by the Ontario government to start to really focus on these kinds of cases and fund [new strategies]" (participant 15). Indeed, in 2016, the province of Ontario appointed six Crown attorneys to specialize in human trafficking cases. According to the Ministry of Community Safety and Social Services (2017), Ontario's Strategy to End Human Trafficking includes "Creating a Provincial Human Trafficking Prosecution Team that will ensure the provincial coordination of an enhanced prosecutorial model across Ontario and work collaboratively with police and the Victim Witness Assistance Program to improve and enhance human trafficking investigations and prosecutions. The ministry has recruited a Provincial Crown Coordina-tor to lead the team and specialized Crowns with expertise in prosecut-ing human trafficking cases. Once fully implemented, there will be six new Crowns on the prosecution team." As one Crown attorney put it, human trafficking prosecutions are becoming a "big ticket item…. [T]he message from the boss is, take it very seriously" (participant 8). This pressure to take trafficking "seriously" seems to also come from the police. As one officer stated, "For the most part, we have a really good relationship with some of the Crown attorneys, we are trying to estab-lish, what I was talking about earlier, assigned courts, and one thing we wanted was assigned Crown attorneys. So, they were in tune with some of the nuances with a human trafficking case, so they wouldn't get frustrated or reluctant or even discard a case because the victim didn't seem like they had strong credibility or whatever the case may be. We wanted them to understand the psychological impact factors to which their statement was received" (participant 3). The combination of these pressures, funding increases, and the allocation of certain Crowns as specializing in human trafficking prosecutions will undoubtedly result in more aggressive prosecution strategies and increased numbers of convictions and guilty pleas in trafficking cases going forward. As noted in the introduction of this book, the Ontario government is allocating another $307 million into anti-trafficking strategies, with $70 million of this going towards Crown training and improving police intelligence-gathering strategies. What we see, then, is Crown attorneys following the footsteps of specialized anti-trafficking police, gaining "expertise" in the area, and providing exclusive focus on the crime.

The task of the defence counsel is not to prove the innocence of the accused but "to ensure that individuals are not convicted improperly and that the principles of fundamental justice enshrined in the *Charter of Rights and Freedoms* are not overlooked" (Comack and Balfour 2004, 24). To achieve this, defence attorneys focus on raising "reasonable doubt" by "exploiting different properties of prosecution stories" (Bennett and Feldman 1981, 98). Paul Drew explains that defence attorneys under common law justice systems, such as the one we have in Canada, use particularly hostile cross-examination techniques to challenge the cred-ibility of the Crown's evidence and witnesses "with questions which are designed to discredit the other side's version of events, and instead to support his or her own side's case" (1992, 470). Given the lack of an established legal framework for prosecuting a human trafficking case, defence attorneys tend to rely on the familiar, namely, the usual defence strategies of discrediting complainants in sexual assault cases, introduc-ing alternative stories that draw on extra-legal ideals of race, class, gen-der, and sexuality (see also Roots and Lockhart 2021). As one defence lawyer contends, "It [the trial] is the story that gets told. It's the reality [of what happened] that's changed. And that reality is changed based on the attack on credibility, this is what we do. I'm sorry for the people who think the justice system is about truth and justice. I'm sorry. It's not. It's about how you can affect the testimony of a witness so as to affect their credibility" (participant 14). The attacks by defence lawyers on the cred-ibility of complainants in sexual assault trials is well documented by feminist scholars (Backhouse 2008; Bakht 2012; Craig 2015; 2018; Ehrlich 2012; Gruber 2020; Johnson 2012; Sheehy 2012). This is despite feminist efforts to change the practice during the 1980s and 1990s by successfully lobbying for a number of legislative amendments to sexual assault laws (Comack and Balfour 2004; Bonnycastle 2000; Sheehy 2012a; 2012b). The goal of these amendments was to eliminate gender discrimination and the use of rape myths against complainants in sexual assault cases, to refocus police attention from the sexual nature of the offence to the harm done by the offender, to eliminate the link between women's sexual history and their credibility as witnesses, and to increase reporting of sexual offences (Comack and Balfour 2004; Sheehy 2012a; 2012b). Yet, as scholars have extensively demonstrated, in many ways these amend-ments have failed to transform the treatment of complainants in sexual assault cases (Backhouse 2012; Comack and Balfour 2004; Comack and

Peter 2005; Craig 2015; 2018; DuBois 2012; Ehrlich 2012; Gotell 2008; 2012; Johnson 2012; Larcombe 2002; Odette 2012; Randall 2010). For instance, the implementation of the rape shield provision, which aimed at protecting women from being discredited based on their sexual history, was challenged by defence lawyers for its violation of the accused persons' rights to present a full defence. Failure to strike down the provision led defence attorneys to resort to another strategy for access – the use of private records held by third parties, including psychiatrists, counsellors, clinics, and others (Comack and Balfour 2004, 115). According to Comack and Balfour, many lawyers took on sexual assault cases to challenge what they perceived to be politically motivated restrictions on their clients' constitutional rights (Comack and Balfour 2004, 144). The continued disregard of these legislative changes in sexual assault cases has been well established (Comack and Balfour 2004; Craig 2015; Gotell 2008; Larcombe 2002; Randall 2010; Sheehy 2012a).

As Bakht notes, in the context of sexual violence trials, "the adversarial nature of our criminal justice system has often made women complaints feel as though they were on trial for their non-criminal behavior" (2012, 595). These same strategies are seemingly becoming a part of the human trafficking matrix by being adopted in trafficking trials. As the above-quoted defence lawyer further explains, "Victims don't have rights. Sorry. In the criminal justice system, and by that, I mean they have no voice. There's nobody advocating for victims. There [is] no place in the trial for a victim or the Crown to advocate for the human rights of the victim. That's not the issue. The issue is, are they credible, not what rights they have" (participant 14). As a result, in the trial process, where both defence and Crown attorneys pose carefully scripted questions to elicit answers that will support their version of events, the complainant becomes a pawn in the legal game of presenting the most convincing narrative (see Craig 2018; Ehrlich 1987; 2012; Estrich 1987). This strategy was even identified by a complainant in one of the cases examined in this study, who was particularly vocal in her objection: "I'm not the accused and, like, everyone is turning the camera on the victim. Like, it should be the other way around. I shouldn't feel like the accused" (R. v. Beckford, audio of trial, 5 March 2013). She goes on to lament, "you may as well put cuffs on me and throw me in jail with the accused because you are acting like I am the accused" (ibid.). While somethings may have changed through measures "designed to make testifying less traumatic for victims and other vulnerable witnesses" (Public Safety Canada 2012, 8), the complainant's clear frustration suggests that they may not have changed enough.

One enduring feature of criminal justice trials around contested sexual activity is the use of a complainant's sexual behaviour to undermine her credibility based on the stereotyped and misogynistic assumption that consent to one sexual activity must extend to all sexual encounters. This approach is enabled by the almost exclusive focus of Canada's anti-trafficking efforts on cases involving sexual exploitation. Evidence of defence's use of sexual activity to undermine the credibility of complainants can be seen in the case of *R. v. (Gregory) Salmon* (2014), where the defence attorney focused on the complainant's sexual relationship with the accused's friend by asking, "that's when this fooling around with [the best friend of the accused] took place?" When she answered in the affirmative, the defence asked, "that was right after you got here [to the city where the two met]?" When she confirmed, he verified, "within days?" (Audio of trial, 4 March 2014). These questions were intended to show that the complainant had sexual relations with the accused and his best friend within days of her arrival to the new city and without knowing either of the men beforehand. This line of questioning was followed by further interrogations of the complainant's sexual history, which revealed that the complainant had sex with, got pregnant by, and moved in with her boyfriend by the time she was fourteen years old. With such questions, the defence attorney attempted, throughout the cross-examination process, to demonstrate that the complainant was sexually promiscuous and of suspicious moral character, therefore undermining her credibility as a witness.

The defence strategy evident in *R. v. (Gregory) Salmon* is not an isolated example. In fact, similar patterns are evident across a range of cases. For example, in *R. v. Beckford* (201), the defence focused on establishing the complainant's sexual promiscuity, and thus lack of credibility, by suggesting that she had been engaged to a woman while simultaneously dating several men at the same time, without their knowledge. This is a common strategy used in sexual assault trials where complainants are portrayed as having questionable morals. Clearly then, the "rape shield" provision, which was put into place to restrict legal counsel from using women's sexual history to undermine their credibility, has been less than effective. The use of these tactics in trafficking cases demonstrates that despite the emphasis on protection of the victim in trafficking policies and mandates, legal actors are relying on familiar "slut-shaming" strategies to bring doubt to the complainant's alleged lack of consent to the activities under question.

While defence attorneys inserted tactics adopted from sexual assault trials into the human trafficking matrix, Crowns employed their own special strategies, focusing on the vulnerability factors (outlined in chapter one) to shape the complainants into "true" victims. Trafficking scholars have argued that for a human trafficking case to be prosecuted, the complainant must fit into the cast of the "ideal trafficking victim," characterized by innocence, vulnerability, and passiveness (Doezema 2000 2001; 2010; Hua 2011). The characteristics of the "ideal victim" in trafficking cases parallel those of other forms of gendered violence, including domestic and sexual assault, who are expected to be "not only ... morally and sexually virtuous (read white), but also cautious, unprovocative and consistent" (Bakht 2012, 591; see also Bumiller 2008; Craig 2015; Gotell 2008). And while Canada's dominant trafficking narratives uphold the image of the "girl next door" as the "ideal victim" of domestic trafficking, examination of trafficking prosecutions in Ontario reveal a different kind of victim.

Indeed, complainants in trafficking trials align more frequently with the second prominent image of the victim, the Canadian woman or girl from a marginalized background. While there is evidence that prosecutors view complainants from marginalized backgrounds as less likely to be credible at trial (Lindberg et al 2012; Ruparelia 2012), for example, as a street person, alcohol- or drug-dependent, sex-working, mentally unwell, or otherwise distanced from normative white femininity, in trafficking trials, Crowns often focus on these very features precisely because they are seen as vulnerabilities that are easy to exploit. As outlined in chapter one, pre-existing vulnerabilities, which include young age, illness, gender, poverty, drug and alcohol use, and involvement in sex work, have become a part of the human trafficking matrix and play an important role in expanding the application of the trafficking label. Using a complainants' drug use, mental health issues, family problems, economic needs, and other pre-existing vulnerabilities, Crowns in trafficking cases argue that the complainant is in a position of heightened vulnerability which in itself automatically transforms the complainant into a ready-made victim of trafficking. Indeed, perhaps uniquely to domestic trafficking prosecutions, the more troubled she appears the stronger the case.

Consider the following roster of the complainant's suffering and tribulations provided in the Crown's closing submission in *R. v. Byron* (2014), where he not only verbally describes her many sources of vulnerability, but presents an actual photograph of the complainant taken from her Facebook page, which he says displays her susceptibility to exploitation:

> I'll start with a photo of [the complainant] from Facebook. Looking at her.
> *It's hard to picture a more vulnerable* person in our society. You heard a lot
> of evidence about [the complainant]. You know that she is a ward of the
> Crown. Her mother passed away. She suffers from fetal alcohol spectrum

disorder. She's been diagnosed with a bipolar disorder. There's a very serious learning disability and she needs help to do just about anything. One of the last exhibits filed demonstrates how she had to be helped through various public systems, such as school, housing. She can't really get by on her own.

(*R. v. Byron*, audio of trial,
17 May 2013; emphasis added)

In *R. v. (Gregory) Salmon* (2014), the Crown paints a similar picture of the complainant's vulnerabilities: "First, if you look at her background, her parents split up when she was quite young, she lived in foster care for years and left home returning briefly at 13–14 and then back out on her own in her early teens. She had her first child at the age of 18. In her evidence, she presents as a very immature person. She presents as a naïve person" (*R. v. Salmon*, audio of trial, 25 May 2014). In these detailed enumerations of the complainants' "problems," sometimes punctuated by visual evidence, Crowns construct a trafficking prosecution's version of the "ideal victim," whose vulnerability is so evident that the case for exploitation almost builds itself.

The complainants however, do not always agree that they are vulnerable to the point of helplessness. For instance, although the Crown in *R. v. Byron* (2014) (see above) painted a picture of the complainant as one of the most vulnerable types of people in our society, her demeanour on the stand did not match assumptions of what vulnerability looks like. Instead, she presented herself quite confidently, assertively, and at times even forcefully. Consider, for example, her response to the defence attorney repeating questions about why she did not leave the situation when her friend did: "I don't know. That's a ridiculous question! It's pissing me off that I have to get into details like this" (*R. v. Byron*, audio of trial, 13 May 2013). In another instance, when the defence attorney circled back to the same question about why she did not leave the suggestively exploitative situation, the complainant snapped: "if her [her friend] dad wasn't going to pay for me, where else was I going to go? There's your answer. Now move on from the question" (*R. v. Byron*, audio of trial, 10 May 2013). While the tough exterior that may have been developed as a survival mechanism in no way denies the underlying vulnerabilities, this behaviour may nonetheless challenge the Crown attorney's depiction of her as vulnerable in light of the courtroom expectations for complainants.

Similar behaviour was also exhibited by the complainant in *R. v. Beckford* (2013), who expressed frustration and anger with another standard trick used especially well in sexual assault trials around chronologies and timelines in an effort to draw out inconsistencies between the initial police report and the testimony. In response to defence counsel's repetitive questioning, she exclaimed, "ok, this is irrelevant to everything, why don't you start moving on to the evidence instead of just simple little facts that have nothing to do with this at all.... [Y] ou're really starting to frustrate me, you know that?" (*R. v. Beckford*, audio of trial, 5 March 2013). When pushed further, the complainant loudly responded, "I DON'T REMEMBER THIS INCIDENT, SO WHY YOU KEEP ASKING ME ABOUT IT? I DON'T KNOW BUT YOU'RE REALLY STARTING TO GET ON MY NERVES. HOW MANY TIMES DO I HAVE TO TELL YOU THAT I DON'T RECALL SO IT WOULD STICK TO YOUR HEAD, SIR? I'M TELLING YOU, I DO NOT RECALL THIS INCIDENT" (*R. v. Beckford*, audio of trial, 5 March 2013).[3] This example is one of several that indicate how complainants in trafficking trials are not the passive victims portrayed in popular discourse but, in fact, challenge defence attorneys' version of events and call out their focus on minor details in an effort to discredit them, rather than looking at the harm that was caused to them. The diverging images of the victim as, on the one hand vulnerable to exploitation and simultaneously confident, assertive, and even aggressive reveal the paternalistic nature of the law and the ways women's "realities" are co-opted to make a discourse work, thereby strengthening, rather than challenging, the very hierarchies that distinguish between the "girl next door" and the "marginalized woman."

Mental health is another factor used by defence attorneys in sexual assault cases to undermine the credibility of the complainant. As feminists have documented, psychiatric ("psy") discourses have become a prevailing influence in the legal terrain, particularly with respect to women as victims and perpetrators of crime (Comack and Balfour 2004; McGillivray 1998; Smart 1989; 1995). Women with developmental and psychiatric disabilities, especially with brain injuries, have a hard time accessing the justice system as sexual assault complainants (Benedet and Grant 2007, 517). If they do arrive in court, their mental ill-health is often used by defence attorneys to discredit their testimonies, and they are treated either as asexual and child-like or oversexed and promiscuous (ibid.). In trafficking cases however, mental ill-health enters the trafficking matrix as a vulnerability factor, which means it can also serve as an advantage to the prosecution in establishing exploitation. In the Beckford case, as I demonstrate below, the mental health of the complainant served both narratives as the defence and Crown counsel attempted to illustrate very different pictures of the complainant.

According to Benedet and Grant, disabled complainants and witnesses in sexual assault cases are particularly disadvantaged by the lack of flexibility in court procedures but also by the legal system's "blind faith in the importance of repeatedly accusing women of lying about sexual assault as a means of getting at the 'truth'" (2007, 530). Both of these approaches to disability were clearly evidenced in the Beckford case where the complainant's mental health challenges were central to the Crown's case. The complainant in the case displayed aggression and defiance that did not fit the normative understanding of a sexual violence survivor and women more generally (Comack and Balfour 2004). To bridge this gap, the Crown attorney relied on the "psy" discourse, making mental health the ulnerability factor that strengthened the Crown's case. In trafficking trials, Crowns routinely suggest that complainants who exhibit such behaviour are unstable and therefore unable to control their emotions and demeanour in a socially acceptable manner, thus, from a Crown's perspective, making the complainant susceptible to exploitation. The Crown's reliance on the "psy" discourse in the Beckford case infantilized the complainant throughout the trial, where he continuously expressed concern over her mental health: "I am concerned about this witness … knowing what we know about her mental health condition and the way that she is presenting at this time" (*R. v. Beckford*, audio of trial, 5 March 2013). The Crown's "coddling" of the complainant, as one of the defence attorneys called it, even led to an objection by the defence: "I certainly understand my friend's[4] desire to calm the witness down, but she has another cross-examination ahead and I find it difficult to understand how you can calm the witness down without getting into what happened in court, and I would suggest that the support person can perform that function. I have concerns of my friend doing it because it would naturally lead to, 'oh, I don't like those questions, or I don't like what this lawyer is saying and I don't like what's happening in court'" (*R. v. Beckford*, audio of trial, 5 March 2013). By emphasizing the complainant's vulnerability allegedly caused by mental health concerns, the Crown constructed her as a "real" victim of trafficking. He achieved this through a series of slowly evolving questions to the complainant, which first revealed the mental health conditions she had been diagnosed with: "bipolar, clinically depressed, anxiety, ADHD [attention deficit hyperactivity disorder], OCD [obsessive compulsive disorder]." This was followed by questions that revealed the complainant had taken illegal drugs given to her by the accused. She was then offered a ride by the accused, yet rather than taking her home, she was allegedly taken to various cities and eventually raped, beaten, and forced to provide sexual services (*R. v. Beckford*, audio of trial, 4 March 2013). Taken together, this paints a damning picture of a young woman with mental health challenges being sexually exploited and trafficked.

In contrast to the image of innocence and vulnerability being painted by the Crown, defence attorneys in the Beckford case pointed to these mental health challenges in an effort to characterize the complainant as hypersexualized. Specifically, they drew out an argument which focused on the fact that, despite her young age, she had been in numerous romantic relationships with men and women, even suggesting that she engaged in sex work. The complainant lashed out at these suggestions:

> DEFENCE: You posted yourself in the Craigslist postings, correct?
> COMPLAINANT: Are you stupid?
> JUDGE: No [complainant's name].
> COMPLAINANT: Sorry, but we went over this enough times. Yeah, I'm 16 years old and I really want to be opening my legs to all pervs like your client and the people that like to rape and the people that like to kill.
> (*R. v. Beckford*, audio of trial, 6 March 2013)

While the complainant was clear in rejecting the version of events put forth by the defence, the structure of cross-examination allowed the defence attorney to, in effect, testify, rather than inquire about her character:

> DEFENCE: You understood that people wanted to come after you because you lied to them, correct?
> COMPLAINANT: Because I messed people over.
> DEFENCE: And you lied to them.
> COMPLAINANT: NO, I MESSED PEOPLE OVER.
> DEFENCE: And you would lie to people about things that you did in the community?
> COMPLAINANT: NO! NOT CORRECT. NO!
> (*R. v. Beckford*, audio of trial, 5 March 2013)[5]

Furthermore, the complainant's anger and frustration with the questions worked to undermine her image as rational and ultimately led to a mistrial due to the perceived prejudice against the accused's ability to have a fair hearing caused by her testimony.

We see a similar use of the "psy" discourse by the Crown in *R. v. Byron* (2014), who also relied on the complainant's mental health concerns to make his case. In characterizing the complainant, the Crown noted that "it is hard to imagine a more vulnerable person in our society," due to the various mental health conditions she suffers from (Audio of trial, 16 May 2013). Indeed in this case, the Crown went so far as to make the argument that the complainant was specifically targeted "because she has limitations" (*R. v. Byron*, audio of trial, 13 December 2013). The complainant was described as "an orphan who had diagnosed as bipolar and possibly with fetal alcohol spectrum disorder; she also had a learning disability ... and a ward of the Children's Aid Society" (*R. v. Byron*, audio of trial, 13 December 2013). On this account, we see the prosecution strengthening their case based on the complainants' vulnerabilities to argue that the accused's actions were predatory because they targeted a very vulnerable young person. Unlike sexual assault trials, mental health concerns in trafficking trials can be an asset for the Crown to show vulnerability, while for defence attorneys the familiar framework of discrediting mentally challenged witness/complainants is all too evident. We see a similar pattern of multivalent discourses when the complainant is substance-dependent which can, in the hands of a skilful Crown, be transformed into a story about the vitiation of consent.

As with mental health concerns, Crown and defence attorneys also utilize complainants' drug use in their widely varying case-building strategies, where the same evidence of drug use is used to construct significantly different narratives by Crown and defence counsel. In laying out a case for trafficking, the Crown is motivated, where relevant, to establish that the complainant had consumed drugs during the events in question to show that the accused drugged the complainant in order to exploit her non-sober or addicted state. Consider for instance, the case of *R. v. Dagg* (2015), where the accused managed the sex work operations of the complainant and received half of her income as a result of this labour. As part of this business exchange, the complainant expected access to drugs, hotel rooms, and protection. Despite this contract-like agreement, it was her drug dependency that allowed the Crown to argue that "They [the accused] start off by giving her as much crack cocaine that she can consume. They know that she's just came out of rehab, she's told them that.... So part of the lulling her into the prostitution services is to hook her into needing all that crack cocaine" (Audio of trial, 7 April 2015). The Crown further argued that "because Mr. Dagg is aware of what's going on during that time [regarding her addiction] and he continues to pimp her out after that point that, he is ultimately exploiting her" (*R. v. Dagg*, audio of trial, 13 April 2015). The Crown's focus on the complainant's drug use as a vulnerability factor thus allowed her to argue that the complainant's consent to sex work was a product of her drug dependency which was being exploited by the accused to achieve their own (financial) interests. The judge, however, rejected this argument, holding the complainant responsible for her own fate: "[the accused] are not taking some vulnerable young person, addicting them and then putting them into prostitution; quite the opposite, she's a prostitute, who is an addict who found these people" (*R. v. Dagg*, audio of trial, 7 April 2015). Despite the judge's rejection of this argument in this particular case, the patterns in trafficking cases analysed here suggest that Crowns tend to cleave closely to this strategy, arguing often across multiple cases that the complainant's drug habit should be treated as a pre-existing vulnerability that the accused is able to exploit.

R. v. Beckford (2013) offers another example of this strategy. Here, the Crown elicited questions about the way in which drug use impacted the complainant's memory:

CROWN: How would you describe your memory about the events you are here to testify about?
COMPLAINANT: It's not perfect.
CROWN: Why not?
COMPLAINANT: Because of the street drugs and my prescribed drugs – I have gaps in my head.
CROWN: Are you referring to gaps in your memory?
COMPLAINANT: Yes.
CROWN: Do you have gaps in your memory about other things too?
COMPLAINANT: Yes.
CROWN: Is there any other reason that may have affected your memory about the details of the events you are here to testify about?
COMPLAINANT: Yeah, the fact that I try to block it out.
CROWN: How do you do that?
COMPLAINANT: I try to forget.

(*R. v. Beckford*, audio of trial, 4 March 2013)

This examination of the complainant's drug use and its impact on her memory by the Crown is curious at first glance. Presumably, it was the Crown's attempt to control the use of potentially damaging information, which the defence could, and in this case did, use to suggest that the complainant was a liar (see discussion below) and that her testimony was unreliable due to her memory gaps. Instead, the Crown shifted the narrative around the complainant's memory gaps away from the drug use and onto the trauma of the ordeal/events that contributed to the memory loss. The Crown's approach of trying to establish trauma is in juxtaposition to sexual assault trials, where trauma, especially if it results in inconsistent memories and testimony, works to undermine the complainant's testimony. In this case, we see the complainant being given leeway as the Crown tries to use such arguments to their advantage.

Furthermore, although the complainant admitted to recreational drug use outside of the incident at trial, the Crown suggested that drugs were provided to the complainant by the accused with the intent of kidnapping, assaulting, and exploiting her:

> CROWN: Describe any interaction you had with him [the accused] around that [drugs]?
> COMPLAINANT: He offered me some, so I took some.
> CROWN: Do you know how much ecstasy you took *from [the accused]*?
> COMPLAINANT: I think four double stacks.
> CROWN: What does that mean?
> COMPLAINANT: Drugs are regular size, double stack, which is double the pill, or triple stack, which is triple the pill.
> CROWN: And did the drugs have an effect on you?
> COMPLAINANT: Yeah, they got me all messed up.
> CROWN: How were you feeling?
> COMPLAINANT: Not good.
> CROWN: How so? Can you describe what you mean by not good?
> COMPLAINANT: Especially with drinking that night too – I just felt messed up, I wanted to go home.
>
> (*R.v Beckford*, audio of trial, 4 March 2013)

The complainant's assertion that the accused offered her drugs was used by the Crown to argue that he did so in order to stupefy her and subsequently kidnap and exploit her – a strategy that is aimed at showing the absence of consent since, as outlined by the governments of British Columbia and Ontario, a victim's (involuntary) drug use is one indicator of trafficking (Government of B.C. 2014; Government of Ontario 2020a). This narrative also aligns with the trafficking panics – drugged, kidnapped, and prostituted – the perfect trifecta of trafficking, peddled in movies such as *Taken* (2008), where the main character's (played by Liam Neeson) daughter – the victim – is kidnapped, then drugged and trafficked for sex. Similar storylines playing out in other movies, such as *I Am Still Here* (2017), which tells the story of a very young victim who is suggestively drugged, kidnapped, and sex trafficked, and *Angie: Lost Girls* (2020), in which a middle-class young American woman is kidnapped and forced into the sex trade. These are only a few out of many movies on human trafficking that tell parallel storylines. Such depictions of drug use and dependency feed into the human trafficking matrix to shape the meaning of trafficking and go a long way to explaining its importance for the Crown's case, allowing for some blending of fact and fantasy.

At the same time, drug use among women complainants is used by defence counsel to treat them as non-credible witnesses to their own alleged exploitation, for reasons that are not dissimilar to the ways sexual assault victims are treated in court. We see this in the case of *R. v. Dagg* (2015), where the defence successfully showed that the complainant used drugs voluntarily and that such extensive drug use rendered her testimony unreliable. The defence pointed the complainant to her testimony to the police, where she noted: "yeah I just feel bad because like my memory, it's blotched, right, like it's true memory but the time frames keep blending" (Audio of trial, 1 April 2015). We then see drug use as an indicator of trafficking being mined by the Crown to tap into the trafficking panics and to construct a narrative of the complainant as drugged and prostituted against her will, while the defence counsel, using legal strategies of sexual assault cases, rely on the very same factor of drug use to undermine her credibility. Given the conflation of sex work and trafficking, the question of whether the complainant engaged in sex work voluntarily is allocated significant attention by both Crown and defence attorneys. Unlike in sexual assault, domestic violence and other gendered violence cases, the Crown's case in domestic human trafficking trials examined in this study often hinged upon the testimony of complainants who work in the sex trade. Crown attorneys typically took the position that the complainant was forced to provide sexual services to establish a case of human trafficking. In the case of complainants who were already engaged in sex work, the argument relied on the assumption that sex work is a pre-existing vulnerability, as captured by the Crown's comment in *R. v. Byron* (2014): "Prostitution becomes the activity that is degrading to the individual dignity of the prostitute which is a vehicle for 'pimps' and customers to exploit the disadvantaged position of women in our society" (Audio of trial, 17 May 2013). The Crown's argument reveals the assumption that no self-respecting (dignified) woman would engage in sex work; therefore, it either is, or is an indication of, some flaw – vulnerability – in the "victim." Here, the sex worker is understood as a vulnerable person – a victim of sorts – a position which is very much in line with the post-Bedford sex work laws that see sex workers as victims.

Yet, this view of sex workers as victims is fragile, as seen by the pattern of defence attorneys in the cases I studied trying to demonstrate that the complainants' engagement in sex work was voluntary and, as such, no trafficking can be said to have occurred. The central aim of the defence in trafficking cases was to undermine the complainant's assertion that they were forced or coerced into the sex trade, which is frequently and effectively achieved by deploying sexist and misogynistic stereotypes that construct her as an irresponsible and risky individual (see also Roots and Lockhart 2021). As Gotell notes, careless disregard for personal safety, which is assumed when engaging in sex work, "becomes a site for an altered form of victim-blaming" (2008, 880). The condemnation of a woman's sexually risky behaviour is exhibited in the following exchange between the defence counsel and the complainant In *R. v. Greenham* (2015):

> DEFENCE: *So, you're taking in these men in your room – I told you before I'm not criticizing at all for what you are doing.*
> COMPLAINANT: No, I understand.
> DEFENCE: But you took in strange men in a hotel room all by yourself.
> COMPLAINANT: Yes.
> DEFENCE: Locked the door behind you?
> COMPLAINANT: Yes.
> DEFENCE: Takes a fair amount of courage to do that.
>
> (*R. v. Greenham*, audio of trial,
> 25 August 2015; emphasis added)

While the defence attorney was seemingly admiring the courage of the complainant in engaging in sex work, he was also highlighting the risky behaviour in which she was engaged. Indeed, he went on to point out that the accused, who was acting in the role of the complainant's protector, was in the next room ready to assist if anything went wrong. In this way, the defence re-constructed the events under question in a way that moved away from the dominant narrative about trafficking, in which the complainant is a helpless victim, turning it instead into a story in which the complainant voluntarily assumed the risks associated with sex work. In this narrative, the accused becomes a hero, rather than a villain, offering protection against "bad" risks undertaken by a consenting sex worker. The implication is that if anyone has been irresponsible, it is the complainant herself, who has made dangerous (courageous) choices of her own accord. Such consent to sex work, however, vitiates the argument about trafficking.

While such defence strategies may sound, on the surface, a lot like sex work–positive arguments about the capacity of individuals to make their own choices about their bodies and sexual labour, there is also a danger of using this argument as a defence against trafficking charges. Specifically built into this strategy is an assumption that once an individual – typically a woman – has engaged in voluntary sex work, she can no longer be forced into it. This is similar to the victim-blaming logic seen in sexual assault cases where the existence of one's sexual history, especially if it is extensive, is taken as a sign of consent (Craig 2018). And while, as discussed above, Canadian law has put into place rape shield provisions and affirmative consent requirements to protect survivors from these assumptions, they continue to problematically emerge in sexual assault cases (ibid.). Similar troubling assumptions are being woven into trafficking cases where complainants engagement in sex work prior to meeting the accused is often constructed by the defence counsel into a situation akin to an ongoing contractual agreement between two parties. This was the argument of the defence in *R. v. Dagg* (2015), who suggested that "This was an agreement. She got into this because she was going to be making more money on Backpage than she would've on the street" (Audio of trial, 7 April 2015). In effect, the defence argued that the complainant had exercised her own agency in seeking to improve her earnings by entering into an agreement with the accused. The implication is that trafficking is, thus, not possible, given the complainant's extensive experience in sex work and drug and alcohol addictions.

More generally, given the importance of the relationship between consent (or more precisely, lack of) and the legal definition of exploitation, defence attorneys in the majority of the cases studied went to great lengths to present any and all evidence that might signal the complainant's voluntary participation in the sex trade. In *R. v. Beckford* (2013), the defence attorneys brought an application requesting the court's permission to question the complainant about her potential involvement in sex work before the incident at trial (Audio of trial, 22 February 2013). When the judge denied this application, the defence used a less-direct approach to accomplish the same objective, questioning the complainant about her relationship with a young woman whom she had met at a juvenile detention centre and who was involved in sex work. The defence's questions suggested that the complainant had been introduced to sex work by her friend from the juvenile detention centre and that she had engaged in the practice. In effect, the defence was aiming to discredit the complainant's testimony that she was forced into the sex trade by suggesting that she had already engaged in it voluntarily and thus tapping into the assumption that consent to sex work means that one can no longer be forced into it (*R. v. Beckford*, audio of trial, 5 March 2013).

Similar efforts to draw a picture of complainant's consent to sex work was put forth by the defence in *R. v. Oliver-Machado* (2013):

DEFENCE: At some point, you thought about doing something.

COMPLAINANT: Can you be more specific?

DEFENCE: The foot massage?

COMPLAINANT: Yeah, it was in my mind cause $150 is a lot of money for a kid but it's only questionable. I was there, but it's not something I would actually go and do.

DEFENCE: But you were thinking about it.

COMPLAINANT: Yeah.

DEFENCE: And you and [another complainant] talked about doing it.

(*R. v. Oliver-Machado*, audio of
trial, 10 September 2013)

The defence attorneys in the above exchange cleverly work to associate the complainant's actions with voluntary involvement in sex work. The suggestion underlying the above set of questions was that the complainant's knowledge – that the accused was a "pimp" – and the conversation she had with her friend about giving foot rubs for money followed by her subsequent decision to meet the accused, amounted to consent to engage in sex work.

Crowns divergently used the argument that sex work, which they tended to present as frequently accompanied by violence by clients and "pimps," is a pre-existing vulnerability that makes it easier for traffickers to exploit the victims. For example, in *R. v. Dagg* (2015), the Crown attorney lamented:

she [the complainant] talked about how she prostituted herself on other occasions but she wasn't aware of Backpages, she never described having a pimp like this before so this is a new situation for her. She talked about driving [name of another sex worker] around prior to [center for addition recovery] and she would prostitute herself on [name of] Road but she's never had business arrangement like this before. So, like she comes into that situation being naïve and well she's been a crack addict before and a prostitute before this. She also talked about long stretches that she wouldn't be and I would suggest when she came out of [center for addition recovery] she fell hard, really hard. And that Marshall [nick name of accused] ultimately took advantage of that hard fall.

(R. v. Dagg, audio of trial, 14 April 2015)

The defence attorney pushed back on this argument and took the position that because of the violence experienced by sex workers on a regular basis, the complainant could not have been made fearful by name calling and insults directed at her by the accused:

> when she [the complainant] was mentioning the reason she felt fearful was because [accused 2] would call her names and [accused 1] called her a crack hoe, I put to her that people on the streets aren't the nicest, it's not something that was new to her. It's not something that would instill fear in her and I felt like she was trying to twist it…. And I distinctly told her at the cross [examination], I'm not saying that it's okay but you would agree with me that on the streets, you've been called names before. And she agreed. And you never run to the police about that – no.
>
> (R. v. Dagg, audio of trial, 14 April 2015)

Because violence was a frequent part of the complainant's life due to her extensive and voluntary engagement in sex work, the defence believes it can be considered neither coercive nor exploitative. What we see then is Crown attorneys working to establish the post-Bedford understanding of sex workers as victims – a position which is easily substituted for that of sex workers as criminals, while defence attorneys are relying on the well-established pre-Bedford arguments premised on the assumption that consenting sex workers cannot be trafficked.

The testimony of young people is especially complicated in trafficking trials. On the one hand, the discursive importance of the "girl next door" and the consequent need to aggressively protect young women especially from trafficking gives urgency to cases involving the sexual exploitation of minors. On the other hand, young people are often seen as poor witnesses in criminal trials, making their testimony difficult to elicit and establish as credible. As Comack and Balfour observed, lawyers portray young complainants as "liars, fabricators, provocateurs or attention seekers" (2004, 134). This tendency makes the testimony of youth very complicated.

The complexities around the role and treatment of youth complainants in legal processes are evident in R. v. Beckford (2013), where the defence attorney attempted to establish that the young complainant's story of exploitation was a fragment of her imagination, made up to save herself from getting in trouble for having gone missing for several days: "I'm going to suggest to you that you were just making things up as you went along, is that not fair to say?... I'm going to suggest to you that you lied to [your mother] about this entire affair about you being in a strip club at all" (*R. v. Beckford*, audio of trial, 6 March 2013). The defence placed particular focus on the complainant's claim that she did not sustain any physical injuries from being sexually assaulted: "I'm going to suggest that that would be impossible for you to be forcefully anally raped and not have any physical injuries" (*R. v. Beckford*, audio of trial, 6 March 2013). The defence further asked the complainant a series of detailed questions about the incident under examination, at the end of which he concluded, "you have no idea what you are talking about" (*R. v. Beckford*, audio of trial, 6 March 2013), suggesting that the reason she had no recollection of the event in question was "because it never happened" (ibid.).

In cases involving young women as complainants, it is not uncommon for their mothers to testify ostensibly in order to help establish their daughter's credibility. Putting mothers on the stand, however, allows defence attorneys to also place the mother's credibility on the stand and draw out distinctions between "good" and "bad" motherhood (Thurer 1994). The good/bad mother dichotomy has been operating in Western societies for a long time. Mothers have been the centre point of the family since the Victorian era, contributing to the governance of society through their focus on the family, the microcosm of society (Giles 2012). As Molly Ladd-Taylor and Lauri Umansky explain, over the last century, the "bad mother' label has been generally applied to any woman who falls outside traditional middle-class white norms. These women typically fall under three categories: (1) women who live outside of the nuclear family, (2) women who were unable to protect their children from harm, and (3) women whose children "went wrong" (1998, 3).

Questioning of the mother's credibility can be evidenced in the Beckford case, where the defence constructed the incident as a "stunt" pulled by a sixteen-year-old girl:

DEFENCE: Would it be accurate to say that you didn't know whether it was another stunt your daughter is pulling?

WITNESS: No, that would not be accurate because my daughter has never pulled a stunt, as you say. This is not a stunt why we're here today. There's no history of this situation, so I wouldn't agree with that.

DEFENCE: And, you would not have used those words to describe that phone call, correct?

WITNESS: No.

DEFENCE: At the preliminary hearing, you were asked by the Crown, what your son said to you, and you indicate he told you she was out in [name of city] with some guy. You say that you felt something wasn't right about that and you say, "I didn't know what to do at the time, I wasn't sure if she was just pulling a stunt but I knew that she wasn't high and I knew that she was scared so something wasn't right." Do you recall being asked that question?

(*R. v. Beckford*, audio of trial, 25 January 2013)

The defence attorney's emphasis on the word "stunt" is noteworthy, as it undermines the seriousness of the events as a joke played by a child and stands in contrast with the seriousness of the charge of human trafficking. The above exchange also reveals the defence attorney's suggestion that the mother's inability to tell the difference between a stunt her daughter was pulling and real fear, exposes her subpar parenting. The complainant's mother in this case lived outside of the traditional nuclear family setting as a single mother – that, combined with her daughter's "rogue" behaviour, made her an easy target to be categorized as a "bad mother."

This categorization was continued in another exchange between the same parties regarding the complainant's attempts to reach out to her family for help:

WITNESS: Initially when she [complainant] said I'm sorry and I love you mommy, I was like, I don't want to hear it, and I passed the phone.
DEFENCE: You didn't want to hear it and you didn't believe that there was something wrong, or you didn't want to hear what was wrong at that time?
WITNESS: I didn't want to hear anything that she had to say at that moment.
DEFENCE: I'm going to suggest to you that you said to her, you are full of shit.
WITNESS: Yes.
DEFENCE: So, she calls you up and says I love you mom and you say, you're full of shit and you pass the phone to [name of son], and [name of son] is closer in age to [name of complainant].

(*R. v. Beckford*, audio of trial, 25 January 2013)

The defence attorney is thus suggesting that she is a "bad" mother due to her failure to respond to her daughter's call for help. Ladd-Taylor and Umansky explain that class is an important factor in determining who gets labelled as a "bad" mother. Since the 1990s, there has been a shift away from the glamourization of the working mother and a move back to the "cult of domesticity" (Giles 2012, 124), participation in which is heavily dependent on financial security. Those who cannot abide by this shift are now often categorized as bad mothers. The complainant's mother in this case was a single, working mother, yet the challenges she faced in juggling childcare, work, and other obligations are not taken into consideration in the defence's suggestion that she failed in her role as a mother by not believing and not responding to her daughter's plea for help. The defence counsel's ultimate goal is to propose that a "bad" mother raised a "bad" daughter who is not naïve, innocent, and blameless but is instead drug-addicted, unruly, and not a victim of trafficking.

When complainants displayed aggressive responses to authority and attempts to control, defence attorneys often delineated this to mean that such complainants could not have been controlled and victimized by the accused because of their defiant and aggressive personality/demeanour. As such, defence attorneys explore complainants' histories of violent behaviour whenever available to suggest that it is unreasonable to propose that a complainant, who behaves in an inappropriate manner, in court or other situations in their life could be forcibly confined or made to do something against their will. This suggestion relies on the stereotyped assumptions of what trafficking victims are like – coy, passive, and easily controlled. Complainants' past violent behaviour and criminal histories are also mined by the defence for evidence of moral depravity "to contrast them with" the image of the "ideal victim" and therefore to show that they are not a "real" victim. This is seen in an exchange between the complainant and the defence attorney in *R. v. Beckford*:

> DEFENCE: *And you'd agree with me that when your mother tries to get you to do something and you don't want to do it you react by raising your voice like you did at me yesterday for asking the questions, correct?*
> COMPLAINANT: No, incorrect.
> DEFENCE: *And I'm going to suggest that when the police ask you to do certain things, you respond by raising your voice and getting aggressive, correct?*
> COMPLAINANT: Incorrect.
> DEFENCE: You've been convicted of assaults in the past?
> COMPLAINANT: Correct.
> DEFENCE: *You actually hit somebody as a result of an interaction you had with them.*
> COMPLAINANT: I punched somebody because that somebody cut off my cat's toe and the cat had to have twelve stitches, so yeah, I punched them out.
>
> (*R. v. Beckford*, audio of trial,
> 6 March 2013; emphasis added)

The defence attorney's suggestions that the complainant is defiant, aggressive and therefore, not a "true victim" continues as follows:

> DEFENCE: Essentially, when you feel that if somebody is doing something you don't like you can get aggressive?
> COMPLAINANT: Doesn't mean that I will be aggressive.
> DEFENCE: *But you can be aggressive.*

COMPLAINANT: Anyone can be aggressive.

DEFENCE: *In cases where you feel that somebody is telling you to do something that you don't feel is right you can get aggressive, right?*

COMPLAINANT: I can, yeah.

DEFENCE: *You can raise your voice?*

COMPLAINANT: Not every time. I do have self-control.

(*R. v. Beckford*, audio of trial,
6 March 2013; emphasis added)

The defence attorney's intent here is to undermine the possibility that the complainant could have been victimized, given her tendency to "get aggressive" and "raise her voice," therefore, making her victimization very difficult for the accused.

Defence emphasis on the aggressive behaviour of the complainant is also demonstrated in *R. v. Oliver-Machado* (2014), as seen in an exchange by the defence attorney and the mother of one of the complainants:

DEFENCE: You called 911 because of an assault complaint you had.

WITNESS: No, that's not the reason I called. I called because she [the complainant] was out of control and smashing the walls, not for an assault.

DEFENCE: She kicked holes in the drywall?

WITNESS: Yes, underneath her window.

DEFENCE: You were afraid of getting hurt by your daughter?

WITNESS: Yes, I didn't want her to hit me. The female officer that responded suggested I charge her with mischief. That would open up doors for her to get help. I didn't know she was charged with assault.

(*R. v. Oliver-Machado*, audio of trial,
26 April 2013)

The image of the complainant as smashing walls, kicking holes into drywall, and endangering the physical well-being of her own mother, created by the defence, stands in stark contrast to the image of the "ideal victim" who needs protection and thus undermines the position of the Crown that she was forced into an exploitative situation.

Another way in which defence attorneys separated complainants from the "ideal victim" narrative was through a focus on their criminal records. In *R. v. Beckford* (2013), the defence attempted to construct the complainant as dangerous by pointing out her extensive criminal record and suggesting that a tattoo she had on her body indicated a gang affiliation:

DEFENCE: I'm noticing that on your right side there appears to be some ... tattoos?

COMPLAINANT: Yes.

DEFENCE: You agree with me that that is a reflection of gang culture – that you've been involved in some sort of murder or request for...
COMPLAINANT: No, I disagree – I strongly disagree.
DEFENCE: I'm going to suggest to you that you are still involved in the gang and drug culture now.

(R. v. Beckford, audio of trial, 5 March 2013)

By using a set of controlled questions, the defence attorney developed an impression of the complainant as a gang member involved in murders. He goes on to point out that the complainant's extensive criminal record, which is "18 offenses long" and includes "robbery, drugs, theft" (R. v. Beckford, audio of trial, 25 January 2013), suggests she is a hardened criminal with violent tendencies who is far from the vulnerable victim the Crown is trying to present.

Similar to the above situation, one of the complainants in R. v. Oliver-Machado (2014) also had a criminal record, which the defence attorney gladly explored with her mother in an effort to construct an image of the complainant as a criminal, rather than a victim:

DEFENCE: Many instances where the police came to your house in response to a complaint against your daughter?
WITNESS: Some yes, some correct, and a number of them weren't...
DEFENCE: She was issued a number of YCJA [Youth Criminal Justice Act] warnings. How many? Six?
WITNESS: I'm not aware of six; I received something twice.
DEFENCE: Warning your daughter for criminal conduct?
WITNESS: I'm not sure it was criminal; it was minor, not criminal.
DEFENCE: Do you recall receiving one for shoplifting?
WITNESS: Yes.
DEFENCE: Would you consider that criminal?
WITNESS: I'm not sure for youth.

(R. v. Oliver-Machado, audio of trial,
26 April 2013)

The defence's emphasis on the criminal past of the complainant was intended to discredit her testimony by portraying her as morally deprived and therefore not trustworthy. It was also used to suggest that she is not an innocent victim, but more like the accused herself, revealing an operating reliance on the binary construction of victim/perpetrator. This denies the complainant her victimhood due to her history of behaviours and characteristics that align her with the perpetrator.

To prove the presence of consent to activities under question, defence counsel often work hard to show that the complainant was able to leave the situation – often hinging on the idea of common sense that once in a dangerous situation, common sense surely dictates that she would do what she could to get out of jeopardy. If the complainant does not follow this common-sense strategy of leaving the situation, then they must be consenting to it (see also Roots and Lockhart 2021). For instance, in *R. v. Burton* (2016), the defence counsel challenged the complainant's inability to leave through the following questions,

> DEFENCE: I'm going to try and jog your memory by suggesting that on the days that you were at [the accused's] house, he wasn't always there with you, correct?
> COMPLAINANT: Correct.
> DEFENCE: He would leave that resident for several hours at a time, correct?
> COMPLAINANT: Correct.
>
> (Audio of trial, 31 January 2014)

The suggestion by the defence in the case above was that since the accused was not physically holding her down, she was able to leave, and since she did not leave, it must mean that she chose to stay and consented to what was happening. The complainants' ability to leave the physical situation was also questioned by the defence in *R. v. Oliver-Machado* (2014). Consider the following exchange:

> DEFENCE: You step into his [client's] vehicle, he doesn't force you to get in there.
> COMPLAINANT: No.
> DEFENCE: [accused #1] doesn't force you to get in there.
> COMPLAINANT: No.
> DEFENCE: [accused #2] doesn't force you to get in there.
> COMPLAINANT: No.
> DEFENCE: You don't try to walk away.
> COMPLAINANT: No, I didn't want to try. I thought I was going to get beat up.
> DEFENCE: But you don't try to run away.
> COMPLAINANT: No.
> DEFENCE: It's a well-lit, busy area. You didn't try running out and flagging someone down?
> COMPLAINANT: The streets were clear, there was no cars at all.
> DEFENCE: When you get in the car with the first male, you have a polite conversation with him?
> COMPLAINANT: Yes.

DEFENCE: He doesn't make any threats to you.

COMPLAINANT: No.

DEFENCE: You have a conversation with him about what you do for a living. He makes small talk.

COMPLAINANT: Yes.

DEFENCE: You talk about having done this once or twice before.

COMPLAINANT: Yes.

DEFENCE: There's a conversation about money.

COMPLAINANT: Yes.

DEFENCE: He stops at a bank machine, goes in, and takes out a certain amount of money. When he does that, you are in the car by yourself?

COMPLAINANT: Yes.

DEFENCE: You don't get out of the car and walk away.

COMPLAINANT: No.

DEFENCE: You don't get out of the car and run away.

COMPLAINANT: No.

DEFENCE: You never asked the man if you can not do this.

COMPLAINANT: No.

(*R. v. Oliver-Machado*, audio of trial, 22 April 2013)

The defence thus points to the fact that the complainant was not physically forced into the car and had several opportunities to escape the situation by simply walking or running away. If she did not do so, then she must be consenting. This is despite the complainant's indication that she was being threatened by the accused and was feeling scared, to which the defence attorney suggested that "smoking marijuana is having the effect of making you paranoid" (*R. v. Oliver-Machado*, audio of trial, 22 April 2013; see also Roots and Lockhart 2021). The implication is that if the complainant truly wanted to leave, there were opportunities to escape. Based on the fact that she did not leave, the assumption was that she did not really want to leave and was therefore not trafficked. This argument ignores the psychological fears being expressed by the complainant which go beyond the physical ability to leave the situation, as well as the Criminal Code definition of trafficking, which does not require that the victim subjectively fear for their safety. Instead, the fear of safety standard is objective based on the "reasonable person standard" (see chapter one for discussion). In this case, the complainant testified that they did indeed fear for their safety, thus surpassing the legal requirement necessitated for human trafficking, a determination also made by the court (see also Roots and Lockhart 2021).

As scholars have extensively documented, this line of questioning is common in trials dealing with sexual assault where evidence of resistance is paramount to legitimizing the complainant's claim, a point also made by the Crown counsel in *R. v. Dagg* (2015):

> JUDGE: I would ask you this, here she is at the [name of location], early on, I think this is very early on in her interplay with these people when she says things are pretty good. So here she is at the [name of location] and here's [another woman] being beaten up by [accused 2]. Why wouldn't she just say, "I'm out of here"? You're trying to turn it around to say "oh no she's confined by this conduct"? A thirty-five-year-old woman?
>
> CROWN: Well, Your Honour, this is the same question we've been asking in rape and domestic violence cases forever. The domestic violence victim is beat up by her husband; why would she stay with her husband, you know?
>
> (Audio of trial, 7 April 2015)

Such arguments, commonly seen in domestic violence and sexual assault cases, are weaving their way into the human trafficking matrix and shaping the way trafficking is coming to be understood. In the absence of clarity on the elements of trafficking, especially consent and exploitation, court agents rely on other familiar frameworks, notably ones from sexual and domestic assault cases, which do, but also do not, fit with this particular offence. In contrast, and as demonstrated throughout this chapter, the prosecution's argument is premised on the idea that the coerciveness of these situations is much more subtle and is often dependent on complainants' pre-existing vulnerabilities.

Conclusion

The concept was officially reintroduced by the Trafficking Protocol due to fierce and seemingly successful efforts of pro–sex work feminists, aimed at establishing a distinction between sex work and trafficking. And as this chapter has shown, the consent factor is central in prosecution and defence strategies in Canadian human trafficking trials studied here – a finding which should come as no surprise, as international and Canadian laws establish that one cannot consent to human trafficking, even as one can consent to sex work. Lack of consent is central to the establishment of the offence of human trafficking, yet, as discussed in chapter one, the concept is not straightforward and is influenced by a number of factors including mental health, drug use, youth, sex work, and other factors that are used by Crown and defence attorneys to establish different narratives that support or undermine the case for human trafficking. Rather than simply prosecuting human trafficking, this chapter has shown that the legal strategies used by Crowns and defence attorneys for other crimes have become a part of the human

trafficking matrix and are in fact shaping the crime of human trafficking on the ground. The legal narratives reveal both the use of pre-
established sexual assault frameworks in the trying of trafficking, as
well as attempts by Crown attorneys to establish new lines of arguments that sometimes tap into the stereotyped narratives around the
offence of trafficking and its victims. In essence, evidence outlined in
this chapter reveals that the offence of trafficking does not have a uni-
form applied definition and continues to be shaped through actions of
police (as seen in chapter three), as well as those of Crown and defence
attorneys.

Chapter Five

The Villain

The myth is that these girls come across in containers from these Third World countries, they get to Canada, and they're spread out throughout Canada and they're trafficked. Whereas I can tell you that 98–99 per cent of the girls that we get are born and raised in Canada. It doesn't mean that it doesn't happen that girls come here from other countries. We haven't seen very much of it. All the girls that we have are domestic.

(participant 1)

As with the victim of trafficking, the image of the "trafficker" plays a crucial role in confirming Canada's national imaginary and draws (thinly coded racially defined) lines between "barbarism" and "civilization," both transnationally and domestically, thus making it a crucial factor to examine. This chapter explores the development of trafficker discourses and the ways in which it shapes Canada's national imaginary at the level of public and political discourses. As the Canadian human trafficking focus shifted from transnational migration to a "home-grown problem," the villain of the story – the trafficker – also underwent changes, shifting from a Russian or Chinese mobster to that of a racialized Canadian immigrant. In Canada, the two most common images of the "trafficker" are (1) the foreign, often Russian or Chinese, mobster who operates or works for a transnational organized crime ring and has no respect for women; and (2) the individual, often Black, "pimp" who exploits his friend or girlfriend in the sex trade. These two images, as I discuss below, are products of two very different discourses around international and domestic trafficking.

The first part of this chapter explores the ways in which the "foreign" trafficker is discursively linked to the problems associated with transnational organized crime, the War on Terror, and national security. The second part focuses on the way in which the discourse of the "foreign" trafficker is combined within the human trafficking matrix with that of the local "pimp," an image which mobilizes the associated issues related to sexual and domestic violence, child sexual exploitation, and sex work to shape the figure of the domestic trafficker. Drawing on the findings of my research data, this chapter focuses more specifically on the construction of Black men as traffickers, who are overwhelmingly the accused in trafficking cases. To make sense of this racializing construction, this chapter draws on critical race literature to explore how the Black "pimp," who has been a longstanding target of the procuring provisions in Canada (s. 286.3 [1] of CCC), has re-emerged as the main target of anti-trafficking enforcement and prosecution. This chapter illustrates the ways in which Crown and even defence attorneys draw on racialized stereotypes of Black men as always and already suspect, threatening and criminal, despite their engagement in rather common activities that would not otherwise raise suspicion. The chapter examines how characteristics and activities stereotypically associated with "pimps" and "pimping" are recrafted to fit the legal requirements of human trafficking and contribute to the formation of the human trafficking matrix, thus folding the exceptional into normal. In the process, those accused of trafficking are routinely represented as "monsters," "parasites," and "animals" who not only pose a threat to members of the public but also, by virtue of their imputed "gangsterism," pose a larger threat to national security and public safety. These findings reflect and contribute to what Robyn Maynard calls Canada's "anti-blackness" that "continues to hide in plain sight, obscured behind the normal commitment to liberalism, multiculturalism and equality" (2017, 3). The chapter elucidates the racial politics that operate within these discourses and exposes the ways in which various "racialized practices regulate the boundaries of citizenship" (Murdocca 2004, 154). In the context of trafficking, we can look to how the racialized and ethnicized category of the "trafficker" is produced through knowledge making by policymakers and criminal justice actors and how this is in turn produces the boundaries of citizenship and national belonging.

Linking Trafficking with Terrorism

The discursive combination of the War on Terror with human trafficking was enabled by the spectre of organized crime and threats to national security, along with the representation of a mutual enemy in the form of a "dangerous foreigner," both inside and outside borders. One profound effect of this combination is that it provides the War on Terror with a human face. As Kempadoo explains, "the breadth and scope of the war [on terror] remain undefined and ambiguous. It would include a situation where, if terrorism was defined as a transnational crime, then by merely committing the crime of seeking illegal movement and illegal entry these people [migrants] could be defined as terrorists" (2005, 34). In the United States, the past twenty years has seen the proliferation of law and policy measures designed to act upon terrorism and organized crime threats posed by the crime of human trafficking. On 16 December 2002, then US President George W. Bush signed National Security Directive 22, which specifically linked human trafficking to terrorism and public health (Rizer and Glaser 2011, 70). As Soderlund explains, Bush, in part motivated to respond to criticisms of the US occupation of Iraq, drew on historically and institutionally embedded rhetoric to move "effortlessly from the war on terrorism to the evils of global sex trafficking," symbolically linking the United States to "the broader moral agenda embodied by the new 'War Against Trafficking'" (2005, 77; see, too, Aradau 2008). This linkage between the War on Trafficking and the War on Terror was further cemented in 2004, with the passage of the US Intelligence Reform and Terrorism Prevention Act, which led to the establishment of the Human Smuggling and Trafficking Center to study human trafficking, smuggling, and "criminal support of underground terrorist travel." The following year, the Trafficking Victims Protection Reauthorization Act mandated the formation of an interagency task force to study the relationship between trafficking in persons and terrorism (Rizer and Glaser 2011, 70).

International efforts to link the War on Terror with human trafficking were evident as early as 2004 when the UNODC wrote "*with deep concern*" of "the growing links between transnational organized crime and terrorist crime" and called upon: "*all States* to recognize the links between transnational organized criminal activities and acts of terrorism, taking into account the relevant General Assembly resolutions, and to apply the United Nations Convention against Transnational Organized Crime in combating all forms of criminal activity, as provided therein" (2004, 2; emphasis in original). The strength gained by this link between the War on Terror and trafficking at the international level is revealed through the UN Security Council's meeting held in December 2015, the expressed purpose of which was to discuss the connection between human trafficking and terrorism, a connection which Yuri Fedotov, the executive director of UNODC, calls the "crime-terrorism-conflict nexus" (UNODC 2015a). The following year, the Security Council adopted Decision 2331, which provided international recognition of the "connection between human trafficking, sexual violence, terrorism and other transnational organized criminal activities" (OSCE

2017, 42). At the 2015 meeting Fedetov maintained that "human trafficking during armed conflict ... could be part of the strategic objectives and ideologies of certain terrorist groups" and suggested that "victims of trafficking and sexual violence should be categorized as victims of terrorism" (UNODC 2015a). This position was supported by Ban Ki-Moon, the secretary-general of the United Nations who, during the same Security Council meeting, held that terrorist organizations use "trafficking and sexual violence as a weapon of terror and an important source of revenue" (UNODC 2015a). The special representative of the secretary-general on sexual violence in conflict, Ainab Hawa Bangura, called the use of sexual violence and trafficking "new tactics of terrorism" and encouraged a rethinking of responses to these issues (ibid.). These recent actions by the UN Security Council evince the strength of this association between trafficking and terrorism at the international level.

In the Canadian context, the reconfiguration of organized crime as a threat to national security was most notable with the 2002 enactment of the IRPA. According to Pratt, the IRPA was first drafted in response to perceived Canadian national security threats posed by organized criminal networks (2005, 3). US criticism of Canada's porous borders and lenient immigration policies following 9/11 led the government to bring in "sweeping new legislation targeting the terrorist threat within" (Pratt 2005, 3; see also Oxman-Martinez et al. 2005). The ensuing Anti-Terrorism Act (2001) "dramatically expanded the powers of law enforcement and national security agents to target, monitor, arrest, and detain without warrant Canadian citizens on the basis of suspicions relating to terrorist activity" (Pratt 2005, 3). The IRPA and the Anti-Terrorism Act "were promoted as Canada's hard-hitting, two-pronged contributions to the post-September 11th 'War against Terrorism'" (Pratt 2005, 4).

At the same time as the War on Terror maintained its global face, it, like trafficking, simultaneously expanded into the domestic terrain. The War on Terror's turn to domestic criminal activities has been captured in the work of Jeffrey Monaghan, who argues that in Canada, discourses of radicalization and violent extremism have led to the War on Terror becoming increasingly focused on activities and individuals within Canada (2014, 489). The expanded threat environment means that the War on Terror "can comprise threats based domestically or abroad. It can include direct violence or the support of violence. It can include participation in extremist activities or providing forms of material support for violence abroad. It can be applied to direct violence against civilians or activities that can be understood by authorities as threatening 'Canadian interests'. It can include events that have happened, would have happened, or events that may happen" (Monaghan 2014, 489). This expanded field of action, and the vagueness with which it is applied, works to link Canada's war against domestic terrorism with simultaneous efforts to combat human trafficking within the matrix. Indeed, evidence of this linking of terrorism and human trafficking can be seen through the suggestion that the proceeds of trafficking support terrorism and can be tracked through domestic banking activities of Canadians. The connection between these "wars" can be observed, in part, through the established partnership between the RCMP and the Financial Transactions and Reporting Analysis Centre of Canada (FINTRAC), an organization which works to "establish links between individuals and groups in Canada and abroad who engage in money laundering and support terrorism" (2016, 13). Specifically, FINTRAC and the RCMP launched Project Protect, an initiative that enables Canadian financial institutions to track money laundering associated with human trafficking and alert FINTRAC of any suspicious activity. The expansion of the linked issues of terrorism and trafficking into the domestic terrain is captured by the comments of Luc Beaudry, the assistant director of collaboration, development, and research at FINTRAC, who explains, "To put a human face on this initiative, it has led directly to dozens of young Canadian women being rescued from the most deplorable conditions imaginable over the past year" (Government of Canada, 2018). Whether this is true is unknown, but the promise put forward by Beaudry serves well to justify the bank's role as the scout for the police. Beaudry's remarks draw an explicit connection between domestic exploitation of Canadian women and girls in the sex trade and international terrorist activities. Linking human trafficking with the War on Terror enables the imagination of a potentially catastrophic future, akin to the enormity of 9/11 in the past, to translate the fear of terrorism into proactive strategies against traffickers, who are always foreign and racialized and exploiting Canada's daughters.

The Problem of International Trafficking

The shift from international to domestic trafficking has transformed the imagination of the villainous trafficker and the way they are spoken about, both in parliamentary debates and among those interviewed for this study. In contrast with constructions of trafficking victims as "our girls" and "our women," we see contradictory discourses focused on the racial and ethnic Otherness of the traffickers. As Carmella Murdocca contends, "in the context of a white settler society such as Canada, the historical production and reproduction of racist discourse operate as an unfixed set of ideological and narrative formations that emerge from, respond to, and help construct changing historical conditions in order to legitimize racial categories and racial delineations" (2004, 155). To examine the ways in which the boundaries of citizenship are shaped within the trafficking matrix through the "trafficker" as a representative of "uncivility," we can first look at the case of *R. v. Dagg* (2015). Taylor Dagg is a racialized man who at the age of twenty-three was arrested for trafficking a thirty-two-year-old woman. During his interrogation, the two police officers asked Dagg why human trafficking charges are "more sensitive" than other charges, elucidating the following exchange:

> ACCUSED: Because it's a person's body and it's sex and uh...
> OFFICER: Yeah.
> ACCUSED: Uh, free will and...
> OFFICER: Yeah. It's against a person's free will.
> ACCUSED: I understand that.
> OFFICER: See, *this country prides itself on something called free will.*
> ACCUSED: Free will, yeah.
> OFFICER: Free (inaudible)
> ACCUSED: And I understand that.
> OFFICER: And *you two*[1] *come here and cut apart everything that we stand for.*
>
> (*R. v. Dagg* 2015, police interview,
> part 6; emphasis added)

The interaction between the officers and the accused shows a prevailing sense of moral superiority attributed to Canada as a nation that prioritizes and defends human rights and stands in opposition to the barbarism that human trafficking represents. Trafficking, then, is anathema to Canadian values and freedoms, and therefore the state has the moral authority to defend against it. And while the accused in this case was a Canadian resident, he was nonetheless a racialized man born outside of Canada and therefore Othered as someone who "comes here and harms people." In this construction, Dagg's crime highlighted, at least for the police investigators, the harms of migration, implying the need for greater border control. Cases such as that of Dagg demonstrate the mobilization of tropes around trafficking made available by the expansive trafficking matrix as a distinctly un-Canadian crime, something carried across borders by migrants who undermine Canadian civility as evidenced by our adherence to human rights. In this way, the trafficker remains a foreigner/outsider in the public and political imagination, whose moral turpitude has the ability to infect the Canadian society.

"Foreign-ness" was also a strong element in the labour trafficking case involving the Kolompar and Domotor families, originally from Hungary. The families were found to have formed a criminal organization that facilitated the trafficking of nineteen other Hungarians to Canada for work in their construction business. In this case, all the elements of a more "traditional" trafficking case were in play, including migration across international borders, forced labour, exploitation, restrictions on movement, and withholding of documents. Court evidence revealed that upon arrival, the complainants' passports were taken and withheld by the employing family, and they were forced to work long hours at construction sites with very little or no pay. When not working, the complainants were confined to the family's home basement and fed once a day with scraps. The family also forced the complainants to apply for social assistance – money that the family took from the complainants.

The members of the Domotor and Kolompor families were charged with human trafficking (s. 279.01), withholding identifying documents (s. 279.03), receiving material benefits by failing to pay the workers for their labour (s. 279.02), defrauding the City of Hamilton through payments made to the complainants under the Ontario Works Act (s. 380.1[b]), taking part in a criminal organization (s. 467.11[1]), and criminal conspiracy (s. 465[1][c]) (Hastie and Yule 2014). And while Gyongyi Kolompar, Ferenc Domotor, and Ferenc Domotor Jr. were also charged with section 126[2] of the IRPA, with the latter two also charged with section 124(1)(c)[3] of the IRPA, it is interesting to note that none of the accused were charged with section 118 of the IRPA, which governs transnational human trafficking. The reasons for this are curious given that the case contains elements of transnational trafficking and in the context of a notable absence of convictions under this provision of IRPA. In fact, CBSA records show there have been only eight charges laid under section 118 of the IRPA between 1 January 2006 and 13 July 2020, and none of these have ended in successful prosecutions.[4] The vast majority of the trafficking cases in Canada, are domestic and do not involve migrants, organized crime, or cross-border transportation of victims. All but two members of the families pled guilty to trafficking or related offences and were sentenced to jail and subsequent deportation.

While this case aligns with the elements of transnational trafficking and was seen as providing evidence that transnational trafficking exists in Canada, it is worth noting that this case was an exception in the Canadian anti-trafficking landscape since migrant trafficking and involvement of organized crime are rare (see also Hastie and Yule 2014).

It was, in part, the exceptional nature of the crime that led to significant media coverage of the Domotor–Kolompar case. In a well-publicized speech marking their deportation, then Public Safety Minister Steven Blaney released the names of nine of the individuals convicted of what he called "the most heinous of crimes" and declared, "We are sending a clear signal that there is no room in Canada for those who are committing the heinous and despicable crime of human trafficking" (Carter 2014). Blaney's deportation announcement, which highlights the fact that Canada is "intolerant" of this behaviour, draws a clear line between this type of barbaric crime and Canadian values. As Jeffrey explains, Canada's identity as a morally superior nation tasked with solving "many of the world's problems" is carefully upheld by constructing human trafficking as an "innate object beyond the government's control, which it is then forced to confront" (2005, 39). Such national moral superiority was evident in Justice Glithero's judgment hearing for three of the accused in the case of *R. v. Domotor* (2012): "this country has a long and strong tradition of respecting human rights and dignity, and a strong tradition of providing assistance to those who require it, and a strong tradition of being welcoming to people from other lands. As Canadians we are proud of these values that are central to our being and when our values are abused, flagrantly, as they were by these three individuals, we are offended and intolerant to those who behave in this fashion. Modern day slavery is disgusting to us and it offends our core values" (*R. v. Domotor* 2012). Justice Glithero's judgment strongly echoes Blaney's statements one year earlier. Together, these kinds of declarations serve as a "grand performance of the sovereign authority of the Canadian nation-state to coercively control its borders in the name of protecting the public and nation from the crime-security threats posed by dangerous outsiders" (Pratt 2005, 276). Convicting migrants for trafficking offers the perfect opportunity for such "grand performances."

In his decision, Justice Glithero also used the language of modern-day slavery to describe the actions of the Domotor–Kolompar families. The equation of trafficking with slavery provides powerful support for the humanitarian framework and helps further the anti-trafficking agenda. The Domotor case is as close as we come to human trafficking as defined by international law and provides the most support for the categorization of trafficking as modern-day slavery. The image of slavery is a powerful tool which, according to Kamala Kempadoo, evokes images of the worst known treatment of humans associated with the cross-Atlantic slave trade of African people (2005, xix). This discursive link between human-trafficking-as-slavery also employed during the white slavery panics at the turn of the twentieth century, conjures up images of suffering and horror that require immediate intervention. As such, the anti-trafficking and slavery cause has received widespread support across a variety of political spectrums, which, according to Bunting and Quirk, creates the impression that these issues are "non-ideological and removed from 'normal' politics" (2017, 19). In Canada, this translates in specific ways. In particular, rather than focus on the plight of the exploited migrants and/or trafficking victims, we see modern-day slavery and trafficking rhetoric being used to support an anti–sex work agenda and to justify aggressive criminalization and even deportation of non-citizens who "traffick" Canadian women.

Framing trafficking as a human rights issue exists alongside a simultaneous focus on organized crime. The links between trafficking and organized crime were materially and discursively consolidated when the international Trafficking Protocol (2000) emerged as part of the Convention against Transnational Organized Crime (2000). As John Ferguson explains, the Trafficking Protocol "was presented to the international community as a new tool, an internationally sanctioned instrument for governments to use in their fight against the threat of rapidly expanding transnational organized crime groups that were believed to be profiting from the formed movement of, and abusive exploitation of, enslaved people across national boundaries" (2012, 68).[5] The emphasis on human trafficking as one of the new threats of transnational organized crime reveals the intersecting objectives of securing borders and criminalizing the accused while simultaneously emphasizing the need to protect victims of trafficking.

The linking of trafficking with organized crime has shaped the official mandates of a wide range of international organizations, including not only the UN but also transnational policing agencies such as FRONTEX, the European Border and Coast Guard Agency, the European Union's law enforcement agency, EUROPOL, and the International Criminal Police Organization (INTERPOL). In 2016, the UNODC emphasized that the intent of human trafficking campaigns is to raise awareness about transnational organized crime, a priority also shared by INTERPOL, which affirmed that "trafficking in human beings is a multi-billion-dollar form of *international organized crime, constituting modern-day slavery*" (2016; emphasis added). Concerns over wealth accumulated by transnational organized crime groups through human trafficking activities enables trafficking to be constructed as an economic and moral imperative.

Like their international counterparts, Canadian policing organizations have also raised concerns over the involvement of organized crime in human trafficking and the threats posed by organized crime to Canada's economic security and national integrity. For instance, according to a 2016 RCMP report, entitled "Human Trafficking in Canada: A Threat Assessment," "many human trafficking suspects have been linked to other organized criminal activities, such as conspiracy to commit murder, credit card fraud, mortgage fraud, immigration fraud, and organized prostitution, in Canada or abroad" (RCMP 2016a). The Ontario Association of Chiefs of Police similarly noted that Ontario is a "home to organized crime groups who profit from the huge global market in trafficking human beings, and to its victims" (n.d., 22). As detailed in chapter three, the sophisticated cross-border elements that are seen as inherent to the specific crime of trafficking have motivated police to enjoin, at least in reports and talking points, multi-jurisdictional efforts that transcend local policing practices.

This construction of human trafficking as a form of organized crime threatening the economic security of Canada is also echoed in parliamentary debates about trafficking laws and in interviews with criminal justice actors conducted for this study. For example, during a debate on Bill C-310, MP Fin Donnelly (NDP) described traffickers as "often highly sophisticated, multinational criminal organizations that are experts at trading humans, just as they would weapons, drugs or firearms" (House of Commons, 12 December 2011, Bill C-310). In addition to the references involving multinational organized crime, evoking the transnational trafficking discourse and sending a message that trafficking comes from outside Canada's borders, the statement by MP Donnelly also frames the issues within a modern-day slavery framework where victims are dehumanized and treated as commodities such as drugs and guns. The ways in which various threats come together under the umbrella term "human trafficking" is paradigmatic of the human trafficking matrix in operation.

In court cases, we see characteristics of domestic trafficking being used to build discursive connections to (transnational) organized crime discourses. This is demonstrated in the highly publicized case of Kailey Oliver-Machado – a fifteen-year-old labelled as a human trafficking ringleader for her part in forcing other underage girls into sex work. She and two of her accomplices were found to have lured three of their peers to parties and outings with the intent of carrying out criminal activities. According to the Crown in summation, the accused "was essentially the ringleader of the enterprise and that was a criminal enterprise that sought to capitalize on the innocence of other young girls through violence and exploitation in a common pursuit of instant financial gain." The Crown went on to note that "while there were three co-accused, it appeared to be the collective impression of almost all of the victims who testified that Ms. Oliver-Machado was, in fact, the ring-leader" (*R. v. Oliver-Machado*, audio of trial, 30 September 2014). The crimes of Oliver-Machado and her co-accused were presented by the Crown as a form of organized criminality since they appeared to be well-planned and organized: she had a list of "johns'" numbers, access to "underground taxis," and the participation of two other teenagers. Using the language of organized crime, the prosecution carefully and systematically constructed (then) fifteen-year-old Oliver-Machado as a leader of a criminal organization, arguing that her acts "were well planned, well organized, pre-meditated and executed with a degree of precision much to the detriment of her intended victims" (*R. v. Oliver-Machado*, audio of trial, 30 September 2014). Oliver-Machado's small operation thus attains the moniker of "criminal enterprise" – a strategy which, in this case, was successful. What we see then is the collapsing of "criminal organization," which Oliver-Machado engaged in and "organized crime," two concepts which, while sounding similar, are actually quite distinct. The success of this strategy may be, in part, because unlike in most Canadian trafficking cases where the complaints are marginalized women and girls, often working in the sex trade, in the Oliver-Machado case, the victims fell into the category of the "girls next door, thus making conviction and harsh punishment more urgent and necessary."

With the exception of a few cases where organized crime links were successfully made, as with Domotor and Oliver-Machado, empirical evidence does not support the presumed connection between organized crime and trafficking (see Aradau 2008; Bruckert and Parent 2004; Feingold 2005; Kapur 2005; Kempadoo 2005; Millar et al. 2015; Roots 2013; Sanghera 2005). The few Canadian studies that exist on criminalization of trafficking show that most of those charged in trafficking cases have no confirmed connections to criminal organizations. Instead, the vast majority of human trafficking cases in Canada deal with low-level domestic, largely racialized, poor and not terribly well organized or sophisticated offenders (see also Ferguson 2012; Millar et al. 2015; Roots 2013). That this has not diminished the significance of criminal organizations within the human trafficking matrix is, itself, testimony to its significance in the construction of Canadian domestic trafficking.

Evidence that a few Canadian trafficking cases involve sophisticated enterprises has not diminished the discursive reliance on the policing of criminal organizations. The bridge between small-time criminality that is typically targeted by anti-trafficking efforts, and actual organized crime, is provided by the term "street gang," which is used fluidly and interchangeably with the term "organized crime." For instance, according to information provided by Criminal Intelligence Services Canada (CISC):

> A number of the organized crime networks assessed, some that have been involved in the illicit sex trade for decades, have evolved from individuals involved in street-level pimping (characteristic of the mid-90s) to well-organized networks that have shifted toward less visible environments, such as strip bars, massage parlours, hotel/motels, the Internet, and private residences. These networks operate within cell-based structures that allow degrees of independence for individual members to have control of their own prostitutes. Most of these networks maintain tight bonds between members, making law enforcement access difficult. The majority of networks identified are street gangs, particularly located in Ontario, Quebec, Nova Scotia, and New Brunswick.
>
> (2008, 2)

The quote shows how organized crime becomes transliterated as a "street gang" and enables the synonymous use of the two terms. The RCMP draws a similar link between small-scale criminality and transnational organized crime syndicates, noting that transnational organized crime groups are increasingly involved in human trafficking and explaining that transnational crime networks also rely on "*smaller, decentralized criminal* groups that may specialize in recruiting, transporting or harbouring victims" (RCMP 2022; emphasis added). As Anna Pratt (2014) has shown, the term "street gang" emerged as a key target of police in the 1990s, when shifts in the governance of crime and immigration resulted in organized crime becoming loosely defined, including within its ambit violent street crimes, gun crimes, and sex work by smaller, decentralized criminal groups. This variance in the organization of crime groups is captured by the comment of one Crown attorney I spoke to: "Either officially gang-related or there's a group, like, they're [the women are] passed on from one to another sometimes. Even though it may not be like the Crips or the Bloods, in some cases it is, but a group of individuals who are involved in it together and passing girls among each other, so officially and unofficially gangs, I guess" (participant 15).[6] The Crown depiction of "groups of individuals" passing women around also draws on a longer tradition of understanding sex work as an activity controlled by – indeed existing for the purpose of enriching – gangs (Brock 1998; Jeffrey and MacDonald 2006; Smith 2000).

The crafting of trafficking cases in courts is also heavily shaped by an implicit understanding that organized crime threats intersect with small-scale criminality within the trafficking matrix. Indeed, Crown attorneys seem particularly preoccupied with the question of "gang" membership, as evidenced by the case of *R. v. Byron* (2014), where the complainant travelled from Windsor to Toronto to meet the accused and was found in court to have been forced into the sex trade by the accused. In this case, the Crown advanced the argument that "Byron [the accused] was within a network akin to a criminal organization.... Mr. Byron was running a sophisticated organization that was exploiting a young person sexually" (Audio of trial, 13 December 2013). This conclusion was drawn once again based on criminal organization, including arranging hotel rooms, recruiting clients, managing money, etc., rather than involvement in organized crime. The Crown's attempts to establish this connection were rejected by the judge who found that "there was no evidence to suggest that he was operating as a part of an organized crime syndicate in human trafficking" (*R. v. Byron*, audio of trial, 13 February 2014). Nonetheless, the judge convicted Byron of human trafficking . The discourses of organized crime activity may have had an impact on the lengthy sentence of six years of incarceration, along with a number of conditions which stipulated that he must place himself on the sex offender registry and comply with the Sex Offender Registration Act for a period of twenty years, a mandatory weapons prohibition for ten years, and a mandatory DNA order (*R. v. Byron*, audio of trial, 13 February 2014). The harsh sentence indicates that, despite lack of conviction on organized crime–related charges, Byron – a black man – was nonetheless deemed dangerous.

In *R. v. Burton* (2016), we see "gang membership" being presumed from the accused's wardrobe, particularly his loose clothing and backward hat:

CROWN: Can you describe what the gentleman looked like that you observed with [the complainant]?

WITNESS: The person was medium build, dressed in loose clothing, I think he had a backwards hat on, he was dressed like a gangster right out of a movie.

CROWN: So, he was wearing a hat backwards?

WITNESS: Yeah, normal *gangster like garb*.

(*R. v. Burton*, audio of trial,
17 December 2013; emphasis added)

In addition to calling on this witness's subjective interpretation that the accused was wearing "normal gangster garb," the Crown also tried to create an organized crime connection based on the colour of clothing the complainants were prohibited from wearing:

> CROWN: Was there any indication from [the complainant] about any affiliations he had?
>
> WITNESS: Yes, that may have come from [one of the complainants], but they believe that he was a Crips *gang member*.
>
> CROWN: Why did they believe that?
>
> WITNESS: They weren't allowed to wear red because that was the opposing gang members' colour.
>
> (*R. v. Burton*, audio of trial,
> 16 December 2013; emphasis added)

The cultural stereotypes at play in this curation of "evidence" paint a readily accessible and widely familiar picture of a racialized street level "gang banger" (Hill Collins 2004; hooks 2006; Quinn 2000). Such lines of inquiry by legal actors demonstrate the ease with which criminality, dangerousness, and association with gangs are read into Black personhood. Burton's Blackness and non-Canadian origins shore up the idea that trafficking is something that comes from "outsiders," whose criminal associations undermine law-abiding Canadian sensibilities and laws.

The Domestic Trafficker

According to the UNODC, "for a universally condemned, but globally evident issue, surprisingly little is known about human traffickers – those who enable or partake in the trade and exploitation of individual human beings" (2008, 2). As the UNODC outlines, traffickers "can be men or women," "some traffickers are former victims," "a/the majority of offenders are nationals of the country in which the trafficking case is investigated," they can be "children to elderly adults," and some "are married or in domestic partnerships, others are single" (2008, 5–8). The profile of the trafficker, then, is very wide ranging and could be anyone: young, old, single, married, foreign or domestic residents, male or female, victims or villains. The international discourse has tended to place trafficking outside of Canada, focusing on the trafficker as a Russian or Chinese foreigner involved in transnational criminal organization and possibly terrorism – an offence that is not only very serious, but also poses a threat to Canada's national security. This is reflected in the seriousness with which these charges are treated by Canadian courts. This is reflected in the comments of one interviewed Crown attorney: "when I stand at a justice bail hearing two weeks ago, for example, and say, this is a human trafficking case, that resonates now in a way that it wouldn't have necessarily five years ago … that has meaning and content and that increases the seriousness of the case" (participant 6). Using the same logic, we should also expect that those criminalized for human trafficking should be terrorists, transnational organized crime syndicates, and foreign "others." This, however, is not the reality reflected in Canadian court cases.

Because the above-described international figures tend not to present themselves in Canada, Canadian police and legal actors have gone to significant lengths to link them to domestic practices. In so doing, they have worked hard to transform the domestic "pimp" into a human trafficker. This transformation takes place through the human trafficking matrix, where racialized stereotypes are redeployed as indicators of trafficking activities and characteristics of traffickers. The urgency of these indicators and characteristics is amplified by the transnational trafficking discourses which link them with larger concerns over public safety and national security.

While there are no official statistics that can be used to determine the race of those charged with human trafficking in Canada or elsewhere, this study gives a small glimpse into who is being charged with trafficking offences in Ontario, the province with the largest number of trafficking charges in Canada (Maisie 2016; Ibrahim 2018). As outlined in the Introduction, 123 cases of individuals charged with human trafficking under the Criminal Code in Ontario from 2005 to 2016 (as well as noteworthy and precedent-setting cases following the conclusion of the study and until 2021) were analysed for this study, recording not only charges and outcomes but also age, race, and gender, wherever possible. The race of the accused was able to be determined in 89 out of 123 cases examined. Of these eighty-nine individuals, fifty-six (63 per cent) were visible minorities[7] (see Appendix A for breakdown), fifty-one were men (57 per cent of all charges), and only thirty-three individuals (37 per cent) were visibly white,[8] with nearly half of the 37 per cent (fifteen out of thirty-three) being ethnic minorities from two large Romani families, the Domotor and Kolompar families from Hungary, whose case received significant public attention as an example of transnational labour trafficking in Canada. This leaves us with only nineteen out of eighty-nine (21 per cent) other visibly white accused. In effect, 78.5 per cent of those charged with trafficking in my study were racialized and/or ethnic minorities, a number that becomes even more noteworthy when we place it in the context of the fact that only 25.9 per cent of the population identify as visible minorities in Ontario, and

19.1 per cent in Canada overall (Statistics Canada 2016). These findings are also consistent with studies in the United States. For instance, Elizabeth Bernstein found that 62 per cent of those suspected of sex trafficking in the United States were African American, while 25 per cent of all suspects were Hispanic/Latino (2012, 253).

In addition to being a highly racialized offence, trafficking charges are significantly skewed in terms of gender and age. As this data shows, 99 out of 123 (80 per cent) of those charged with human trafficking were men, with the average age of 27 years (see Appendix A for details). If we remove the Hungarian family members from the data set, most of whom were between thirty and sixty-eight years of age, then the average age of the accused during the period under study goes down to twenty-five years. In providing this data, I am not making definitive claims about the demographics of the accused in human trafficking cases, particularly given the relatively small and Ontario-focused sample of a large and growing number of trafficking cases in Canada. Instead, the findings are meant to provide a glimpse into the profile of those criminalized under Canada's human trafficking provisions and to suggest, given the troubling findings, that a more comprehensive study is needed.[9]

The criminalization of racialized and, especially Black men, is nothing new (Alexander 2012; Browne 2015; Chan and Chunn 2014; Davis 2017; Hill Collins 2004; James 2012; Jeffries 2011; Maynard 2017). As Angela Davis contends, young Black men are much more frequently charged and imprisoned than young white men for engaging in similar behaviour (2017, xiv; see also Browne 2015). Davis's observations are made in the context of the United States, but overcriminalization of Black people, particularly Black men, is certainly not exclusively an American issue and is also confirmed by numerous reports and studies in the Canadian context (Chan and Chunn 2014; Mullings et al. 2016; Ontario Human Rights Commission 2020; Wortley 1996). Human trafficking, historically known as "white slavery," has been one of many ways in which racialized men were criminalized. For instance, Jack Johnson, the first Black man to win the world heavyweight boxing champion in 1908, was convicted of "white slavery" for travelling across a state border with his ex-girlfriend (a sex trade worker) and several of her friends, who were also sex trade workers. Johnson was sentenced to five years in prison (Doezema 2010, 89). As this, and other similar cases show, and as academics have extensively documented, efforts against "white slavery" specifically targeted racialized men who were in any way associated with the sex trade (see Doezema 2010; Donovan 2006; Valverde 2008). Jo Doezema goes further to argue that the racist discourse of "white slavery" is a "perverse inversion of the historical reality of black slavery in America, an attempt to reconfigure its horrifying meaning by recasting the sexual violation of white women in the hands of dark men as 'more terrible than any black slavery that ever existed in this or any other country'" (2010, 83). This type of targeting of racialized and especially Black men also took place during the 1980s and 1990s panics over youth involvement in the sex trade in Canada, during which the police continued to use the language of "white slavery" (Brock 1998, 123; Jeffrey and MacDonald 2006). The criminalizing focus of these panics was on young Black men who engaged in the "pimping" of white women and girls (Brock 1998; Jeffrey and MacDonald 2006; Smith 2000). As I discuss in chapter three and elsewhere, the discourses and knowledges of this historical panic have become a part of the human trafficking matrix to be redeployed by police and legal actors in anti-trafficking efforts in Ontario (Roots 2019).

Black men have historically, and continue to be, disproportionately arrested for violence, drugs, and sex trade–related crimes. This pattern continues to be sustained by the enforcement of human trafficking laws, which, fuelled by transnational trafficking discourses, evoke a much larger public safety and national security threat implied by the imported connection of "street gangs" with organized crime. As one Crown attorney explains, traffickers are "youngish, they are in their 20s generally, some are involved in gangs, the majority of the people, if not all. There's ones who's not – they're Black – young Black males have been – from my experience" (participant 15),[10] thus confirming the targeting of young racialized men through anti-trafficking enforcement.

Even though human trafficking takes many forms – from labour to debt bondage and organ trafficking. The vast majority of human trafficking cases, as discussed in chapter one, involve charges of sexual exploitation. This focus on sexual exploitation is enabled by various factors operating within the human trafficking matrix, including prevailing prohibitionist rhetoric, legal changes that criminalize trafficking with a focus on the term "exploitation," but also recent legal changes in Canada's sex work laws, which have enabled a redirection of sex work–related offences into the legal realm of trafficking. Given the limited number of transnational trafficking cases (Ferguson 2012), the front line of domestic law enforcement and courts have refocused on the prototypical Black "pimp" who can be "easily resurrected and redeployed as part of anti-trafficking efforts" (Roots 2019, 104). As Jeffrey and MacDonald note, the "pimp" mythology is based on the presumption sometimes, although not often, borne out that "some men pressure women into the sex trade and/or run women in the trade in order to make a profit for themselves" (2006, 95). In contrast to this mythology, Chris Bruckert found in her research that third-party work in the sex trade is more often carried out by women than men. The boundaries are also exceptionally porous with sex workers and third-party actors moving in and out of both roles and disrupting the strictly established division between the predator and the victim (2018a, 36; see also Gilles and Bruckert 2018). Nevertheless, the racialized, classed, and gendered image of the "pimp" reinforces the stereotypical popular mythology of Black men in connection with Black sexuality and crime (Kalunta-Crumpton 1998, 567; see also Bruckert 2018a; 2018b; Hill Collins 2004; Jeffrey and MacDonald 2006 Mensah 2018).

Racialization of trafficking is most evident through media portrayals of the accused. Many accused in trafficking cases have their names and pictures displayed in newspapers with screaming titles, such as "Human trafficking suspect accused of exploiting girls as young as 14 arrested in Bowmanville" (Mitchell, 14 March 20179), and "Toronto police arrest 4 men in human trafficking probe involving teen victims" (*The Canadian Press*, 12 February 2018). These sensationalist headlines that often link sexual exploitation with discourses of youth and/or child protectionism are often accompanied by mug shots of the arrested suspects, along with vivid descriptions of their horrific actions, not yet verified in court. As Jonathon Finn explains, a police mug shot, which permeates people's daily lives through the news media "is an image that is taken to indicate criminality" (2009, 1). A mugshot of the accused in a news outlet therefore establishes their guilt even before the evidence is reviewed and evaluated by the court, which, as Finn notes, works to document criminal identity (ibid., xviii). Importantly, as Finn points out, despite being as much cultural as they are natural, pictures are seen as more objective in contrast with other forms of visual representation, therefore guilt is once again more easily established (ibid., xii).

Unsurprisingly, a large portion of the pictures of accused traffickers published in newspaper articles are those of racialized men. Of the 123 individuals whose cases were examined in this study, 73 had their picture published in various news outlets. Of these seventy-three pictures, fourteen were women,[11] eleven were visibly white (five of the eleven white women were members of the two Hungarian Roma families convicted of human trafficking in 2012). Of the seventy-three pictures, nineteen were of visibly white men and, once again, nine belonged to the Hungarian family of traffickers. This leaves only ten other white men, which constitutes 8 per cent of the total number of cases, one of whom contacted the media himself to provide his side of the story. There were three pictures published of racialized women accused of trafficking, while forty pictures, or 55 per cent of all pictures published, were of racialized, and most often Black, men. It is noteworthy that pictures of racialized men accused of human trafficking were published more frequently than the other three groups, including racialized women and visibly white men and women, combined.

Racialized, particularly Black, men are depicted in particular ways that result in the visualization of them as dangerous and criminal. Consider for instance the case of Yul Styles-Lyons, a Black man who was charged with human trafficking in 2011 and whose mugshot accompanied a *Hamilton Spectator* article entitled "Jail escapee faces Hamilton human-trafficking charge" (7 December 2011). The note underneath the picture warns the public of his dangerousness, a message also conveyed through the depiction of Yul Styles-Lyons in a standard repertoire mugshot foregrounded by a height chart, which connotes criminality and with which young Black men are frequently burdened (Stevenson 2017, 4). Despite the grave written warning and visual depiction of this Black man's dangerousness, the human trafficking charges were withdrawn by the Crown less than a year later. Yul Styles-Lyons's name, however, will remain associated with human trafficking accusations as a result of these media reports, which are easily accessible in the age of the internet and social media. The Black male's guilt is therefore existential.

Newspaper articles covering trafficking-related arrests also provide brief summaries of the incident provided to them by police. These summaries, however, are based on police theories of what occurred and are not yet verified in court, at times also departing from the events as they are later revealed. For instance, CTV news reported that Daryn Leung, another Black man, was charged with human trafficking along with a string of other charges after an "18-year-old woman contacted them [the police] with allegations that she had been forced into the sex trade and violently assaulted" (*CTV News*, 2 April 2014). In court, it was revealed that the complainant had entered the sex trade voluntarily rather than being forced into the trade; that the two were in a romantic relationship where the complainant was giving the accused money from her proceeds; and that the police had made the initial contact with the complainant after they found her advertisement on the escorting site Backpage.com, rather than her contacting the police, as reported by the media. Despite these important differences between the story told by the media and the evidence presented in court, these corrections rarely, if ever, become a part of the official story.

The impressions left by inaccurate reporting are especially troubling given the seriousness of the charge and the findings of this study that human trafficking charges are often withdrawn or stayed. In particular, in fifty-five[12] out of eighty-four (65 per cent) cases for which a disposition was available by the conclusion of research time, trafficking charges were withdrawn, stayed, or acquitted by a judge (see Appendix B for a breakdown of case outcomes; see also Maisie 2016). The suggested reasons for this varied widely among criminal justice actors interviewed for this study and include challenges with cooperation of complainants, lack of Crown familiarity with the offence, and poorly conducted investigations. Some defence attorneys, however, attribute the high numbers of withdrawn and stayed charges to overcharging practices. In relation to police enthusiasm in laying human trafficking charges, one defence lawyer states, "In my mind, they're just charging everybody with human trafficking now"[13] (participant 10).

In 25 per cent of the cases,[14] the accused pled guilty to human trafficking charges. This is surprising given the statements of defence attorneys interviewed that they would never let their client plead guilty to a charge as serious as human trafficking. One defence attorney expressed his dismay at the idea of anyone pleading guilty to human trafficking: "as regards to human trafficking, I can guarantee you no matter what the circumstances are I would never plead a client to human trafficking, never ever. Before I plead a client to human trafficking, I'm going to exhaust everything, I'm going to attack the case from an attack on the law, I'll argue the exploitation issue, I'll argue everything before I plead someone guilty to this nonsense. Plead to human trafficking?" (participant 14). Similar sentiments were conveyed by another defence attorney, who noted that if "you don't do a good job, your client's facing mandatory minimums…. He's going away for a very long time. Like you don't take a case like this and half-ass it ever" (participant 13). According to yet another defence attorney: "The reality is on those cases so often we're going to work out a deal, they're going to plead to something less rather than human trafficking, right, unless it's a really compelling human trafficking case" (participant 10). Thus, as the defence attorney noted, while plea deals in trafficking cases may be frequent, they usually involve pleading to a lesser charge. According to this study however, only 8 per cent of cases ended in accused pleading to a lesser charge. And despite the sentiments of these defence attorneys and the severity of the charges, 25 per cent of accused in this data set pled guilty to trafficking-specific charges. This rather surprising finding could be attributed to ineffective legal representation since the accused in these cases are often poor and likely rely on legal-aid lawyers who are inadequately paid for the work. It may also be a result of defence lawyers' lack of knowledge about the seriousness of human trafficking charges, as the offence (at the time of research) was new. These guilty pleas to human trafficking offences, however, may seem like self-fulfilling prophesies confirming the white public's racist beliefs that racialized people are indeed criminogenic.

Legal Strategies and Racialization in Trafficking Trials

In her study of drug trials in the United States, Anita Kalunta-Crumpton (1998) illustrates how lawyers produce crime and criminality at trial by placing evidence within social contexts and relying on extra-legal factors. In particular, she found that in order to build a story that would resonate with the jury, evidence against the accused was embedded within racial stereotypes related to poor Black men who were most commonly the accused in the drug trials she analysed. For instance, Black men who owned expensive items were suspected of getting those items through criminal activities. Similar uses of racialized stereotypes of Black criminality were also commonly seen in the strategies of Crown and even defence attorneys in my own study of trafficking trials. For example, in *R. v. Beckford* (2013), the Crown's questioning led one witness to indicate that they had seen the two Black accused persons with pizza boxes entering the hotel where they believed the complainant was being held and found the accused suspicious:

CROWN: Did you make any observations?
WITNESS: We witnessed three coloured men carrying a pizza box into the hotel.
CROWN: What colour?
WITNESS: Black.

(*R. v. Beckford*, audio of trial, 27 January 2013)

The emphasis on the "colour" of the accused with the explicit question "what colour [were they]?" and the coding of the accused's ordinary behaviour of carrying a pizza box up to their hotel room as somehow suspicious confirms the argument made by Hill Collins that the sheer physical presence of a Black male can be "enough to invoke fear, regardless of his actions and intentions" (2004, 153). Emphasis on the accused's race in the same case was exemplified several more times as the Crown posed the following questions: "when did you see *this Black man*?"; "with regard to *those Black men* that you saw, did you ever see them prior to ever coming to court?"; "The person with the hat was [accused 1], *the bigger Black man*"; "on how many occasions did you see *these Black males* around the hotel?" (*R. v. Beckford*, audio of trial, 26 February 2013; emphases added). It is important to note that there were no other suspects in the case, therefore, emphasizing the race and gender of the accused was not a matter of accurate identification. Such emphasis on the accused's race is rarely, if ever, evidenced in the case of white people accused of crimes. It is hard to imagine a Crown posing the following questions: "when did you see this white man?" or "the person with the hat was the bigger white man?" or "on how many occasions did you see these white males around the hotel?" This emphasis on the whiteness of the accused would be unnecessary since "whiteness" is the standard against which all others are measured and therefore deemed as a redundant identifier.

In contrast, Blackness not only needs to be identified, but is also relied on to enact the persistent cultural myth that Black people and especially Black young men are more criminogenic than other groups (Alexander 2012; Chan and Chunn 2014, 17; Davis 2017a; 2017b; Hill Collins 2004; Jeffries 2011). As Ronald Jackson explains, once Black people have been deemed criminal, they are treated as "throwaways"; they become nothing more than bodies in need of containment for the sake of justice (2006, 80). Inscriptions of Black people, and especially men, are so pervasive that "even when a Black body has not been criminalized, he is suspect" (ibid., 80). Indeed, the suspiciousness read into the conduct of the accused above did not appear to be based on anything other than the accused's Blackness, as uncovered by the following exchange between a defence attorney and a witness:

DEFENCE: You said that there is something suspicious about them [the accused]?
WITNESS: They were checking me out as intense as I was checking them out.
DEFENCE: And you thought these two Black individuals walking around one o'clock or three o'clock in the morning look suspicious to you?
WITNESS: The way they were looking at me was suspicious. And there was enough thickness in the air to cut it with a knife. There was just a certain vibe that was in the air.

(R. v. Beckford, audio of trial, 25 February 2013)

As the exchange reveals, the witness believed that the two accused were "checking her out," which one can presume to mean glancing or looking at her, rather than any real or uttered threat-based behaviour. The act of "looking" would likley not elicit the same assumptions around dangerousness or suspiciousness had the accused been white. The interpretation of mundane or ordinary behaviour when exhibited by Black people as somehow suspect is not new. In his study of Black surveillance, Fiske notes "street behaviours of white men (standing still and talking, using a cellular phone, passing an unseen object from one to another) [are often] coded as normal and thus granted no attention, whereas the same activity performed by black men [is] coded as lying or beyond the boundary of normal, and thus subject to disciplinary action" (2000, 71). Fiske's point is well exemplified by the following exchange in *R. v. Beckford* (2013),

> WITNESS: Closer towards the end of us walking around we saw two of the three Black males we saw earlier come out of the elevator and walk to their room.
> CROWN: Did you make eye contact with either of them?
> WITNESS: No, I was too uncomfortable to make eye contact.
>
> (Audio of trial, 27 January 2013)

Presumably the witness's reluctance to make eye contact due to discomfort was, at least in part, because the accused were Black and therefore feared as dangerous. Interestingly in this instance, the defence attorney pointed out the way in which race (or, more specifically, Blackness) was being used as an index of criminalities:[15]

> DEFENCE: And you are indicating that at that point you had already seen these suspicious Black men?
> WITNESS: Yes.
> DEFENCE: What was so suspicious about the Black males?
> WITNESS: I didn't point out that they were suspicious, I had pointed out that we saw three people walking into the hotel. We were just looking to see people walking around.
> DEFENCE: You didn't think they were suspicious?
> WITNESS: I didn't really know who to think was suspicious. I was just looking and observing people to see if I can see [the complainant].
> DEFENCE: There is nothing suspicious about a Black male walking with a pizza box, right?
> WITNESS: I agree.[16]
>
> (*R. v. Beckford*, audio of trial, 27 January 2013)

The defence thus highlights the racist assumptions underlying the witnesses' statements that the accused going to their hotel room with a pizza box at night while Black was suspicious. As Lois Wacquant explains, "the formula 'Young + Black + Male' is now openly equated with 'probable cause' justifying the arrest, questioning, bodily search and detention of millions of African-American males every year" (2002, n.p.; see also Wacquant 2005).

While Crown strategies tended to draw on racist stereotypes to construct an image of the accused as dangerous, these same stereotypes were also at times put to use by defence attorneys, albeit for different reasons. For instance, in *R. v. Greenham* (2015), the defence attorney focused his argument on the protection offered to sex workers by third-party security – a common business relationship in the sex trade industry where the manager and the sex worker are in a reciprocal arrangement, with the former offering a variety of services, including the prevention of violence to the latter (Gilles and Bruckert 2018). In doing so, however, the defence continued to draw on white fantasies about Black propensities for effective violence and intimidation:

> DEFENCE: I'm going to ask you about [the accused], he's a big guy, what 6'4", 250 lbs. – *big Black guy?*
> COMPLAINANT: Yep.
> DEFENCE: So, you felt safe that if one of these clients got out of line that you could call him, he would come to the rescue.
>
> (*R. v. Greenham*, audio of trial,
> 26 August 2015; emphasis added)

Despite the defence counsel's presumably good intentions, the submission that the accused – as a "big Black guy" – would have been able to protect the complainant from potentially violent clients nonetheless signals problematic assumptions about the potential for dangerousness and violence of Black men, since the ability to inflict violence, even if not against the complainant, remains unchallenged.

The racialization of the human trafficker is also brought to light through an association of trafficking offences with hip-hop culture by criminal justice actors. As Alridge and Stewart note, hip-hop has been commodified and distributed in ways that emphasize sexism, misogyny, and nihilism, thus reinforcing historical stereotypes about African Americans (or Canadians) (2005, 193). This, as Michael Render writes, has "the potential to silence a generation of artists who are exercising their First Amendment right to express themselves" (2019, IV). According to Render, the influence of hip-hop has been particularly important in the Black community, allowing many Black people upward mobility, especially at a time when many factory jobs were disappearing. Hip-hop is also a form of art that enables Black people to celebrate their culture and provides a form of therapy to "express even our rawest feelings" (Render 2019, IV). This very culture, however, has become the target of surveillance and harassment by the police and the justice system.

The hip-hop performer constructed as a "violent Black supercriminal bent on capital accumulation and personal gratification [who] began as a figment of the white racist imagination now thrives as a commoditized sign of immoral rebellion and masculine strength" (Jeffries 2011, 77). Taking on the "thug image," the hip-hop performer celebrates aggression and hypersexuality, citing lyrics that refer to a "thug," "ruffneck," "pimp," "mack," "playa," "big baller," "dog," "several of which refer mainly to his acquisition of cash, in addition to the male's sexual conquest of women and/or the whole mystique of his genital enormity," in songs such as "Thug Life" and "Bitch Better Have My Money" (Jackson 2006, 111). The "thug," Jackson explains, "is a modern brute," known for his volatile, violent, and sexually exploitative behaviour (2006, 112), thus linking Black men with criminality.

In the criminal justice system, Black men's engagement in hip-hop culture is used to stereotype, demonize, and construct links with criminality, As Nielson and Dennis show in their book *Rap on Trial: Race, Lyrics and Guilt in America*, rap lyrics have been used in hundreds of criminal court cases to prove criminality (2019, 13), either as "evidence indicating motive, confession or violent character or state of mind" (Khan 2021, 250). Nelson and Dennis' (2019) research further suggests that police are suspicious of hip-hop artists at the outset and thus target and surveil hip-hop communities as sources of potential criminality (see also Khan 2021). According to this research study, the association of hip-hop culture and criminality has extended to the crime of human trafficking. We can see this explicit connection drawn in an intelligence brief from 2008 by the Criminal Intelligence Service Canada (CISC), entitled "Organized Crime and Domestic Trafficking in Persons," which states that "hip hop music, clothing, and prostitution are popularized" in mainstream culture, helping to lure potential trafficking victims (2008, 2). Nearly a decade later, a Crown attorney interviewed for this study made the same link while describing how traffickers meet their victims: "there have been [human trafficking] cases where the accused is a low-level rapper and has a bunch of loser videos on YouTube and people are posting saying 'I like your video' or whatever ... and that's how people meet" (participant 15). The comment not only links human trafficking to hip-hop culture and subsequently to Black men, but the reference to "loser videos" also demonstrates a disapproving attitude towards the value of hip-hop music (and those who like it).

Another interviewee, a police officer, revealed that his knowledge about human trafficking was gained from reading "pimping books, breaking down hip-hop culture, listening to the lyrics, understanding what they are saying"[17] (participant 3). The production of knowledge about human trafficking from music embedded with racist stereotypes of, as Jeffries describes it, "the ghetto-poor Black male" as "a heartless criminal" (2011, 77), reveals the highly troubling racialization of the accused in human trafficking cases. The same police officer went on to note that when look-ing at suspected traffickers' tattoos, he looks for ones that say "thug, nigga, riches … bitches and game" since "when people talk about game, or he's got this, it's like charisma, male charisma in hip-hop culture, it's Black male charisma" (participant 3). In other words, Black men are depicted as physically powerful, hypersexual, and hyper-masculine (read: violent and dangerous), therefore posing a threat to society and particularly white women – a threat that must be neutralized through physical removal from society, either through imprisonment or if possible, deportation.

Moreover, the word "thug" used by the officer above has, accord-ing to Boyd, "come to stand in for 'nigger' as an epithet for crimi-nally inclined Black men. 'Thug' can be spoken in the public sphere without rebuke because it is ostensibly racially neutral" (as cited in Jeffries 2011, 86). And yet, as Boyd points out, the re-appropriation of racially insulting words such as "thug" by Black communities is done as a form of resistance against this racism and "to affirm Black self-worth" (as cited in Jeffries 2011, 87). This however, was not the way in which the term was taken up by the officer, who himself was not Black. The police officer's comment, that he looks for tattoos with the words "bitches and game" demonstrates a continuation of the race-based controlling narrative of Black men as hypersexual and speaks to the way in which objectification, degradation, and insulting of women within hip-hop music (Jeffries 2011, 154) are seen as innate character-istics of Black men more generally. Moreover, as Hill Collins explains, the essence of the identity of the "gangsta" "lies in the inherent vio-lence associated with his physicality" (2004, 159). At the most basic level, this cements a discursive relationship between "pimping," hip-hop and Blackness. The police officer, who was attempting to display his "street smarts" for looking in these places, is instead substituting fiction for fact in his own knowledge production, verifying what he thinks he already knows, rather than actually going out to learn about it. The commodification of gangsta rap, which is distinct from rap's origins as a particularly Black form of political expression of dissent, is therefore reconstituted as a source of information for criminal activ-ity. This subsequently becomes a self-fulfilling prophecy as trafficking activity is read into Black men's tattoos and the music they listen toand "and generate," while white men get to re-affirm their position as the heroes of rescue in this story.

The use of these racial stereotypes to construct Black men as human traffickers is painfully evident in trafficking trials, as seen in the follow-ing exchange between a defence counsel and a young, white, female complainant in *R. v. Burton* (2016),

DEFENCE: He [the accused] wasn't just Black but he had sort of a gangster
   persona.
COMPLAINANT: Yeah.
DEFENCE: He spoke differently, in patois.
COMPLAINANT: Yes.
DEFENCE: It was difficult for you to understand him.
COMPLAINANT: Yes.
DEFENCE: You thought he might have a gun.
COMPLAINANT: I never saw it.
DEFENCE: But all these things affected your impression of him?
                                  (*R. v. Burton*, audio of trial, 2 November 2013)

The lawyer's claim that the accused "wasn't just Black" reveals the
underlying assumption that the accused's Blackness was in and of itself
dangerous and was intensified by his simultaneous "gangster persona."
And while the above exchange was meant to suggest that the complainant feared the accused due to her unfamiliarity with Jamaican culture,
and embedded racialized stereotypes that fail to hold merit rather than
any tangible reason, his line of questioning, instead, constructed an
image of the accused as doubly dangerous. The danger of the accused's
Jamaican-ness and Blackness, when combined with his "gangster persona," operationalized the transnational discourses, linking the accused
with foreign criminals and transnational criminal "gangs," despite a
lack of evidence to support either connection. Here we see a legal actor
unintentionally operationalizing transnational discourses of trafficking
by drawing connections between the activities and characteristics of
what are essentially poor Black men engaged in domestic "pimping,"
with broader fears around transnational "gangs," national security, and
public safety.

Black men's sexuality forms another source of fear mined in criminal
court proceedings. As bell hooks explains, regardless of external factors, such as education, income, and occupation, "for many black men
sexuality remains the place where dysfunctional behaviour first rears
its ugly head. This is in part because of the convergence of racist sexist
thinking about the black body, which has always projected onto the
black body a hypersexuality" (20036, 67; see also Jackson 2006). In line
with this, Crown attorneys in trafficking trials frequently focused on
the rapacious sexual appetite of the often-racialized accused. Consider
for instance, the case of *R. v. Greenham* (2015), where the racialized stereotypes of hypersexualized Black men were evoked by the Crown's
questioning around the accused's practice of having sex with the various sex workers he was managing:

CROWN: But it was a problem that [the accused] would have sex with the girls who were working for him, correct?

WITNESS: It bothered me.

CROWN: And one of those girls that he had sex with while she was working for him was [name of complainant].

WITNESS: Yes.

CROWN: And that was what caused your relationship with [name of complainant] to fall apart when you found out that the two of them had been having sex behind your back?

WITNESS: Yes.

(*R. v. Greenham,* audio of trial, 26 August 2015)

The above exchange suggests that the accused's uncontrollable sexual urges, reflected in his need to have sex with the women who worked for him, caused significant problems in his relationship, demonstrating the way in which even the heterosexual relationships entered into by Black men are negotiated by the prevailing stereotypes of promiscuity as a defining feature of Black masculinity. The way in which legal actors tap into these stereotypes in order to paint the accused's behaviour as criminal was revealed in the Crown's questioning of one of the complainants in *R. v. Burton* (2016),

CROWN: When you were intimate with [the accused], was he using protection?

COMPLAINANT: No.

CROWN: Did you ever ask him to?

COMPLAINANT: No.

CROWN: And you just said that if he was your boyfriend he wouldn't have had relations with your friend – who were you referring to?

COMPLAINANT: [Name of complainant 2].

CROWN: Were they intimate as well that you were aware of?

COMPLAINANT: Yeah.

CROWN: Were you there when that happened?

COMPLAINANT: Yes.

CROWN: Were there any – that you were aware of – any rules around the relationship between [the accused] and [complainant 2] having sex?

COMPLAINANT: Again, not rules that were spoken, it was more just like, when he wanted it, he got it, kind of thing.

CROWN: How often would he want it, do you think?

COMPLAINANT: Usually every night and in the morning.

(*R. v. Burton,* audio of trial, 29 January 2014)

The accused's need for sex "every night and in the morning" with two women, sometimes at the same time, captures the cultural stereotype of

Black man's uncontrolled sexual desire and need for unrestrained access to "the booty." The Crown went further, pointing to the accused's failure to use protection when engaging in sex acts with women working in the sex trade, to establish the accused's sexual recklessness, a feature which is also captured in the investigating officer's statement as follows: "She [complainant 2] talked about having a sexual relationship with him [the accused]. She said she was forced but not held down or anything. She describes it as disgusting. He knew that she had slept with all these men during the day but he wouldn't care. He'd make her have sex anyway" (R. v. Burton, audio of trial, 16 December 2013). In addition to sexual recklessness and an uncontrollable urge, the above statement went further to depict the accused as a sexual predator who forced women to have sex with him. Indeed, as the following statement suggests, he didn't care, and possibly took pleasure from knowing that the complainant "hated him":

CROWN: And what, if anything, did she [complainant 2] say about whether she wanted to engage in this sexual relationship?
WITNESS: She definitely did not want to. And she says that he [the accused] knew that she hated him.
CROWN: Did she tell you how this sexual relationship started and how long it went on?
WITNESS: They had to all sleep in the same bed together and he would just say, hey let's go, let's do it. It was a matter of fact, you have to.
CROWN: Did she say how often?
WITNESS: I believe it was every day.
(R. v. Burton, audio of trial, 16 December 2013)

Although the complainant was not physically forced to engage in sex with the accused, representations of Black men's uncontrolled sexual urges, compounded with stereotypes of the predatory Black male hustlers, were relied upon to suggest that she did so under threat of violence. This is because Black men's predatory skills as hustlers and their association with violence construct a dominant image of Black men as "booty call-seeking rapists" (Davis 1983; Hill Collins 2004, 166; hooks 2003; Jackson 2006), an image which, according to Robyn Wiegman, emerged after the end of transatlantic slavery as a product of "the fault line of the slave's newly institutionalized masculinization by framing this masculinity as the bestial excess of an overly phallicized primitivity" (1993, 458). As Wiegman notes, in the post-slavery period, "The transformation of the image of the Black man from simple, docile Uncle Tom[18] to violent sex offender characterizes the oppositional logic underwriting the representational structure of the Black male image in nineteenth-and twentieth-century United States culture, a logic in which the discourse of sexual difference – from feminized docility to hypermasculinized phallicity – comes to play a primary significatory role" (1993, 459).

The mythology of the Black "pimp" is even further aggravated when the perceived predatory advances of Black men are made towards white women. Emerging during the Jim Crow era, the myth of the Black man as a rapist who lusts after white women became a tool for controlling Black men viewed as "prematurely freed from the civilizing influences of slavery" (Davis 1983; Hill Collins 2004, 166; hooks 2006; Wiegman 1993). The "Black man as rapist" trope has historically functioned in powerful ways to justify racism and the segregation of Black men under the guise of protecting white women (Maynard 2017, 41; Walker 2010). As Maynard points out, in Canada, this trope was effectively utilized to justify the use of capital punishment as a sentence for rape and to exclude Black people from settlement in order to protect the safety of white women (2017, 41; see, too, Walker 2010). Cases of white women's rape by Black men have historically also served as cautionary tales to other white women (Walker 2010).

The image of the prototypical Black "pimp" is a continuation of these historical mythologies and, according to Hill Collins, is redeployed whenever the need arises (2004, 166; hooks 2006; Jackson 2006; Quinn 200017). In this case, they can be seen emerging through anti-trafficking efforts. It is indeed telling that in seven out of eight court transcripts examined for this study, the complainants were white women and girls, while in six of the eight cases the accused were Black men. The racial dynamic is illustrated through the Crown's eliciting of complainant descriptors as small and "blonde" (*R. v. Beckford*, audio of trial, 6 March 2013), "white, pretty, tall, very nice, her hair was long" (*R. v. Oliver-Machado*, audio of trial, 2 May 2013), while another complainant was described as "middle height, blonde hair" (*R. v. Oliver-Machado*, audio of trial, 9 September 2013), which position these girls and women as worthy and indeed deserving of protection. Such imagery of the white female being raped and sexually exploited by the Black male threat is a historically continuing fantasy that horrifies the white community, adding severity and urgency to the need not only to intervene, but to avenge using the full force of the legally sanctioned punishments, thus maintaining domination over Black communities.

In the context of the protectionism that surrounds (especially white) women and particularly children, Black men's violent actions are seen as particularly aggravating and given significant weight in sentencing decisions. One example of this comes from the case of *R. v. R.R.S.*

(Ricardo Spence), where in sentencing yet another Black man for human trafficking, the judge noted, "what I consider particularly aggravating in the circumstances of this case is R.S's lengthy criminal record – particularly in regards to crimes against women. There is no evidence that suggests that R.S's attitude towards women has improved …. R.S. will continue to be a danger to women … therefore protection of society plays a significant role in my sentencing of R.S" (*R. v. R.R.S.*, 29 March 2016, para. 40). The judge's sentencing decision must be read in the context of his Blackness, evidenced by the judge's observations of Spence's upbringing in Jamaica, where violence and poverty prevail, providing another illustration of the way in which severe punishment and exclusion of Black men from Canadian society is justified in the name of white women's protection. Violence, according to the racialized narrative of hyper-sexualized Black men, is a natural extension of their behaviour. One police officer interviewed for this study described his surprise at "the length to which these guys go to and the way they treat these girls. I've never seen anything like it…. [Y]ou can't flower this, you can't flower [make nice] human trafficking. This is an awful criminal offence," explaining further that, "they ['pimps'] have between five and ten girls in that stable. This is how they talk about these women. These girls. It's disgusting. It's plain and simple disgusting" (participant 1).

Crown attorneys in the trafficking cases analysed also paid significant attention to any clear or suggested sign of violence by the accused. In *R. v. Byron* (2014), the accused's violence towards the complainant played a central role as the Crown argued that "The violence which is an essential element of some of the offences cannot be more clearly corroborated. [The complainant] was very clear on a continual violence when she didn't want to give him money" (Audio of trial, 17 May 2013). Even a tenuous connection between populist images of the Black "pimp" and the use of violence in managing transactional sex could be put to use in constructing a case. Consider for instance, *R. v. Greenham* (2015), where the Crown attorney suggested that the accused's violence towards his girlfriend (who was not a complainant in the case) was meant as a veiled threat towards the complainant:

I would ask you to accept [the complainant's] evidence as she testified that she was afraid not to give [the accused] his 40%. She had told this court what she had seen had happened between him [the accused] and [his girlfriend] in the past. She had seen the accused assault [his girlfriend] in the past and the fact that that was corroborated by [name of witness]…. And subjectively speaking, although she doesn't relate the second portion at all to fear objectively Your Honour has to consider that [the accused] had on

two occasions destroyed her personal belongings, her phones, apparently
out of anger with her.

(Audio of trial, 13 April 2015)

While acknowledging that the accused's violence towards his girlfriend
did not cause the complainant subjective fear,[19] the Crown still used the
incident to support the argument that the complainant's decision to
hand over 40 per cent of her income to the accused should have caused
the reasonable person to fear for their safety. The Crown's argument
was rejected by the judge, who in his decision noted: "From an objective
basis, there is no evidence that [the accused] used or threatened to use
force against [the complainant]. The fact that on one occasion she saw
him argue with [his girlfriend] does not support a reasonable belief that
her safety or the safety of a person known to her would be threatened
if she failed to provide the services which she was providing in their
business arrangement" (*R. v. Greenham*, audio of trial, 17 October 2015).
The Crown's efforts to construct the accused as a violent man must once
again be read in the context of stereotyped depictions of Black "pimps"
as violent, which have become a part of the human trafficking matrix
and made the Crown's argument possible even if the accused had not
exhibited violence against the complainant specifically.

Alongside violence, we also see "Romeo tactics," entering into the
human trafficking matrix as indicators created through reliance on the
old familiar figure of the "pimp" and repurposed in anti-trafficking
efforts. The "Romeo pimp" is seen as romancing women and girls in an
effort to manipulate and subsequently lure and trick them into entering
the sex trade. The operation of Romeo pimps is described in a *Globe and
Mail* opinion piece written by the executive director of the Canadian
Center to End Human Trafficking as follows:

"Romeo pimps" are running a multimillion dollar industry in Canada
and most of us haven't got a clue. They are smooth, polished. They find
their victims through friends, relatives or social media. How many of you
have daughters on Instagram, TikTok or Snapchat? They are watching.
They tell her she is beautiful. They tell her she's different than the others.
They promise love, money, safety; a way out to a better life. They prey on
her dreams. They just need a little favour, though. They just need her to
meet up with a couple of their "friends" to help "cover the costs" for some
of their gifts. She's in "love." She wants to be helpful. But she is slowly
drawn into complete and utter dependency, until there is no way out.

(Drydyk, 22 February 2021)

The Romeo pimp then is a "playboy of sorts that uses flattery and promises of love to take advantage of the women. These characters are everywhere and can take advantage of just about anyone unsuspecting. And while the Romeo pimp' strategies are constructed as a new development in trafficking methods, we see similar depictions of "boyfriend pimps" also constructed as a new strategy during the 1980s and 1990s juvenile prostitution panics when police focus remained on Nova Scotia and, in particular, the street gang North Preston's Finest (Jeffrey and MacDonald 2006; see also Roots 2019). Romeo pimp is a racialized term that can seemingly be traced back to the idea of the "pimp" as a trickster who can maintain a certain elevated lifestyle without having to work or use violence (Lawrence 1977; Milner and Milner 1977). The trickster narrative developed from nineteenth-century African American folklore where animal characters like Bre'er Rabbit and Spider Anansi used trickery to achieve their ends (Lawrence 1977; Quinn 2000). As Milner and Milner explain, "Pimps," hustlers, and con men are tricksters in this classical sense, although they note that they cannot argue this to be a continuity from the days of slavery, since evidence to that effect is lacking (1977, 71).

Relying on Romeo tactics allows the police and prosecutors to suggest that while the complainant was not kidnapped and forced into their situation through threats of violence, they did not make their decision voluntarily but were instead lured and exploited through false promises of love. As one police officer described it: "Pimps ... will approach a girl and the way they do it, they will shower her with gifts, that's the process of procurement ... and all of a sudden, boom! Now you're going to work for me. It goes from that starting point of, I'm going to be your boyfriend, I'm going to shower you with gifts and it ends when they say, now you're going to work for me. So, it's not just the act of you're going to work for me, it starts way before that" (participant 1).[20] Another police officer explained that the Romeo tactic is "where they get the girls to fall in love with them and from that position, they exploit their affection to transition them to working in the sex industry." This romancing is seen as a form of manipulation since "he doesn't have to tell you he's going to kick your ass or beat you; he just has to romance you, do whatever, manipulate you" (participant 2).[21] Unlike in the popular imagination of trafficking, where the victims are kidnapped the repurposing of these age-old "pimping" indicators has enabled the police and legal actors to argue that victims are lured, tricked, and manipulated by subtle methods that can be confused with a romantic relationship. In the context of the overwhelming focus on racialized men as accused traffickers, we can turn to Quinn's observation that "the pimp figure has long been associated with the trickster in African American vernacular traditions and it is above all the persuasive power" (2000, 118). As Quinn notes, "Like gangsta rappers, the 'pimp' and the trickster are expert 'mackers': they earn a rich living from their wit, guile, and dextrous language use" (2000, 118). The construction of traffickers as smooth and convincing was captured by the comment of one interviewed police officer who described the accused as "master manipulators. They will see it and seize it…. They will say, 'hey honey, you look great. Don't let anybody tell you you don't look great'. That's how the conversation starts. Now the girl's like, well somebody's paying attention to me. Somebody thinks I'm pretty. That's how they hook them" (participant 1). The concept of the Romeo tactic thus bridges the gap between consent and exploitation by transforming the racially connotative trickster role associated with "pimping" into the sophisticated recruitment tactics of traffickers.

This link was also in evidence in the prosecution's argument in the case of *R. v. Byron* (2014): "there's a certain sophistication executed by [the accused] by posing as a potential romantic relationship with [the complainant], being very nice to her, forwarding her money, arranging her travel, all the while knowing exactly what was going to happen when she got to Montreal" (Audio of trial, 13 December 2013). In this construction, romance can no longer be taken at face value but needs to be treated as a suspect activity that can lead to women's ruination. The argument of "pimps" using Romeo tactics was supported in this case by the cultural narrative of Black men as "pimps" and tricksters who manipulate and lure women for their sexual games.

The image of the Black "pimp" is also embedded with stereotyped depictions of lavishness and wealth accumulated on the backs of exploited women. This well-cemented stereotype emerged from the glamorization of the "inner-city pimp" portrayed in 1970s blaxploitation movies such as *The Mack* (1973) and *Willie Dynamite* (1973), where the "pimp" was portrayed as a petty criminal often associated with drug dealing, exploitation of sex workers, and came from a poor and "ghetto" neighbourhood (Mensah 2018). These racialized stereotypes of Black men as hustlers, gamblers, drug pushers, and "pimps" continue to be used by police and legal actors to convey criminality since having wealth in and of itself is clearly not criminal. The flaunted wealth is understood to be a product of criminal activity gained, at least in part, from the exploitation of women. This conceptualization is in line with the stereotypical image of "pimps" as wearing gold chains and floppy hats, and driving Cadillacs bought with the money earned by their stable of "hoes" (Brock 1998, 96; Mensah 2018). The reliance on and perpetuation of this "pimp/hustler" aesthetic of luxury is seen in the comments of one police officer: "these guys ['pimps'] are very arrogant. They like to show off their money" (participant 1). He adds that "They [the 'pimps'] flaunt it. These guys have money, are driving cars, Ferraris, Benz, BMW, all high-end cars. I know a pimp that's driving 2 Bentleys. $500,000 cars each" (participant 1).

The "pimp-like" luxurious lifestyle as an indicator of human trafficking links the material benefit of a prostitution charge with trafficking, in turn racializing it based on cultural stereotypes. The "pimping lifestyle" is an indicator of a particular kind of exploitation – not like the "earned" luxury lifestyle of Jeff Bezos, since his form of exploitation – of Amazon workers, for instance – is not considered problematic; in fact, it is legal and considered entrepreneurial. In this way, there is good/respectable wealth and there is ostentatious, obnoxious, dubious wealth, and that difference is very much racialized. The "pimp-like" luxurious lifestyle as an indicator of criminality is captured in the interesting reversed use of this racialized stereotype by the defence attorney in *R. v. Byron* (2014), who argued that the accused deserved a lesser sentence because he did not live a luxurious life like another convicted trafficker, Imani Nakpangi:

> Mr. Nakpangi's lifestyle as reported in that decision is also a distinguishing factor from the one we have before the court. It's relayed that Mr. Nakpangi drove around a BMW. Mr. Nakpangi was buying himself jewelry, expensive furniture, nice clothes, pieces of art, a home in Niagara Falls, paid vacations. In terms of the evidence, in this case, there's no indication that Mr. Byron owned or drove himself around in expensive cars, buying himself jewelry, that he was going on paid vacation, or buying himself real estate or pieces of art. As a matter of fact, it appears that at times Mr. Byron was struggling to make ends meet. So, the lifestyle that's exhibited by Mr. Nakpangi, I would suggest, is quite different from the lifestyle that's exhibited in this case by Mr. Byron.
>
> (*R. v. Byron*, audio of trial, 21 April 2013)

While the defence tries to mitigate the accused's guilt by pointing to his lack of riches, he is actually feeding into what Ronald Jackson notes is the stereotype of the Black man as incompetent, irresponsible, and uneducated (2006, 85).

The stereotype of the "pimp" living in the lap of luxury was also evoked by the Crown's questioning in *R. v. Burton* (2016), which led the complainant to tell the court how she had to kiss the accused's "pimp ring":

CROWN: You had to kiss the ring?

COMPLAINANT: Yeah.

CROWN: When did you have to kiss the ring?

COMPLAINANT: At random times.

CROWN: How would you know when you had to kiss the ring?

COMPLAINANT: I don't know, he would say little things and I would do it. I wasn't forced to or anything.

CROWN: I just want to focus on what you were thinking at the time. A couple of times you told me that you reflected on it after the fact, so I'm going to ask you to think about and tell us right now about what you were thinking at the time, ok? What did he say to you to let you know that you had to kiss the ring?

COMPLAINANT: Again, I don't remember what he would say.

CROWN: Do you have an understanding of why he made you kiss the ring?

COMPLAINANT: I googled it, but I didn't really think anything of it at the time.

CROWN: Was there anything about the ring that made it look a certain way?

COMPLAINANT: It was just sparkly I guess – had diamonds on it.

CROWN: You remember what finger he wore it on?

COMPLAINANT: His pinky.

(*R. v. Burton*, audio of trial, 20 December 2013)

The image of the Black accused as requiring his "hoes" to kiss the "sparkling" ring on his pinky finger captures the stereotypical representation of the "pimp" as exploitative, misogynistic, and arrogant almost too well. As such, we see the popular image of the gold chain, floppy hat, and fur coat–wearing "pimps" with sparkling pinky rings to be kissed by "hoes" becoming a part of the human trafficking matrix, an indicator to be called upon as needed. Contradictorily, and in line with the ever-expanding human trafficking matrix, we also see criminal justice actors mining the accused's economic marginalization to prove guilt.

In her study of drug trials, Kalunta-Crumpton (1998) observed that legal actors relied on impoverished socio-economic circumstances of the accused to argue that the crimes they committed were economically motivated. To make sense of the accused's actions in human trafficking cases, legal actors rely on similar socio-economic circumstances where capital accumulation is deemed to be a significant motivating factor. One of the ways in which the accused men's economic depravity and thus motivation is drawn out is through their employment history. The accused in *R. v. Byron* (2014), for instance, was described as having "worked in a variety of positions in the fast food and retail clothing area, as well as for delivery companies." Yet as the judge was quick to note, "he has never been steadily employed. The longest job he has held is for a period of one year at a catering company" (*R. v. Byron*, audio of trial, 13 February 2014). The accused's low-level precarious work situation was highlighted and contrasted in this case with his greed and parasitic actions in forcing the complainant to work in the sex trade.

A similar focus on the accused's low earning ability was also held by the prosecution in the case of *R. v. (Gregory) Salmon* (2014), where a cross-examination of the racialized accused established not only his low income levels several years in a row, but also other damaging information, such as previous imprisonment and not paying taxes – central factors in determining a successful (neoliberal) citizen. The Crown argues that "the dynamic of [the accused] is, he wants to portray himself as a big shot entrepreneur and there's nothing wrong with that, but if you look at his evidence as a whole, he wants to project one thing when the reality is much different. And the reality became much different for him from a number of different angles" (*R. v. [Gregory] Salmon*, audio of trial, 25 April 2014). As bell hooks (2006) points out, Black men's engagement in criminal enterprises is a result of their lack of opportunities in the legitimate labour market. The accused's efforts to "portray himself as a big shot entrepreneur" is therefore a result of this shifted measure of success as exclusively financial, regardless of where the money is coming from, leading, as hooks explains, Black men to flaunt their financial success whenever available (hooks 2006). Yet, in the context of the accused's absence of financial success and indeed evidence of financial struggle, the Crown's statement reveals the way in which racialized poverty – a frequent reality of Black men's lives (hooks 2006) – is used to argue criminal motivation in trafficking cases through a portrayal of the accused's desire for a better life, contrasted with their limited success in achieving it through legitimate means. What we see then is the construction of the accused as yet another low-earning, criminogenic "pimp" materially benefiting from the sex trade and parasitically riding on the earnings of others to survive.

Crown attorneys are not the only ones holding these views. Similar observations were also expressed by defence attorneys, who noted that the accused in human trafficking cases are "mostly low level, Backpage, thug wannabes" (participant 13), and "compromised males, failures at communicating" (participant 12). "Thug," as previously noted, has come to stand in for "nigger" as an epithet for criminally inclined

Black men, thus demonstrating the racialized shaping of the human trafficker. Some criminal justice actors also see the accused in trafficking cases as unsophisticated, uneducated, and unintelligent. As one police officer explains, "We don't catch the smart ones" (participant 1). One defence attorney I spoke to even suggested that the accused men's lack of sophistication is so acute that the roles have reversed, and they are the ones "ripe for exploitation" by women in the sex trade (participant 12). A similar sentiment was expressed by a police officer who noted that in human trafficking cases, "you're not running into a guy whose university educated or who's a professional" (participant 3). Such depictions of young Black men's low earning potential are attributed to Black cultural inferiority or the assumption that Black people are poor "because of deficiencies intrinsic to Black culture" (Maynard 2017, 52). The portrayed lack of education, sophistication, and intelligence on the part of the accused in trafficking cases is therefore attributed to group and cultural differences, which blame the individual for their lack of success (James 2012, 84). These depictions of the unsophisticated Black criminal were also evidenced in the case of *R. v. R.R.S.* (2015), where the judge highlighted the accused's employment history as holding "sporadic employment as a cleaner, forklift operator, and a scrap metal worker arranged for him through his father's employment. Other jobs in the area of framing, construction and renovation work with a local contractor. Most of these jobs have been short-term in nature. During lengthy periods of unemployment, R.S. has relied on social assistance benefits. He lived either with the women in his life or at his father's residence" (*R. v. R.R.S.*, 29 March 2016). The judge's portrayal of the accused ignores the reality of many Black Canadians who, as Maynard points out, are "among the poorest population in Canada, and continue to face discrimination in access to employment, housing, education, wages and positions of public service" (2017, 51). As Maynard further explains, "structurally mandated poverty persists, defines and constrains the lives of significant proportion of Canada's Black population" (2017, 51). Yet in the context of anti-trafficking efforts, such realities are sidelined by inflated and unrealistic concerns over threats posed by the accused to Canada's national security and are instead used as evidence of their motivation to engage in human trafficking. Of course, trafficking cases are not the only place where such efforts are seen. In fact, it is seen in all court cases, which routinely avoid structural inequality precisely because they are mandated to determine individual culpability.[22]

The judge's comments in *R. v. R.R.S* (2015) are an exemplary expression of neoliberal expectations of individual responsibility, the absence of which justifies removal from society: "it is unlikely that any sentence that I may render will promote in R.S. a sense of responsibility and realization of the harm he has done to A.M.C [complainant] and to the community" (*R. v. R.R.S.*, 29 March 2016, para. 15). Notably, in contrast with this neoliberal responsibilization, the judge placed significant emphasis on the fact that R.R.S. grew up in Jamaica, describing it as a community with "violence and unemployment" (ibid.). The accused's cultural background was therefore seen by the judge as the cause of what she saw as irresponsible, lazy, and criminogenic behaviour. But even more than that, it highlighted the ways in which the accused's violence and unemployment – factors made to characterize the Jamaican culture – are antithetical to Canada's values defined by orderly and law-abiding behaviour and Protestant work ethic.

The socio-economic situation of racialized accused is also used as a common-sense explanation for involvement with drug crimes. Drug dealing and use were prominent points of emphasis in human trafficking trials of Black accused. Critical race scholars have well documented the ways in which the war on drugs has created an association between Black people and crime (Alexander 2012; Maynard 2017). As Maynard explains, although profiling and surveillance of Black lives is a continuation from slavery, "the ideologies and practices of drug law enforcement have consolidated, and have given new breadth and scope toward, the criminalization of Blackness" (2017, 92). Indeed, Alexander, writing about the United States, observes that "nothing has contributed more to the systemic mass incarceration of people of colour in the United States than the War on Drugs" (2012, 60). The criminalization of Blackness is also taking place through Canada's anti-trafficking efforts using, in part, similar association constructions between Black accused, drug crimes, and motivation to carry out human trafficking. For instance, in the sentencing hearing in the case of *R. v. Byron* (2014), the Crown relied on a pre-sentencing report to highlight the accused's use of marijuana "2–3 times a day," summarizing it as "a drug habit" (Audio of trial, 13 December 2013). In *R. v. Beckford* (2013), the constructed link between the accused and drugs can be observed in the following exchange:

CROWN: Can you describe the person you call [accused 2]?
COMPLAINANT: He's a male, always wearing a red hat with the letter P on it, facial hair, Black, maybe 5'5", late twenties, early thirties.
CROWN: How about [accused 1]?
COMPLAINANT: He was a male, light-skinned Black, he looked older, shorter, more lanky, he had raccoon eyes.
CROWN: What do you mean raccoon eyes?

COMPLAINANT: I don't know, from drugs or whatever, he had bags under
     his eyes.

                              (*R. v. Beckford*, audio of trial, 4 March 2013)

The Crown's questions drew out two important components – the
accused's dark skin colour and drug use, which stereotypically go hand
in hand. In human trafficking cases, these suggestions of the accused's
drug use are then relied upon to construct a motive for the crime.

   In addition to the accused's own use of drugs, Crown strategies often
included suggestions that the accused offered drugs to complainants to
control them and subsequently force them to work in the sex trade. The
drugging of victims by traffickers to exploit them and gain their compliance is a common stereotyped narrative of human trafficking. According
to the RCMP, drugs are used by traffickers to maintain control over their
victims and increase their dependency on them (2013, 22). Proving the
accused's active role in the complainant's drug use therefore, strength-
ens the Crown's case. Moreover, as the *Crown's Guide to Human Trafficking Cases* suggests, "The use of drugs or alcohol to help maintain control
over the victim can be viewed as an aggravating factor" (Department of
Justice Canada 2015, 70). The mere presence of drugs or alcohol is used
by the prosecution to argue that the accused relied on these substances
to enhance their control over the complainant. The fact that the accused
was racialized in the above discussed cases helped to cement the seams
between fact and fiction.

   The narrative of victim drugging and exploitation is also drawn out
in the case of *R. v. Beckford* (2013), where the complainant made the following statement about the accused: "he had a big black bag filled with
ecstasy and I was offered a bunch of ecstasy" (Audio of trial, 4 March
2013). What is being insinuated here is that in offering the complainant
"a bunch of ecstasy," the accused intended to drug her in an effort to
then exploit her by forcing her to work in the sex trade. And in *R. v.
Greenham* (2015), we once again see the Crown attempting to construct a
narrative of the racialized accused drugging and subsequently exploiting the white complainant, although in this case unsuccessfully:

CROWN: And when you moved in with them [the accused and his girl-
     friend], where were you getting the [drugs] from?
COMPLAINANT: Either clients or [the accused].
CROWN: Was there any arrangement with respect to that?
COMPLAINANT: No arrangement, no.
CROWN: How would you get the drugs from him [accused]?

COMPLAINANT: What do you mean how?

CROWN: Well, for example, was it something that you had to get special arrangements for? For example, did you ask him to get them for you?

COMPLAINANT: Sometimes, yes. He did sell drugs, so he had it on him the majority of the time.

(Audio of trial, 26 August 2015)

Despite the Crown's attempts to elicit a response that would support the narrative of the accused drugging the complainant, here the complainant's responses revealed voluntary efforts of her own to obtain drugs, either from the accused or others. The Crowns' efforts to draw out information about the accused supplying the complainant with drugs were done in an effort to stimulate the historical imagery of Black men drugging and sexually exploiting white women.

Conversely, in cases where the accused did not give drugs to the complainants and indeed discouraged drug use, as in *R. v. Burton* (2016), the Crown suggested that this too was done to maintain control over them:

DEFENCE: In fact, there was evidence that [the accused] didn't want them to use drugs at all.

WITNESS (investigating officer): Because he wasn't in control.

DEFENCE: But the girls didn't say he didn't want them to use because he wasn't in control, correct? That's your opinion.

(Audio of trial, 16 December 2013)

As the defence attorney pointed out, it was the investigating officer's interpretation that the accused's disapproval of the complainants' drug use was an effort to control them, much like encouragement to use drugs is commonly used to argue the same. This is often blamed on the dysfunctional Black family with an absent father and a pre-occupied, overworked, and/or controlling Black mother.

In addition to the long list of indicators that have now entered the trafficking matrix, the human trafficking story was further constructed at trial through an emphasis on the broken families of the Black accused, attributing yet another reason for Black men's criminality. Particular emphasis was placed on absent fathers and overwhelmed mothers. One of the controlling narratives of Black women as mothers is that of the Black matriarch – the "bad" Black mother. As Patricia Hill-Collins explains, the Black matriarch is the mother who spends too much time away from home due to work obligations, therefore being unable to properly supervise her children and contributing in a significant way to her children's failure in school (2000, 75). This narrative is captured in one defence attorney's explanation for why racialized men become involved in trafficking (and other criminal) activities: "The mothers are kind of bitter, understandably, they've got three or four kids and are trying to make it through the day with the crumbs that they're given with public assistance. They are only human, they get ticked off at you, 'Whack! Shut up jr. Whack!' Then you can see when you interview them [the accused], you can see the hostility they have towards women. The main woman figure they have in their life is their mom, right, and the mom doesn't have anyone supporting them and helping them and dealing with them" (participant 12). In the context of this study, the above quote reveals a number of troubling race-based stereotypes, including Black women as having too many children, their reliance on social welfare to support their children, the absence of fathers in Black families, neglect of children, and violence within these homes (Hill-Collins 2004; Jackson 2006; Maynard 2017).

Mother blaming particularly prevalent in these narratives is especially evident in the case of single and/or poor, racialized mothers. Indeed, the singleness, poorness, and Blackness that taps into the stereotyped image of the Black matriarch is suggested to be a result of Black culture's otherness characterized by laziness, violence, and uncontrolled sexuality resulting in multiple fatherless children and posing as a "threat and contamination" (Maynard 2017, 180). The outcome, as Feldstein explains, is that Black mothers are seen as raising "sons who [are] either insufficiently aggressive, inhibited, and sexually passive and repressed; or sons who [are] too aggressive, insufficiently cooperative and violent" (1998, 159). And while the image of Black mothers as "matriarchs" whose actions damage Black men is not new (Feldstein 1998; Hill-Collins 2004; Jackson 2006), it continues to be relied on to serve new purposes. In the context of anti-trafficking efforts, mother blaming is taken up as a possible explanation for the accused's exploitation and suggested hatred of women. Evidence of this can be seen in the psychological information and past risk assessment in the case of *R. v. Burton* (2018), which states:

> Mr. Burton had a difficult childhood that included lack of care by his mother, physical abuse by both his mother and stepfather and a failure by his mother to follow through with recommended treatment. It would appear from the records that many state actors were aware of the physical abuse suffered by Mr. Burton and that his mother refused to get him the necessary treatment, but little was done to intervene – much to Mr. Burton's detriment. For example, in 1992, the Catholic Children's Aid

Society (CCAS) closed their file on Mr. Burton noting that it was clear that Mr. Burton's mother was not going to get the necessary treatment for her son regardless of CCAS's recommendations. Another example is from 1995. There was evidence that Mr. Burton's mother was hitting him with a belt. The police cautioned his mother about this conduct to which she responded that she would nonetheless continue to engage in this kind of punishment. Despite this information, Mr. Burton largely remained in his mother's care. One final example of note is that when Mr. Burton was placed on probation in 1999, the probation officer spoke to Mrs. Burton many times about programs that Mr. Burton should attend, but she failed to take him to these programs and the probation officer failed to take steps to intervene and make sure that Mr. Burton received the counselling that the court ordered.

(para. 29)

Descriptions of Burton's mother as abusive and neglectful incite cultural stereotypes of Black mothers' treatment of their children, and are used to assign blame to this mother for her son's actions. It is not my intent here to excuse or undermine the seriousness of Burton's mother's abuse and neglect towards him, but to draw attention to the larger negative narrative of the Black mother and her presumed role in the criminal behaviour of her child. No blame was attributed to the failure of social safety nets to protect Burton as a child, even though the situation was brought to their attention. Instead, all blame was directed to Burton's mother and her rejection of any intervention.

While mothers of accused take the brunt of the blame for their sons' actions, fathers can also at times come under fire. As Roberta L. Coles and Charles Green (2009) explain, Black men are rarely seen as fathers – they father children, but they are not around to raise them. The dangerousness of young Black men is therefore also attributed to an apparent lack of father figures to act as role models (Coles and Green 2009; James 2012, 79). Indeed, as James explains, violence by young Black men has been blamed explicitly on "the fact that they are 'from fatherless homes'" (2012, 79). In the context trafficking trials, this is captured by the comment of one defence attorney, "I blame a lot on the males. To me, what they should make a criminal offence – child abandonment. I mean a parent leaving and not paying child support. To me, that's the biggest – and men, still, I mean I'd make that criminal. I really would because I find that 90% of my clientele is, I don't know my father, or I haven't heard of him" (participant 12). The suggestion that further criminalization of Black men would somehow benefit Black families is a continuation of racialized surveillance and punishment justified through the cloak of protectionism. The attribution of Black men's criminality to the absence of a male role model is also captured in trafficking trials. In the sentencing decision in *R. v. R.R.S.* (2015), the judge pointed out the absence of the accused's father from his life, noting that "over the years, R.S. has been unable to benefit from his support and direction" (29 March 2016, para. 13), thus suggesting that fatherly support and direction would have prevented the accused from criminal behaviour. The presentencing report in *R. v. Byron* (2014) similarly highlighted the absence of a father in the accused's life:

> The lack of a father figure has certainly affected him [Byron] and drawn him closer to the negative influence that is also spoken of and it's also expressed as a concern by all three individuals here. The fact that [the accused's] father was and perhaps still is incarcerated, the fact that he has not had any contact with him because he is in St. Vincent has left a void in his life and it's been difficult for him and his mother, I'm sure. [The accused] also has a younger brother that his mother currently raises. And as mentioned in the report, it has unfortunately become taboo in the Byron house to speak of where Mr. Byron [the father] is and what has happened with him.
>
> (Audio of trial, 13 December 2013)

The absent father figure in *R. v. Byron* (2014) is given significant weight as a contributing factor to the accused's actions. It is also notable that the mother's decision to ban any conversation about the father is framed as a failure on her part, rather than for any substantive reasons (abuse, neglect, etc.), demonstrating a patriarchal positivist set of assumptions about fathers that is simply astounding.

In the absence of the father figure, negative peer influence is often assumed to have taken hold for the men accused of human trafficking. This assumption is part of a larger discourse that, according to James, assumes the presence of father figures in young men's lives will set them on the right path (2012, 79; see also Alexander 2012). Bad men replace (presumably good) men/fathers who are, themselves, victimized by mothers' "unfortunate" (irrational) refusal to allow their sons to have access to them. This narrative allows for a deflection from so many structural issues, including men's treatment of women, as well as women's struggles as single mothers in a hostile racial system.

Interestingly, despite the clear blame placed on the families of those convicted of human trafficking at trial and the consideration given to complainants' family backgrounds, these elements appear to be insignificant as mitigating factors. This is exemplified in the comment of one police officer: "I don't really dive into their, you know, did my mom beat me or did my dad, you know, didn't love me or any of that. I don't explore that. I could care less. For me, it's about the evidence and challenging them on it and see what they have to say about it" (participant 3). This seemingly neutral approach, which focuses on evidence collection, allows for a simple evocation of the human trafficking matrix and demonstrates the way in which Black people are easily identified as offenders but seen as incapable of being victims (Stevenson 2017, 4), thus ignoring the systemic destruction of Black families that has taken effect through state policies which criminalize poverty through enforcement of welfare fraud, sex work, and drug laws that reproduce Black people's vulnerability (Maynard 2017).

As this chapter up has shown, pre-existing tropes and stereotypes bound into the human trafficking matrix play an important role in the ability of police and legal actors to redefine certain activities and characteristics as indicators of human trafficking. Anti-trafficking efforts, via the human trafficking matrix, combine transnational discourses of organized crime, the War on Terror, and national security with domestic criminality, which folds the exceptional into the normal. The urgency and severity brought to these criminal acts by the effects of transnational trafficking discourses justify the racialized punitiveness of the state through increased criminal justice responses targeting ethnic, racial, and marginalized men as criminals. The consequences of this on racialized groups are significant. As scholars have observed, Canada's immigration history has seen criminality become linked with a wide range of activities and individuals in order to deport those seen as dangerous for "various combinations of moral, racial and ideological reasons" (Pratt and Valverde 2002, 137; Maynard 2017; Pratt 2014, 2005). As Maynard writes, a large number of Black people have been deported from Canada for relatively minor crimes which have been re-inscribed as national security threats (2017, 174).

Anti-trafficking regimes provide yet another avenue through which racialized men become constructed as threats to national security, illustrated, in part, by the fact that of the eleven trafficking trials I analysed, all but one case involved an accused who was a first- or second-generation immigrant and a racialized person. Consider, for instance, the case of *R. v. Byron* (2014), where the accused "was born in St. Vincent in the Grenadines and immigrated to Canada, to Montreal, when he was 13 years old" (Audio of trial, 13 February 2014). In *R. v. (Gregory) Salmon* (2014), the accused's Jamaican background and ties to the community are revealed at the trial through discussions of his inability to attend the funerals of his mother and father in Jamaica due to travel restrictions resulting from a criminal conviction. In *R. v. Burton* (2016), we learn of the accused's background through the complainant's description of him as "5'7, short black hair, from Jamaica" (Audio of trial, 18 December 2013). *R. v. A.A.* (2012) involves an accused who was born in Barbados and immigrated to Canada as a young child. In *R. v. Rasool* (2015), one of the only women accused in trafficking cases I examined, grew up in Pakistan.

More recent cases where this can be observed (not in the original dataset) include *R. v. Ahmed et al.* (2019), where the accused, Amina Ahmed, was born in Kenya and immigrated to Canada at ten years old (para. 59). Her co-accused, Nadia Ngoto, was born in Belgium to Congolese parents and has a precarious immigration status in Canada.[23] The accused in *R. v. Reginald Louis Jean* (2020) is of Haitian decent; the accused in *R. v. D.A.* (2017) is Jamaican and moved to Canada at five or six years of age (para. 5); and in *R. v. N.A.* (2017), the accused is Macedonian and has permanent resident status.[24] The fact that in each case, the legal actors, typically the prosecution, decidedly identified the non-Canadian birth of the accused[25] is in itself evidence of a form of micro-aggression signalling xenophobia that marks the accused as Other to those who are Canadian-born, as an outsider, racialized, or in a way that identifies them as non-white, which needs no signifier. This focus on the "foreignness" of the accused creates what Pratt calls "a conceptual slippage between criminals, refugee and 'foreigners'" (2005, 14), thus perpetuating the myth that all refugees and migrants are criminals (Maynard 2017; Pratt 2005).

Conclusion

The powerful transnational trafficking discourses that emerged out of the UN Trafficking Protocol (2000) and the Convention against Organized Crime, link trafficking with concerns over organized crime, the War on Terror, and national security. The emergence of these diverse concerns within the trafficking matrix has created a powerful framework supported and incited by the image of the white, middle-class daughter of Canadian families as a potential victim of trafficking. These discursive constructions are central to Canada's national imaginary as a civil and moral nation, which is tasked with combating the "foreign" threat from outside. Despite the now widespread consensus that trafficking in Canada is primarily a domestic issue, this threat is constructed as "foreign" and Other through a focus on racialized and migrant populations in Canada as real and potential traffickers.

This chapter has detailed the ways in which racialized stereotypes of Black culture and people, and particularly Black men, as hypersexual, violent, greedy, and controlling are utilized by police and prosecutors in anti-trafficking efforts to construct Black men and their activities as human trafficking. And while the same depictions have historically been used by law enforcement and legal professionals to target "pimping" activities of Black men, we are now seeing not only their re-employment, but also their conceptual linkage with larger concerns over the War on Terror, organized crime, and national security. Thus, in the post-9/11 world, this criminality, which is consistently associated with young, racialized men, is no longer simply a public nuisance but has become linked with much more serious issues and justifies otherwise punitive repercussions, such as the deportation of offenders for serious criminality and long prison sentences. As Maynard notes, "Canada is in the midst of an explosion of Black incarceration" (2017, 109). Anti-trafficking efforts which target racialized young men, and especially Black men, are contributing to this as well as the criminalization of race and poverty through a targeted focus on racialized people from marginalized socio-economic backgrounds.

Conclusion

The objective of this book was to detail the ways in which global anti-trafficking efforts have been domesticated in Canada through law, policy, discourse, and the actions and decisions of police and legal actors. As such, the book has explored the strategies, knowledges, frameworks, and tactics that shape our understanding of trafficking as a crime in Canada and argued that the crime of trafficking is not unique or exceptional, as often made to seem in popular culture and by politicians, police, and the media who emphasize the overwhelming dangerousness of traffickers and the risk of victimization to women and girls everywhere. Instead, the crime of domestic trafficking is a mundane criminal offence that in practice parallels the offence of procuring (s. 286.3 of the Criminal Code), colloquially known as "pimping," that has existed as a crime in Canada since 1913.

The perception of trafficking as an exceptional offence stems, in part, from the UN Trafficking Protocol (2000), which defines human trafficking as a multi-step process crime that involves recruitment, transportation, and exploitation of people and is carried out by transnational organized crime groups. Yet, as detailed in chapter one, the way the offence has been adopted into Canadian law removes many of the requirements that made the offence what it was at the international level. In particular, under Canadian law, trafficking does not have to be a multi-step process, and in fact, the focus of the offence is on the intent to exploit – a very broad requirement that allows for a wide range of activities to be categorized as "trafficking," despite legislative efforts to narrow it through the fear of safety provision. The offence also does not require the involvement of organized crime syndicates, although the presence of this factor makes the offence graver. As such, Crown attorneys often (even if unsuccessfully) attempt to draw out this narrative. Furthermore, there is no transportation requirement to establish the crime of trafficking. Instead, the offence is strikingly similar to procurement but with a focus on real or intended exploitation. Such an adaptation of the trafficking offence must be understood in the political context from which it emerged, including the US Department of State annual evaluations of participating countries' anti-trafficking efforts and the 2013 Supreme Court decision in the Bedford case, which subsequently led to a shift in Canadian sex work laws, bringing them in line with the protectionist sentiments and goals of anti-trafficking efforts (see chapter one).

The domestication of human trafficking in Canada has also resulted in the blending of the international discourses around trafficking with a variety of national domestic trafficking discourses which are an extension of longstanding racialized, gendered, and moralized concerns about female sexuality and sexual violence. Gaining momentum in the 1970s, these include fears around child sexual exploitation and youth involvement in the sex trade that emerged during the 1980s and 1990s and, in the more distant past, the "white slavery" panics of the late nineteenth and early twentieth centuries. This confluence of international and domestic concerns that include migration, youth sexuality, and involvement in sex work, as well as organized criminal activity, national security, and the War on Terror, blend in what I have labelled the "human trafficking matrix." The matrix forms through a web of combined discourses, laws, policies, front-line criminal justice and legal practices, and expert knowledges and technologies collected from a compilation of pre-existing issues. Within the matrix, these factors intersect to assign new meaning and create new threats, shaping, for instance, race-based stereotypes of Black men as "pimps" into characteristics of new and dangerous traffickers.

A number of heterogeneous factors come into play in the shaping of the offence of human trafficking on the front line. Some factors are novel and even surprising, while others are mundane and organizational, and yet others reflect the continuing influence of historical preoccupations. The varying combinations of factors have divergent effects on the approaches of criminal justice actors to, and even their understanding of, the crime of human trafficking. As the evidence of this study suggests, front-line police officers, defence and Crown attorneys, and judges hold varying and sometimes contradictory understandings of the meaning of human trafficking, particularly when it comes to the distinction between human trafficking and procuring (under section 286.3 of CCC). In this muddle, front-line actors draw on class-, race-, and gender-based stereotypes and knowledges from pre-existing concerns to, among other things, (re-)construct and assign new meaning to the familiar scenario of sex worker and "pimp" dynamics as human trafficking. Yet, the fact that the activities being targeted are previously existing sex work–related offences, rather than a menacing new crime, as it is often portrayed, is obscured by the dominance of the human trafficking matrix.

At the centre of anti-trafficking efforts is the victim of trafficking, captured in Canada by three key trafficking victim images: (1) the "girl next door" – imagined as the white, middle-class daughter of a Canadian family; (2) the marginalized girl or woman whose pre-existing vulnerabilities put her at risk; and (3) the Indigenous woman or girl. These victim images are created along racial lines and a spectrum of innocence in which the "girl next door" is presumed to be most faultless because she is lured, and duped, albeit even she, as a responsible neoliberal citizen, is held to account for her actions and decisions. In contrast, marginalized and Indigenous women and girls, while deemed victims through their pre-existing vulnerabilities (poverty, drug and alcohol use, involvement in sex work, etc.), are held responsible in some measure for their "lifestyles" (of risk).

The narrative of the "girl next door" – Canada's ideal trafficking victim – invigorates the urgency of anti-trafficking efforts by raising the omnipresent threat of trafficking for all women and girls. She plays an important role in the construction of trafficking and is often cited in House of Common debates that seek to establish the scourge of trafficking. Yet, she seldom appears on stage in the courtroom dramas that play out as a result of arrests and prosecutions for human trafficking. Instead, it is marginalized women or girls who may be addicted to drugs or alcohol and/or are already involved in the sex trade who are most commonly seen as complainants in trafficking court cases. Despite her youth, naiveté, and often whiteness, the marginalized girl or woman nonetheless departs from the "ideal victim" through her perceived lack of innocence. She is further along the blame continuum, as her victimization is a product of pre-existing vulnerabilities, including her poverty, addictions, and involvement in sex work. As such, her agency, decision-making, and therefore blame is given more emphasis, particularly by defence attorneys at trial.

Similarly, the victimization of Indigenous women and girls by traffickers is frequently emphasized in the media and in discussions among policymakers (in part as an offshoot of public pressure to look like police and the government are doing something about the problem of colonial violence against Indigenous women). But the limited number of studies that exist on the victimization of Indigenous women, including the present one, do not confirm a significant rate of Indigenous women as trafficking victims in the courts (see Millar et al. 2015). Their absence in prosecuted cases raises questions about who qualifies as a victim of trafficking. And while the recognition of Indigenous women and girls' victimization by traffickers in parliamentary debates and reports is seen as a positive development by advocates for women's and Indigenous rights organizations (Government of B.C. 2014a; National Inquiry into the Missing and Murdered Indigenous Women and Girls 2019), critical scholars have pointed out that this focus is a paternalistic and infantilizing one that depicts Indigenous women as victimized through their own doing – by being poor, engaging in sex work, becoming addicted to drugs and alcohol, and therefore in need of rescue from the colonial government (Hunt 2015; 2017; Kaye 2017). This gap between discourse focus on Indigenous women and girls' victimization, and the apparent lack of Indigenous complainants in trafficking court cases, is curious and signals a need for further research.

The victim of trafficking is largely constructed using pre-existing vulnerability factors – in part, a risk-based approach that enables the police to construct women and girls in the sex trade as potential victims of trafficking and bypass the impossible task of finding complainants who abide by the "ideal victim" standards. In this way, these vulnerability factors have become a part of the human trafficking matrix, transforming a wide range of factors that are a normal part of many people's lives into trafficking vulnerabilities. Yet, women and girls who are deemed by police to be victims of trafficking do not always see themselves as such. What is especially troubling is that if women refuse to accept this characterization of their role, they can be subject to criminal charges or threatened with other punitive consequences. In this way, police place pressure on women and girls to take on the victim label and to tell a particular version of events, even scripting their story to fit the legally required narrative of exploitation (see chapter three). The use of this strategy by police enables them to target the sex trade through anti-trafficking efforts while criminalizing those who refuse to take on the victim label. It reveals how the fine line between "at risk" and "risky" victim identified by scholars in sexual assault cases (Gotell 2008; Moore and Valverde 2000) is alive and operational in trafficking efforts.

At the trial stage, Crown attorneys also use these pre-existing vulnerability factors to construct complainants as subject to an increased risk of exploitation to build their case as one of human trafficking. Crown prosecutors' approach to trafficking cases is once again enabled by the trafficking matrix, which, in addition to the pre-existing vulnerabilities, employs a series of race-, class-, age-, and gender-based stereotypes that enable women, often working in the sex trade, to be constructed as vulnerable and therefore suspect as victims of exploitation. In contrast, defence attorneys rely on the very same factors to undermine the complainant's victimhood by drawing out any evidence of possible consent. As detailed in chapter four, defence attorneys have seemingly adopted the sexual assault framework in their legal strategies to suggest that the complainants consented to sex work and therefore that no human trafficking took place. Ironically, in pursuing this line of argumentation, defence attorneys rely on the same vulnerability factors as the Crowns. Thus, in a number of cases discussed (including *R. v. Beckford* [2013] and *R. v. Dagg* [2015]), we saw Crown attorneys constructing complainants' drug and alcohol addictions as vulnerabilities exploited by the accused, while the defence relied on these addictions to engage in victim blaming. By engaging in these adversarial arguments, legal actors actively constitute a working definition of human trafficking relying on discourses, pre-existing knowledges about victimization, sexual assault, gang activity, and "pimps" that have accumulated within the human trafficking matrix to narrate the stories that come before the courts.

These legal strategies are also central in the construction of the offender. The narrative of the accused, who are often young, poor, and racialized men, is built by the Crown through reliance on characteristics and activities stereotypically associated with "pimps" and "pimping." These gender-, class-, and race- based stereotypes have become part of the human trafficking matrix, within which they have taken on new meaning as indicators. In particular, these indicators, including recruitment methods – the more subtle ones, such as expressions of love, called "Romeo tactics," and the less subtle forms, such as "luring" – and control tactics that involve violence and drugs, are presented as new threats to women and girls. Yet, a closer examination of these indicators suggests that they are the same ones identified during the 1980s and 1990s panics about youth involvement in the sex trade, which defined "pimping" activities (see also Roots 2019). As detailed in chapter three, the knowledges and tactics of the historical panics over youth in the sex trade have become embedded within the human trafficking matrix, in part through police efforts to gain knowledge about human trafficking. To fuel urgency and emphasize danger, law enforcement and prosecution go to significant lengths to link accused men with organized crime, despite frequent absence of evidence, thus invoking a larger threat associated with transnational organized crime and national security. As I also detailed in chapter three, police use particularly aggressive investigation tactics, exemplified in the cases of *R. v. Dagg* (2015) and especially *R. v. (Courtney) Salmon* (2013), where the police went as far as to fabricate evidence to increase the chances of conviction.

These aggressive anti-trafficking approaches by the police and, more recently, Crown attorneys are motivated by a variety of factors. While arrest rates remain a key measure of police performance in general, police working in specialized anti-trafficking units are under additional pressure to arrest traffickers to justify the continued existence of the unit and the large amounts of public funds they receive for anti-trafficking efforts. Furthermore, when arrest rates increase, police use numbers of trafficking arrests to demonstrate a need for more resources because they claim that the extent of the problem is beyond what they can combat with existing resources. Yet, these requests for funding also place local anti-trafficking units in competition with each other, further increasing pressure to show productivity by laying charges. More recently, similar pressures have been applied to Crowns through provincial anti-trafficking strategies, such as the one recently put into place in Ontario, which assigned six specialized Crown attorneys to human trafficking cases. Finally, it is also the case that higher arrest rates for trafficking offences are needed to demonstrate the success of Canada's law enforcement and prosecutorial efforts to the US Department of State, which, as discussed in the Introduction, monitors and ranks countries in their anti-trafficking efforts.

In the absence of transnational trafficking cases however, local anti-trafficking police and Crowns turn to easier cases, re-constructing what might previously have been rather common procuring cases into human trafficking cases. To do this, front-line police officers and prosecutors regularly draw from popular culture, as well as historically resilient and deeply moralized gender-, class-, and race-based stereotypes. As such, the problem of trafficking is at least partially constructed by local front-line enforcement practices that enact the problem in their day-to-day work. These specialized human trafficking police and Crown attorneys are now widely regarded as experts on the issue of trafficking and are called on to share their knowledge on the topic with other police and legal actors in court proceedings with NGOs, the media, and the public, therefore disseminating knowledge on human trafficking which they themselves have generated. In doing so, the politicians, lawmakers, police, and prosecutors are able to respond to the pressures of the United States and the international community to arrest and prosecute trafficking cases and demonstrate their effectiveness in combating this crime.

And while anti-trafficking efforts in Canada are in full force with large-scale and costly undertakings at many levels of government, this research has shown in specific empirical detail the ways in which the trafficking matrix has resulted in some troubling effects. These include the aggressive targeting of the sex trade; the (re)victimization of those labelled as trafficking victims by police and legal actors; the criminalization of racialized, impoverished, and other marginalized groups; and a focus on small-time offenders but with increasingly tougher penalties. Similar patterns around localized anti-trafficking efforts have also been observed in other jurisdictions (Gallagher 2016; Gallagher and Surtees 2012; Horning and Marcus 2017; Lester et al. 2017; Swenstein and Mogulescu 2016; Williamson and Marcus 2017).

A conviction for a human trafficking offence in Canada now comes with a mandatory minimum of four years' imprisonment. If the complainant is under the age of eighteen, the punishment increases to a minimum of five years and a maximum of life imprisonment. These tough sentences are particularly troubling given the wide range of conduct that can be categorized as trafficking. Concern over mandatory minimum sentences was also expressed by the court in in *R. v. Finestone* (2017) and led to mandatory minimums being struck down for adult trafficking in the Ontario case of *R. v. Reginald Jean Lous* (2020), and youth trafficking in *R. v. Ahmed et al.* (2019). Despite this, we have seen significant penalties imposed for trafficking convictions, most notably in *R. v. Moazami* (2015), where the Supreme Court of British Columbia imposed a sentence of twenty-three years' imprisonment for Mr. Moazami's role in the sex work activities of eleven girls and women ranging between fourteen and nineteen years of age. Moazami's exceedingly high sentence was a result of the judge's decision to impose consecutive sentences for each incident, enabled by legislative changes enacted in 2015 that allow consecutive sentencing in cases of child and youth sexual victimization where more than one victim exists (MacKay 2014).

The penalties also come with additional consequences, including a lifetime DNA order, registration with the sex offender registry (if the trafficking is for the purpose of sexual exploitation), and possibly long-term and/or dangerous offender designation. While long-term and dangerous offender designations are usually applied in extreme cases and/or in response to an extensive record of criminal offending, the Crown in *R. v. Burton* (2018) brought an application to have all human trafficking convictions deemed as personal injury offences, which open the door for a Dangerous Offender designation. While the Crown's application for this sweeping change was unsuccessful, the mere attempt is alarming, particularly given the mundane crimes that are now being categorized as human trafficking. Furthermore, the Crown can also ask for a section 161 (1) Order, which can be imposed for offences against persons under sixteen years old. If granted, this order would, among other things, restrict the convicted person from being able to go to parks, swimming pools, be near playgrounds, daycare centres or school grounds where children are likely to be, or have any contact with a person under the age of sixteen. The convicted person would also be prohibited from using the internet unless granted under court-imposed rules (CCC, Order of prohibition 161[1]). The inability to engage in common everyday activities, such as using the internet, walking in the park, or swimming at a public pool, demonstrates the severity with which trafficking is treated.

In addition to criminal penalties, permanent residents convicted of trafficking and sentenced to a term of six months or longer in jail are subject to a non-appealable deportation order. Changes to immigration laws have been designed to enable the faster deportation of non-citizens convicted of serious criminality, including human trafficking. The Faster Removal of Foreign Criminals Act (2013) amended the IRPA to reduce the length of the sentence that allows permanent residents convicted of serious criminality to be deported without appeal, from two years to six months' imprisonment in case of a conviction for an offence that comes with a maximum penalty of ten or more years' imprisonment. This is significant, as it allows for the deportation of long-term residents of Canada for a crime that a decade ago was treated as a conventional domestic offence. Those deported are often Black, and specifically Jamaican men. The continuation of this trend under anti-trafficking efforts is part of an ongoing pattern of criminality-based deportations targeted at Black men more than any other group in Canadian society (Burt et al. 2016; Maynard 2017).

In this context, the combined process of reconceptualizing procuring offences as human trafficking and the use of racial tropes to construct racialized men, particularly Black men, as human traffickers is troubling. And although the number of trafficking convictions in Canada remains low, there has been an upward trend in recent years, signalling a need to remain vigilant of these developments. The racial dynamics of this research are particularly pertinent given the heightened racial tensions that have emerged in the United States, but also the UK and Canada at the time of writing in 2021, especially with the acknowledgment of systemic racism, often for the first time, by politicians, police agencies, sports leagues, and major corporations. The focused criminalization of largely racialized men under the justification of protecting the human rights of victims is an extension of the racial discrimination that led to the murder of George Floyd and many other racialized people at the hands of mainly white police officers. The current political situation illuminates the findings of this research and should therefore give us pause, realizing that an offence which up until a few years ago was seen as a mundane and common-place crime, has now been recreated as a transnational and organized crime that poses a risk to Canada's national security and is used to target and criminalize mainly racialized men, imprisoning them for long periods of time and/or deporting those with insecure immigration status. The UN Trafficking Protocol, which was enacted out of a level of concern for human rights, has therefore seemingly had a very different impact once adopted at the domestic level in Canada. Despite the sensationalized media coverage, documentaries, and narratives presented by parliamentarians and police, the on-the-ground criminal justice efforts reveal a very different reality – one that is not nearly as exceptional, instead revealing the poverty, racial inequality, gender discrimination, and colonial legacy that is deeply embedded into Canadian society. And while the protectionist approach of anti-trafficking efforts seems at first sight to exist for the protection of women, this book has revealed the underbelly of these efforts, indicating a need to pay closer attention to the way in which trafficking narratives are being constructed, not only in the media and other public forums but also in court cases where the very offence of trafficking is being shaped.

Human Trafficking Cases:
Race, Age, Gender, and Visual Depictions
of Accused in the Media[1]

Name	Age at the Time of Arrest	Gender[2]	Race[3]/Ethnicity	Picture Released by Media
1. Tyrone Burton	28	M	Racialized/Jamaican	Yes
2. Ferenc Domotor	48	M	Visibly white/Romani, Hungarian	Yes
3. Ferenc Domotor Jr.	21	M	Visibly white/Romani, Hungarian	Yes
4. Gyongyi Kolompar	40	F	Visibly white/Romani, Hungarian	Yes
5. Gizella Kolompar	41	F	Visibly white/Romani, Hungarian	Yes
6. Lajos Domotor	42	M	Visibly white/Romani, Hungarian	Yes
7. Ferenc Karadi	47	M	Visibly white/Romani, Hungarian	Yes
8. Attila Kolompar	35	F	Visibly white/Romani, Hungarian	Yes
9. Gyula Domotor	32	M	Visibly white/Romani, Hungarian	Yes
10. Gizella Domotor	42	F	Visibly white/Romani, Hungarian	Yes
11. Ferenc Domotor Sr.	68	M	Visibly white/Romani, Hungarian (information from descriptions in newspaper articles)	No
12. Jozsef Domotor	43	M	Visibly white/Romani, Hungarian	Yes
13. Gyozo Papai	42	M	Visibly white/Romani, Hungarian	Yes
14. Zsanett Karadi	24	M	Visibly white/Romani, Hungarian	Yes

(continued)

1 Accused from the same case are grouped together through highlighting. Varied shades of grey are used to indicate where individuals were charged together.
2 As noted on Court Information Sheet.
3 I acknowledge that race is a socially constructed category. Efforts to identify the race of the accused were made in order to show that racialized people are more heavily targeted by anti-trafficking police and prosecutorial efforts on the ground.

Name	Age at the Time of Arrest	Gender	Race/Ethnicity	Picture Released by Media
15. Krisztina Csaszar	30	F	Visibly white/Romani, Hungarian	Yes
16. Janos Szanto	37	M	Visibly white/Romani, Hungarian	Yes
17. Robert Colangelo	33	M	Visibly white	Yes
18. Justin Zealand	21	M	Visibly white	Yes
19. Breanna Garrison	20	F	N/A	No
20. Kadeem Truadian Francis	23	M	Racialized/Black	Yes
21. Jesse Scullion	22	M	N/A	No
22. Travis Savoury	36	M	Racialized/Black	Yes
23. Karim Cherestal	21	M	Racialized/Black (information from description of accused in trial transcript)	No
24. Taylor Dagg	23	M	Racialized/Black	Yes
25. Steven McDonald	36	M	N/A	No
26. Kristen MacLean	32	F	N/A	No
27. Tyrone Smith	20	M	Racialized/Black	Yes
28. Lamone Smith	23	F	Racialized/Black	Yes
29. David D'Souza	26	M	N/A	No
30. Kailey Oliver-Machado	16	F	Visibly white/French Canadian	Yes
31. R. v. A.A.(1) (Oliver-Machado co-accused)	15	F	Racialized/Black (information from description of accused in trial transcript)	No
32. R. v. A.A. (2) (Oliver-Machado co-accused)	17	F	Visibly white (information from description of accused in trial transcript)	No
33. Richard Addis	54	M	N/A	No
34. Kareem Watson	30	M	N/A	No
35. Mohamed Ahmed	26	M	Racialized/South Asian (assumption made based on the name of the accused)	No
36. Jerome Barron Dorsey	25	M	N/A	No

Name	Age at the Time of Arrest	Gender	Race/Ethnicity	Picture Released by Media
37. Merrick Anthony Dennis	27	M	N/A	No
38. Imani Nakpangi	26	M	Racialized/Black	Yes
39. Vytautas Vilutis	21	M	N/A	No
40. Jaimie Byron	24	M	Racialized/Grenadines	Yes
41. Everol Powell	45	M	Racialized/Black	Yes
42. Correll Slawter	26	M	N/A	No
43. Shakib Gharibzada	26	M	N/A	No
44. Masood Hejran	26	M	N/A	No
45. Remington Needham	22	M	N/A	No
46. Daryn Leung	25	M	Racialized/Black (participant observation at trial)	No
47. Cheng Ping Liu	40	M	East Asian (based on a sketch by court sketch artist)	No
48. Christopher McCall	43	M	Visibly white	Yes
49. Mark Anthony Burton	42	M	Racialized/Black	Yes
50. Yul Styles-Lyons	25	M	Racialized/Black	Yes
51. Jerome Hines	28	M	Racialized/Black	Yes
52. Anthony Greenham	28	M	Racialized/Black (information from description in trial transcript)	No
53. Stefan Ascenzi	28	M	Visibly white	Yes
54. Lisa M. Ascenzi	46	F	Visibly white	Yes
55. Vanessa Cachia	22	F	Visibly white	Yes
56. Myriam Robert	18	F	N/A	No
57. Derek Bissue	22	M	Racialized/Black	Yes
58. Goran Kakamad	19	M	N/A	No
59. Gregory Salmon	31	M	Racialized/Jamaican (based on information from trial transcript)	No
60. Pawel Michon	42	M	Visibly white	Yes
61. Toofan Charmin	27	M	N/A	No
62. Zainab Rasool	38	F	Racialized/Pakistani (information obtained from trial transcript)	No

(continued)

Name	Age at the Time of Arrest	Gender	Race/Ethnicity	Picture Released by Media
63. Omar McFarlane	31	M	Racialized/Jamaican (based on information from sentencing reasons R. v.McFarlane [2012])	No
64. Jacques Leonard St. Vil	24	M	N/A	No
65. Ken Katalayi-Kassende	27	M	N/A	No
66. Andrew Lewis	23	M	N/A	No
67. Taylor Eibbitt	25	M	N/A	No
68. Solomon Houlder	20	M	Racialized/Black	Yes
69. Yasin Mohamud	26	M	N/A	No
70. Abdirahman Hussain	18	M	N/A	No
71. Lucas Gabrys	24	M	Visibly white	Yes
72. Anthony Putzu	26	M	Racialized/Black	Yes
73. Simeon Harty	21	M	Racialized/Black	Yes
74. Jamie Forbes	32	M	Racialized/Black	Yes
75. Dustin Macbeth	22	M	Visibly white	Yes
76. Ashor Anwia	19	M	Racialized	Yes
77. Jordan Michael Lynch	18	M	Racialized/Black	Yes
78. Aldain Alando Beckford	25	M	Racialized/Black (information obtained from trial transcripts)	No
79. David Mackay Stone	24	M	Racialized/Black (information obtained from trial transcripts)	No
80. Thomas Downey	20	M	Racialized/Black	Yes
81. Spencer Thompson	22	M	Racialized/Black	Yes
82. Anthony Roberts	21	M	Visibly white	Yes
83. Henok Mebratu	23	M	Racialized/Black	Yes
84. Shaun Butler	23	M	Racialized/Black	Yes
85. Jason Bartley	20	M	N/A	No
86. Anthony Talbert	21	M	Racialized/Black	Yes
87. Brian McKenzie	22	M	Racialized/Black	Yes
88. Tchello Whyte	25	M	Racialized/Black	Yes

Name	Age at the Time of Arrest	Gender	Race/Ethnicity	Picture Released by Media
89. Shanicka Providence	18	F	Racialized/Black	Yes
90. Aloma Shermin Providence	38	F	N/A	No
91. Markus Cole	20	M	Racialized/Black	Yes
92. Alia Alexandria Abdellatif	25	F	Visibly white	Yes
93. Natasha Robataille	18	F	Visibly white	Yes
94. Sage Finestone	21	M	Racialized/Black	Yes
95. Nicolas Faria	19	M	Racialized/Black	Yes
96. Nadine Brown	38	F	N/A	No
97. Yolanda Mohabeer	20	F	N/A	No
98. Rory Thomas Mitchell	29	M	Racialized/Black	Yes
99. Kelvin Earl McPherson	36	M	N/A	No
100. Courtney Salmon	39	M	Racialized/Black	Yes
101. Enoch Johnson	25	M	Racialized/Black	Yes
102. Jah-Tyius Joshua Williams	23	M	Racialized/Black	Yes
103. Renardo Cole	29	M	Racialized/Black	Yes
104. Nathan Turnbull	19	M	Racialized/Black	Yes
105. Deshawn Holmes	19	M	Visibly white	Yes
106. Camille Beausejour	19	F	Visibly white	Yes
107. Maziar Masoudi	23	M	Racialized/Black	Yes
108. Michael Hazel	22	M	Racialized/Black	Yes
109. Isaiah Omoro	27	M	N/A	No
110. Chanelle Espinosa	20	F	Racialized/Latina	Yes
111. Alexander Levi	20	M	Racialized/Black	Yes
112. Jerome Tyrele Belle	18	M	N/A	No

(*continued*)

Name	Age at the Time of Arrest	Gender	Race/Ethnicity	Picture Released by Media
113. Hayley McBride	19	F	N/A	No
114. Marcus Cumsille	22	M	Racialized/Black	Yes
115. Joel Edwards	23	M	Racialized/Black	Yes
116. R.v. A.A. (3)	22	M	Racialized/Black/Barbados	No
117. R.v. A.A. (4)	16	M	N/A	No
118. Sahilan Surenddran	24	M	N/A	No
119. Taylor Laughlin	23	M	N/A	No
120. Matthew Cosmo	28	M	Visibly white	Yes
121. Ricardo Spence	33	M	Racialized/Jamaican (description from sentencing decision *R. v. R.R.S.* [2015])	No
122. Brandon Fraser	29	M	Racialized/Black	Yes
123. Jordan Kimmerly	27	M	N/A	No

Summary of Chart

Total of 123 accused persons
   24 women and 99 men.
Average age: 27
   women = 27 years; men = 27 years
Race of accused:
   12 visibly white women, 5 racialized women, 7 unknown
   21 visibly white men, 51 racialized men, 27 unknown
73 pictures released in the media
   14 pictures of women: 11 visibly white women and 3 racialized
      women
   59 pictures of men: 19 visibly white men and 40 racialized men

Human Trafficking Charges and Outcomes[1]

Name	Year Charged	Type of Human Trafficking	Outcome[2]	Sentence
1. Tyrone Burton	2012	Trafficking for the purpose of sexual exploitation	Convicted by judge of the following: 1) Exercising control over victims 2) Trafficking in persons 3) Receiving a material benefit from trafficking in persons 4) Withholding passports 5) Obstructing justice	Sentenced to 10.5 years in prison. Designated long-term offender. Application for Dangerous Offender Designation by Crown denied.
2. Ferenc Domotor	2010	Labour trafficking	Pled guilty to human trafficking, participating in activities of a criminal organization and knowingly counselled a person to misrepresent or withhold material facts relating to a relevant matter that induces or could induce an error in the administration of this Act	Global sentence: nine years (minus two years' credit in respect of the guilty plea[3]) Credit for pre-trial custody for thirty months on the basis of two for one. *Deported to Hungary 10 April 2015.
3. Ferenc Domotor Jr.	2010	Labour trafficking	Pled guilty to 1) conspire to commit an indictable offence of trafficking in persons (s. 279.01[1][b]); 2) participated in the activities of a criminal organization to wit: an extended Hungarian family for the purpose of enhancing the ability of the said organization to facilitate the offence of trafficking in persons (s. 467.11[1] and s. 279.01(1)(b): 36) knowingly counselled a person to misrepresent or withhold material facts relating to a relevant matter that induces or could induce an error in the administration of this Act (s. 126 IRPA)	Count 1: sixteen months in jail (pre-trial credit 1:2); s. 109 order for ten years; s. 487.051 DNA order; count 2: sixteen months concurrent to count 1; count 3: six months concurrent to counts 1 and 2 (from court docs) Note: Sentencing transcript has different info: five years' imprisonment minus two years for guilty plea = thirty-six months minus fifteen months for pre-trial custody = twenty-one months' jail time. *Deported to Hungary.

(continued)

1 Accused from the same case are grouped together through highlighting. Varied shades of green are used to indicate where individuals were charged together.
2 This research was concluded in the summer of 2016. The outcome of any case that was ongoing at that time has been noted as "outstanding."
3 Pre-trial detention credits are an eligibility, not an entitlement.

Appendix B: Human Trafficking Charges and Outcomes (*continued*)

Name	Year Charged	Type of Human Trafficking	Outcome	Sentence
4. Gyongyi Kolompar	2010	Labour trafficking	Pled guilty to count 36) knowingly counselled a person to misrepresent or withhold material facts relating to a relevant matter that induces or could induce an error in the administration of this Act (s. 126 IRPA)	Count 36 (eighteen months of pre-trial custody at 1:2 entitles her to thirty-six months served) *Deported to Hungary.
5. Gizella Kolompar	2010	Labour trafficking	Pled guilty to counts 1 and 2: 1) conspired to commit the indictable offence of trafficking in persons to wit: unlawfully recruit, transport, transfer, receive, hold, conceal and harbour or exercise control, coercion or influence over the movements of various persons (s. 465[1] [s]); 2) did participate in the activities of a criminal organization to wit: an extended Hungarian family for the purpose of enhancing the ability of said organization to facilitate the indictable offence of trafficking in persons (s. 467.11[1]) and s. 279.1[1][b]) By direction of the Crown, count 3 withdrawn: 3) did unlawfully recruit, transport, transfer, receive, hold, conceal or harbour or exercise control, coercion or influence over the movements of a person for the purpose of exploiting or facilitating the exploitation of that person (s. 279.01)	The accused is sentenced to a period of two years' incarceration on count 1 and a period of two years concurrent on count 2 S. 109 order for ten years after release from jail; s. 487.51 DNA order; s. 738; recommendation for early parole in preparation for deportation. (source: handwritten by judge in court file) *Deported to Hungary.
6. Lajos Domotor	2010	Labour trafficking	Pled guilty to conspiring to commit human trafficking, being part of a criminal organization and four counts of possession of stolen cheques from a related mailbox theft ring in London. Died of stomach cancer (source: media)	Sentenced to six years in prison. After time served, had twenty-five months remaining. *Deported to Hungary.

7. Ferenc Karadi	2010	Labour trafficking	Pled guilty to conspiring to commit human trafficking, being a part of a criminal organization, coercing his victims to lie to immigration officials, and fraud	Sentenced to six years' imprisonment. Twenty-five months remaining after credit for time served
8. Attila Kolompar	2010	Labour trafficking	Pled guilty to conspiring to commit human trafficking, being a part of a criminal organization, and welfare fraud	Sentenced to twenty-six months' imprisonment in addition to sixteen months he spent in pre-trial custody *Deported to Hungary
9. Gyula Domotor	2010	Labour trafficking.	Pled guilty to conspiring to commit human trafficking and being a part of a criminal organization	Global sentence 7.5 years; paroled November 2013
10. Gizella Domotor	2010	Labour trafficking	Pled guilty to count 1, conspiring to commit trafficking and count 2, participating in a criminal organization to commit trafficking	Sentenced to time served (nine months: eighteen months on 2 for 1 basis) and one day. Count 1: eighteen months concurrent on count 2; DNA order: weapons prohibition s. 109 (2a) + (2b) for life *Deported to Hungary
11. Ferenc Domotor Sr.	2010	Labour trafficking	Believed to have escaped to Hungary; warrant outstanding	N/A
12. Jozsef Domotor	2010	Labour trafficking	Pled guilty to conspiring to commit human trafficking and being a part of a criminal organization	Sentenced to six years' imprisonment. After pre-sentencing time served, twenty-four months remaining *Deported to Hungary

(continued)

Appendix B: Human Trafficking Charges and Outcomes (*continued*)

Name	Year Charged	Type of Human Trafficking	Outcome	Sentence
13. Gyozo Papai	2010	Labour trafficking	Pled guilty to count 1, conspiracy to commit the indictable offence of trafficking in persons to wit: unlawfully recruit, transport, transfer, receive, hold, conceal and harbour or exercise control, coercion or influence over the movements of various persons (s. 465[1][s]); and count 3, unlawfully recruiting, transporting, transferring, receiving, holding, concealing or harbouring or exercising control, coercion or influence over the movements of a person for the purpose of exploiting or facilitating the exploitation of that person (s. 279.01). Count 2 withdrawn: 2) participating in the activities of an organized crime group	Sentenced to 2 years, less time served on a 2 to 1 basis = 18 months. Leaving 6 months' sentence from the date of sentence. DNA order; weapons prohibition (s. 204(2b) *Deported to Hungary
14. Zsanett Karadi	2010	Labour trafficking	Pled guilty to count 3, stealing $20 from a victim. Counts 1 and 2 withdrawn: 1) conspiring to commit human trafficking and 2) participating in the activities of an organized crime group withdrawn	*Deported to Hungary
15. Krisztina Csaszar	2010	Labour trafficking	Pled guilty to being a part of a criminal organization, welfare fraud, and obstruction of justice	Sentenced to time served (spent eleven months in pre-trial custody) *Deported to Hungary
16. Janos Szanto	2010	Labour trafficking	Pled guilty to count 1, conspiring to commit human trafficking, and count 2, participating in the activities of an organized crime group	Sentenced to two years; count 1: credit sixty-eight days' jail at 2 for 1. S. 109 – life: DNA Order *Deported to Hungary

	Year	Charge	Outcome
17. Robert Colangelo	2014	Trafficking for the purpose of sexual exploitation	Outstanding
18. Justin Zealand	2014	Trafficking for the purpose of sexual exploitation	All charges withdrawn
19. Breanna Garrison	2014	Trafficking for the purpose of sexual exploitation	All charges withdrawn
20. Kadeem Truadian Francis	2014	Trafficking for the purpose of sexual exploitation	All charges withdrawn
21. Jesse Scullion	2014	Trafficking for the purpose of sexual exploitation	All charges withdrawn
22. Travis Savoury	2014	Trafficking for the purpose of sexual exploitation	Found guilty of count 1, assault, and count 4, failing to comply with recognizance; all other counts withdrawn at the request of Crown *no trafficking conviction (source: court docs); victim did not want to testify	Sentenced to six months in jail but was allowed to go free since he spent ten months in custody
23. Karim Cherestal	2013	Trafficking for the purpose of sexual exploitation	Outstanding

(continued)

Appendix B: Human Trafficking Charges and Outcomes (*continued*)

Name	Year Charged	Type of Human Trafficking	Outcome	Sentence
24. Taylor Dagg	2013	Trafficking for the purpose of sexual exploitation	Convicted on count 7: 7) steal a cellphone, value not exceeding $5,000 (s. 334[b]) Acquitted of counts 1–6: 1) did exercise influence over the movements of a person for the purpose of exploiting or facilitating the exploitation of that person (s. 279.01); 2) received financial or other material benefit, namely a sum of money, knowing that it resulted from the commission of an offence (s. 279.01); 3) without lawful authority confined a person (s. 279[2]); 4) did by word of mouth knowingly utter a threat to cause bodily harm to a person (s. 264.1); 5) wrongfully and without lawful authority for the purpose of compelling a person to do something that she had a lawful right to abstain from doing, namely to have sex with men and women against her will, intimidate by threats that violence would be done to, in Canada or elsewhere, that person (s. 423[1]); 6) did by word of mouth, knowingly utter a threat to cause bodily harm to a person (s. 264.1[2])	For count 7, he is sentenced to fifteen days to be credited against time served

25. Steven McDonald	2013	Trafficking for the purpose of sexual exploitation	Outstanding
26. Kristen MacLean	2013	Trafficking for the purpose of sexual exploitation	All charges withdrawn
27. Tyrone Smith	2014	Trafficking for the purpose of sexual exploitation *Trafficking of a person under eighteen years	Outstanding
28. Lamone Smith	2014	Trafficking for the purpose of sexual exploitation *Trafficking of a person under eighteen years	Outstanding

(continued)

Appendix B: Human Trafficking Charges and Outcomes (*continued*)

Name	Year Charged	Type of Human Trafficking	Outcome	Sentence
29. David D'Souza	2014	Trafficking for the purpose of sexual exploitation *Trafficking of a person under eighteen years	Outstanding	
30. Kailey Oliver-Machado	2012	Trafficking for the purpose of sexual exploitation *Trafficking of a person under eighteen years	Verdict by judge [her two co-accused pled guilty]. Thirty-six-count indictment. Found guilty of twenty-four counts, including three counts of trafficking a minor 279.011(1) Also found guilty of: 279(2); 344(1); 266; 264.1(2); 212(1)(d); 279(2); 271(1); 264.1(2); 334(b); 172.1(2); 163.1(2); 163.1(4); 163.1(2); 163.1(4); 152; 163.1(2); 163.1(4); 264.1(2); 266; 279(2); 281 Charges stayed: 212(1)(d); 212(1)(d); 212(1)(2) Acquitted: 264.1(2); 267(b); 279(2); 271(1); 264(b)	78 months' custody [sentenced as an adult] Total sentence 6.5 years less PTC = 2 years +325 days + SOIRA lifetime order + s.109 weapons prohibition lifetime order + DNA order
31. R. v. A.A. (1) (Oliver-Machado co-accused)	2012	Trafficking for the purpose of sexual exploitation *Trafficking of a person under eighteen years	Pled guilty to human trafficking	N/A

32. R. v. A.A. (2) (Oliver-Machado co-accused)	2012	Trafficking for the purpose of sexual exploitation *Trafficking of a person under eighteen years	Pled guilty to human trafficking	N/A
33. Richard Addis	2014	Trafficking for the purpose of sexual exploitation	Count 2 (assault) convicted. Counts 1, 3, 4, and 5 withdrawn by Crown: 1) exercised control over the movements of a person in such a manner as to show that he was compelling that person to engage in prostitution (s. 212[1][h]); 3) for the purpose of gain, did exercise control over the movements of a person in such a manner as to show that he was compelling her to engage in prostitution; 4) recruited or exercised control, direction or influence over the movements of a person for the purpose of exploiting them (s. 279.01); 5) unlawfully received financial benefit knowing that it resulted from the commission of an offence under s. 279.01(1)	Count 2: Total sentence eighteen days (pre-sentence custody twelve days at 1.5 to 1). Probation twelve months
34. Kareem Watson	2014	Trafficking for the purpose of sexual exploitation	Outstanding	

(continued)

Appendix B: Human Trafficking Charges and Outcomes (*continued*)

Name	Year Charged	Type of Human Trafficking	Outcome	Sentence
35. Mohamed Ahmed	2014	Trafficking for the purpose of sexual exploitation	Charged on 3 February 2014; charges withdrawn at the request of the Crown on 13 January 2015	
36. Jerome Barron Dorsey	2014	Trafficking for the purpose of sexual exploitation	Charges stayed half-way through the trial	
37. Merrick Anthony Dennis	2014	Trafficking for the purpose of sexual exploitation	Charges stayed half-way through the trial	
38. Imani Nakpangi	2007	Trafficking for the purpose of sexual exploitation *Living off the avails of a person under eighteen years	Pled guilty to counts 1 and 6: 1) exercise control or direction over the movements of a person for the purpose of exploiting her or facilitating her exploitation (s. 279.01[1]) and 6) did live wholly on the avails of prostitution of a person under eighteen years (s. 212[2]) Counts 2, 3, 4, 5, and 7 withdrawn by the Crown: 2) did live partly on the avails of prostitution of a person under eighteen and for the purposes of profit did compel her to engage in prostitution and used violence in relation to her (s. 212[2.1][b]); 3) did for the purposes of gain, exercise control over the movements of a person in such a manner as to show that he was aiding her to engage in prostitution (s. 212[1][h]); 4) did in person knowingly utter a threat to a person to cause bodily harm (s. 264.1[1][a]); 5) assault (s. 266); 7) did for the purposes of gain exercise control over the movements of a person in such a manner as to show that he was aiding her to engage in prostitution (s. 212[1][h])	Count 1: two years in jail; count 6: three years in jail to be served consecutively. Pre-trial custody of 404 granted

39. Vytautas Vilutis	2008	Trafficking for the purpose of sexual exploitation	Guilty on counts 1, 2, and 5: 1) did exercise control, direction over the movements of a person for the purpose of exploiting her and facilitating her exploitation (s. 279.01); 2) did unlawfully receive financial benefit knowing that it resulted from the commission of an offence under s. 279.01(1), contrary to s. 279.02; 5) assault (s. 266) Counts 3, 4, 6, 7, and 8 withdrawn by the Crown: 3) for the purposes of gain, exercise control over the movements of a person in such a manner as to show that he was aiding the person to engage in prostitution (s. 212[1][h]); 4) did live wholly on the avails of the prostitution of a person (s. 212[1][j]); 6) knowingly utter a threat to a person to cause bodily harm to a person (s. 264.1[1][a]); 7) utter a threat to cause bodily harm (s. 264.1[a]); 8) unlawfully possess a controlled substance (s. 4[1] of the Controlled Drugs and Substance Act)	Count 1: 156 days of pre-trial custody, plus 417 days in jail. Count 2: concurrent to count 1; count 5: concurrent to count 1.
40. Jaimie Byron	2011	Trafficking for the purpose of sexual exploitation *Trafficking of a person under eighteen years	Convicted by court's verdict on counts 2–9: 2) lived wholly or in part on the avails of prostitution of another person who was under the age of eighteen and for the purpose of profit aid that person to engage in prostitution with another person or generally use violence, intimidation or coercion in relation to the said person (s. 212[2.1]); 3) exercised control over the movements of a person who was under the age of eighteen for the purpose of exploiting or facilitating exploitation of that person (s. 279.01);	Count 2: 1,341 days in jail; count 3: 1,341 days in jail concurrent; count 4: 1,341 days in jail concurrent; count 6: 1,341 days in jail concurrent; count 7: 1,341 days in jail concurrent; count 8: 1,341 days in jail concurrent; count 9: 1,341 days in jail concurrent; SOIRA Order – 20 years; DNA primary; noncommittal order; weapons order – 10 years

(continued)

Appendix B: Human Trafficking Charges and Outcomes (continued)

Name	Year Charged	Type of Human Trafficking	Outcome	Sentence
			4) received financial or other material benefits, namely a sum of money, knowing that it resulted from the commission of an offence (s. 279.011); 6) committed assault (s. 266); 7) failed to comply with recognizance entered into (s. 811); 8) failed to comply with recognizance entered into (s. 145 [3]); 9) failed to comply with recognizance (s. 145[3]) Counts 1 and 5 stayed: 1) for the purpose of gain, exercises control, direction or influence over the movements of a person in such a manner as to show that he was aiding, abetting or compelling that person to engage in prostitution (s. 212[1] [h]); 5) procured, or attempted to procure and or solicit a person, to have illicit sexual intercourse with another person (s. 212[1][a])	
41. Everol Powell	2014	Labour trafficking	Outstanding	
42. Correll Slawter	2012	Trafficking for the purpose of sexual exploitation	Pled guilty to Count 1: 1) exercised control over the movements of a person for the purpose of exploiting or facilitating the exploitation of that person (s. 279.01) Counts 2 and 3 withdrawn by the Crown: 2) received financial or other material benefits knowing that it resulted from the commission of an offence under s. 279.01(1), contrary to s. 279.02; 3) did by threats of violence, without reasonable justification or excuse and with intent to obtain money induce a person to engage in prostitution and provide him with the money from said activity (s. 346)	Count 1: sixty days' pre-sentence custody time served (1:1); two years less a day in jail; probation two years; S. 109 – life; DNA – twenty years

43. Shakib Gharibzada	2015	Trafficking for the purpose of sexual exploitation	Outstanding.	
44. Masood Hejran	2015	Trafficking for the purpose of sexual exploitation	Outstanding	
45. Remington Needham	2014	Trafficking for the purpose of sexual exploitation *Trafficking of a person under eighteen years	Convicted of Count 4: 4) did transfer the possessions of or otherwise deal with property with an intent to conceal or convert that property knowing or believing that all or part of that property was derived directly or indirectly from the commission of the offence of living off the avails of prostitution of a person under eighteen (s. 463.31[2][a]) Counts 1, 2, and 3 withdrawn by the Crown: 1) exercise control, direction or influence over the movements of a person for the purpose of exploiting them (s. 279.011[1][b]); 2) did live wholly or in part on the avails of prostitution of a person under eighteen years (s. 212[2]); 3) did receive financial or other material benefit knowing that it resulted from exercising control, direction or influence over the movements of a person under the age of eighteen for the purpose of exploiting them or facilitating their exploitation (s. 279.02)	Pre-sentence custody 106 days (1.5 for 1) = 159 days; custody 381 days; probation 2 years.

(continued)

Appendix B: Human Trafficking Charges and Outcomes (continued)

Name	Year Charged	Type of Human Trafficking	Outcome	Sentence
46. Daryn Leung	2014	Trafficking for the purpose of sexual exploitation	Convicted of counts 1, 2, and 4–16: 1) did steal money of a value not exceeding $5,000 (s. 334); 2) did by deceit, falsehood or other fraudulent means defraud a person of money not exceeding $5,000 (s. 380[1]); 4) sexual assault (s. 271); 5) sexual assault (s. 271); 6) sexual assault (s. 271); 7) procurement (s. 212[1][d]); 8) did exercise control over the movements of a person for the purpose of exploiting or facilitating the exploitation of that person (s. 279.01[1]); 9) did receive financial or other material benefit knowing that it resulted from the commission of an offence (s. 279.01[1]), contrary to s. 279.02; 10) did by word of mouth and texting knowingly utter a threat to cause death (s. 264.1[1][a]); 11) assault (s. 266); 12) assault (s. 266); 13) assault (s. 266); 14) assault (s. 266); 15) assault causing bodily harm (s. 267[b]); 16) robbed a person of a sum of money (s. 343) Acquitted on count 3: 3) sexual assault (s. 271)	Sentence: 8.5 years' imprisonment. With 3 years served, 5.5 years remaining (source: media)
47. Cheng Ping Liu	2012	Trafficking for the purpose of sexual exploitation	All charges withdrawn by the Crown	
48. Christopher McCall	2012	Trafficking for the purpose of sexual exploitation	Accused acquitted on all charges	

| 49. Mark Anthony Burton | 2011 | Trafficking for the purpose of sexual exploitation | Pled guilty to count 18 (possession of stolen property) and 21 (breach of court order). Guilty on charges 17 (attempt to procure), 20 (breach of court order), and 23 (breach of probation). Not guilty of counts 1, 2, 3, 4, 5, 6, 7, 8, 9, 10, 11, 12, 13, 14, 15, and 16: 1) procured a person to become a prostitute (s. 212[1][d]); 2) for the purpose of gain, did exercise control, direction or influence over the movements of a person in such a manner as to show that he was compelling her to engage in prostitution (s 212[1][h]); 3) did live partly on the avails of prostitution (s. 212[1][j]); 4) committed assault on a person (s. 266); 5) did by word of mouth knowingly utter a threat to a person to cause serious bodily harm to her, contrary to (s. 264[1][a]); 6) did by word of mouth knowingly utter a threat to a person to cause the death of another person (s. 264.1[1] [a]); 7) did commit a sexual assault on a person (s. 271); 8) did unlawfully recruit, or exercise control, direction or influence over the movements of a person, for the purpose of exploiting her, or facilitating her exploitation (s. 279.01); 9) did unlawfully receive a financial or other material benefit, knowing that it resulted from the commission of an offence under s. 279.01 (1), contrary to s. 279.02; | Count 17 (procuring): two years in jail; count 20: two years concurrent; count 21: one year concurrent; count 22: one year concurrent; count 23: one year concurrent; count 18: one year concurrent. Pre-trial custody twenty-three months; three years' probation; DNA registry; not permitted to communicate directly or indirectly with his victims or anyone under eighteen, except his daughter |

(continued)

Appendix B: Human Trafficking Charges and Outcomes (continued)

Name	Year Charged	Type of Human Trafficking	Outcome	Sentence
			10) procured a person to become a prostitute (s. 212[1][d]); 11) did live partly on the avails of prostitution (s. 212[1][j]); 12) for the purpose of gain, did exercise control, direction or influence over the movements of another person in such a way as to show that he was aiding, abetting or compelling her to engage in prostitution (s. 212[1][h]); 13) did procure a person to have illicit sexual intercourse with unknown males (s. 212[1][a]); 14) did commit a sexual assault on a person (s. 271); 15) did unlawfully recruit, or exercise control, direction or influence over the movements of a person, for the purpose of exploiting her, or facilitating her exploitation (s. 279.01); 16) did unlawfully receive a financial or other material benefit, knowing that it resulted from the commission of an offence (s. 279.01[1]); contrary to s. 279.02	
			Count 19 withdrawn by the Crown:	
			19) did have in his possession property, to wit: a license plate, of a value not exceeding $5,000, knowing that all the property was obtained by the commission in Canada of an offence punishable by indictment (s. 354[1]	
50. Yul Styles-Lyons	2012	Trafficking for the purpose of sexual exploitation	All charges withdrawn by the Crown	

51. Jerome Hines	2014	Trafficking for the purpose of sexual exploitation	Outstanding	
52. Anthony Greenham	2014	Trafficking for the purpose of sexual exploitation	Guilty of mischief charge *charge not on court documents nor read out in court (*R. v. Greenham* 2015, audio of trial). Not guilty of all other charges: 1) procure a person to have illicit sexual intercourse with another (s. 212[1][a]); 2) procure a person to become a prostitute (s. 212[1][d]); 3) for the purpose of gain, exercise control, direction or influence over the movements of a person in such a manner as to show that he was aiding, abetting or compelling that person to engage in prostitution (s. 212[1][h]); 4) assault (s. 266); 5) recruit a person for the purpose of exploiting or facilitating the exploitation of that person (s. 279.01[1]); 6) received financial or other material benefit, knowing that it resulted from the commission of an offence (s. 279.01[1]); 7) steal money of a value not exceeding $5,000 (s. 334[b])	The sentence is time served (fifteen days pre-trial custody) plus one day, which is deemed served by lppearance here today; ninety days to pay the victim fine surcharge
53. Stefan Ascenzi	2012	Trafficking for the purpose of sexual exploitation	All charges withdrawn by the Crown	

(continued)

Appendix B: Human Trafficking Charges and Outcomes (*continued*)

Name	Year Charged	Type of Human Trafficking	Outcome	Sentence
54. Lisa M. Ascenzi	2012	Trafficking for the purpose of sexual exploitation	All charges withdrawn by the Crown	
55. Vanessa Cachia	2012	Trafficking for the purpose of sexual exploitation	Charges dismissed	
56. Myriam Robert	2014	Trafficking for the purpose of sexual exploitation	All charges withdrawn	
57. Derek Bissue	2014	Trafficking for the purpose of sexual exploitation	Outstanding	
58. Goran Kakamad	2015	Trafficking for the purpose of sexual exploitation *Trafficking of a person under eighteen years	Outstanding	

59. Gregory Salmon	2013	Trafficking for the purpose of sexual exploitation	Guilty by verdict on counts 3, 7, 8, 12, 13, and 14: 3) assault using a weapon, namely, a knife (s. 267[a]); 7) assault (s. 266); 8) assault with a weapon, namely, a shoe (s. 267[a]); 12) violation of peace agreement; 13) violation of peace agreement; 14) violation of peace agreement Not guilty of counts 1, 2, and 11: 1) 1) exercised control over the movements of a person for the purpose of exploiting or facilitating the exploitation of that person (s. 279.01); 2) received financial or other material benefits knowing that it resulted from the commission of an offence under s. 279.01(1) or 279.011(1), contrary to s. 279.02; 11) violation of peace agreement Counts 4, 5, 6, 9, and 10 withdrawn: 4) utter a threat (s. 264.1); 5) assault with a weapon, namely, a plastic spatula (s. 267[a]); 6) assault (s 266); 9) utter a threat to cause bodily harm (s. 264.1); 10) assault (s. 266)	Count 3: 143 days in jail (pre-trial custody: 1.5 days to 1); DNA primary: OPS – 10 years; probation 18 months; count 7: jail time served 143 days (1.5 to 1); probation 18 months concurrent; count 12: jail time served 30 days; probation 18 months; jail 1 day; counts 13 and 14: jail time served 30 days; jail 1 day; probation 18 months concurrent
60. Pawel Michon	2011	Trafficking for the purpose of sexual exploitation *Trafficking of a person under eighteen years	Counts 1 and 2 withdrawn by the Crown: 1) 1) unlawfully recruit, exercise control, direction, influence over the movements of a person under eighteen years of age (s. 279.011[1]); 2) unlawfully received financial benefit knowing that it resulted from the commission of an offence (s. 279.01), contrary to s. 279.02	

(continued)

Appendix B: Human Trafficking Charges and Outcomes (*continued*)

Name	Year Charged	Type of Human Trafficking	Outcome	Sentence
			Not guilty of counts 3–6: 3) did procure a person to become a prostitute (s. 212[1][d]); 4) for the purposes of gain did exercise control over the movements of a person in such a manner as to show that he was aiding that person to engage in prostitution with unknown persons (s. 212[1][h]); 5) did live partly on the avails of prostitution (s. 212[1][j]); 6) with intent to obtain $2,400 induced a person by threats to cause harm to her or her two-year-old daughter (s. 346[1.1])	
61. Toofan Charmin	2015	Trafficking for the purpose of sexual exploitation	Outstanding	
62. Zainab Rasool	2012	Labour trafficking	Day 2 of trial accused entered into a peace bond, in turn the Crown withdrew all charges *Complainant filed a civil suit against accused	
63. Omar McFarlane	2012	Trafficking for the purpose of sexual exploitation	Pled guilty to two counts of kidnapping using a firearm, human trafficking, and dangerous operation of a motor vehicle	Sentence: eight years' imprisonment; prohibited from having a firearm for ten years; prohibited firearm, restricted firearm, prohibited weapon, prohibited device, prohibited ammunition for life; Sex Offender Registry order for life; DNA order

64. Jacques Leonard St. Vil	2007	Trafficking for the purpose of sexual exploitation	Pled guilty to count 1 and count 9: 1) did exercise control, direction over the movements of a person for the purpose of exploiting her and facilitating her exploitation (s. 279.01); 9) did live wholly on the avails of prostitution of another person (s. 212[1][j]).	On counts 1 and 9 = one day, in addition to the eighteen months and seventeen days' pre-sentence custody, for which he is credited thirty-seven months; thirty-six months' probation; DNA order
65. Ken Katalayi-Kassende	2013	Trafficking for the purpose of sexual exploitation	Outstanding	
66. Andrew Lewis	2015	Trafficking for the purpose of sexual exploitation *exercise control, direction or influence over the movements of a person under 18 (s. 286.3)	Outstanding	
67. Taylor Eibbitt	2015	Trafficking for the purpose of sexual exploitation	Outstanding	

(continued)

Appendix B: Human Trafficking Charges and Outcomes (*continued*)

Name	Year Charged	Type of Human Trafficking	Outcome	Sentence
68. Solomon Houlder	2014	Trafficking for the purpose of sexual exploitation *Trafficking of a person under eighteen years	Outstanding	
69. Yasin Mohamud	2014	Trafficking for the purpose of sexual exploitation	All charges withdrawn by the Crown	
70. Abdirahman Hussain	2014	Trafficking for the purpose of sexual exploitation	All charges withdrawn by the Crown	
71. Lucas Gabrys	2014	Trafficking for the purpose of sexual exploitation	All charges withdrawn by the Crown	
72. Anthony Putzu	2014	Trafficking for the purpose of sexual exploitation *Living on the avails of a person under eighteen	All charges withdrawn by the Crown	

73. Simeon Harty	2014	Trafficking for the purpose of sexual exploitation	Outstanding	
74. Jamie Forbes	2014	Trafficking for the purpose of sexual exploitation *Trafficking of a person under eighteen years	Pled guilty to counts 10 and 11: 10) did commit an assault on a person (s. 266); 11) assault (s. 266) All other counts withdrawn by the Crown: 1) assault on a police officer (s. 270[1]); 2) received financial or other material benefit, namely a sum of money, knowing that it resulted from the commission of an offence (s. 279.01) contrary to s. 279.011; 3) did receive financial or other material benefit, namely a sum of money, knowing that it resulted from the commission of an offence under s. 279.01, contrary to s. 279.02; 4) procured a person to become prostitute (s. 212[1]; 5) procured a person to become a prostitute (s. 212[1][d]); 6) for the purpose of gain, exercised control, direction or influence over the movements of a person, in such a manner as to show he was aiding, abetting or compelling that person to engage in prostitution (s. 212[1][h]); 7) for the purpose of gain, exercise control, direction or influence over the movements of a person, in such a manner as to show that he was aiding, abetting or compelling that person to engage	Suspended sentence and 18 months' probation in view of 115 days' pre-trial detention at 1 to 1.5 days

(continued)

Appendix B: Human Trafficking Charges and Outcomes (*continued*)

Name	Year Charged	Type of Human Trafficking	Outcome	Sentence
			in prostitution (s. 212[1][h]); 8) did live wholly or in part on the avails of prostitution of a person that was under eighteen years (s. 212[s]); 9) did live wholly or in part on the avails of prostitution of another person who was under eighteen years old (s. 212[2]); 12) assault an officer (s. 270[1][b]); 13) assault an officer (s. 270); 14) assault an officer (s. 270); 15) recruit a person under the age of eighteen for the purpose of exploiting or facilitating the exploitation of that person, contrary to s. 279.011; 16) recruit a person under the age of eighteen for the purpose of exploiting or facilitating the exploitation of that person (s. 279.011); 17) exercised control over the movements of a person for the purpose of exploiting or facilitating the exploitation of that person (s. 279.01); 18) exercise control over the movements of a person for the purpose of exploiting or facilitating the exploitation of that person (s. 279.01); 19) without lawful authority confined a person, contrary to section 279(2); 20) did without lawful authority confine a person contrary to section 279(2)	
75. Dustin Macbeth	2015	Trafficking for the purpose of sexual exploitation	All charges stayed by the Crown	

	Year	Charge	Outcome	Sentence
76. Ashor Anwia	2014	Trafficking for the purpose of sexual exploitation	Outstanding	
77. Jordan Michael Lynch	2012	Trafficking for the purpose of sexual exploitation	Pled guilty to counts 8 and 9: 8) committed assault (s. 266); 9) stole property to wit, a laptop computer, of value not exceeding $5,000 (s. 334[b]) All other counts withdrawn by the Crown. Human trafficking charges were dropped at the preliminary hearing: 1) procure a person to become a prostitute (s. 212[1][d]); 2) did live wholly or partially on the avails of prostitution (s. 212[1][j]); 3) did for the purpose of gain, exercise control, direction or influence over the movements of a person in such a manner as to show that he was aiding, abetting or compelling that person to engage in prostitution (s. 212[1][h]); 4) sexual assault (s. 271); 5) utter threats, attempt by use of hands to choke another person contrary to s. 246(a); 6) did by word of mouth knowingly utter to cause death (s. 254[1][a]); 7) without lawful authority confined a person (s. 279[2])	Count 8: three months' pre-trial custody, resulting in time served and suspended sentence: one year probation with terms and conditions; DNA order; Section 110 for ten years; concurrent suspended sentence for count 9 with same terms and conditions on the one-year probation order.
78. Aldain Alando Beckford	2012	Trafficking for the purpose of sexual exploitation	7 March 2013 – mistrial declared; 15 November 2013 – Crown directs a stay of proceedings based on the amended condition of the complainant, making her unable at present	

(continued)

Appendix B: Human Trafficking Charges and Outcomes (*continued*)

Name	Year Charged	Type of Human Trafficking	Outcome	Sentence
		*Trafficking of a person under eighteen years	to testify. It is the position of the Crown that a reasonable prospect of conviction remains. In accordance with the position taken by the Crown, all counts on this indictment are stayed	
79. David Mackay Stone	2012	Trafficking for the purpose of sexual exploitation *Trafficking of a person under eighteen years	7 March 2013 – mistrial declared; 26 March 2013 – Crown withdraws all charges	
80. Thomas Downey	2008	Trafficking for the purpose of sexual exploitation	Jury found Downey guilty of kidnapping, unlawful confinement, sexual assault, assault, sexual assault with weapon, and aggravated sexual assault; acquitted of count 3: trafficking in persons; count 4: theft of identity documents; count 6: sexual assault with another person; count 7: sexual assault with weapon	Sentenced to ten years on count 1; fourteen years on count 10 to be served concurrently; to be credited with pre-sentencing custody of five years and four months, leaving approximately eight years and eight months to serve; DNA order and lifetime weapons prohibition under s. 109
81. Spencer Thompson	2008	Trafficking for the purpose of sexual exploitation	Jury found Thompson guilty of kidnapping, unlawful confinement, four counts of sexual assault, one count of sexual assault with a weapon, assault, and aggravated sexual assault. Acquitted of count 3: trafficking in persons; count 4: theft of identity documents; count 7: sexual assault with a weapon	Sentenced to ten years for kidnapping, ten years concurrent for sexual assault; fourteen years concurrent for aggravated sexual assault; ten years concurrent for sexual assault; DNA order: life-time weapons prohibition; credited with pre-sentencing custody of five years and five months, leaving approximately eight years and seven months to be served

82. Anthony Roberts	2008	Trafficking for the purpose of sexual exploitation	At the conclusion of the Crown's case, Roberts brought a motion for a direct verdict of not guilty on all counts. For written reasons released 30 October 2009, the motion was granted and he was found not guilty on all charges
83. Henok Mebratu	2015	Trafficking for the purpose of sexual exploitation *Trafficking of a person under eighteen years	Outstanding
84. Shaun Butler	2014	Trafficking for the purpose of sexual exploitation	Outstanding
85. Jason Bartley	2014	Trafficking for the purpose of sexual exploitation *Trafficking of a person under 18 years	15 December 2014 – charges stayed at the request of the Crown

(continued)

Appendix B: Human Trafficking Charges and Outcomes (*continued*)

Name	Year Charged	Type of Human Trafficking	Outcome	Sentence
86. Anthony Talbert	2014	Trafficking for the purpose of sexual exploitation *Living on the avails of and prostitution of a person under eighteen years	Charges stayed at the request of the Crown	
87. Brian McKenzie	2014	Trafficking for the purpose of sexual exploitation *Living on the avails of and prostitution of a person under eighteen years	Charges stayed at the request of the Crown	
88. Tchello Whyte	2014	Trafficking for the purpose of sexual exploitation	Convicted of count 4: 4) did for the purpose of gain, exercise control, direction or influence over the movements of a person in such a manner as to show that he was aiding, abetting or compelling that person to engage in prostitution (s. 212[1][h]) Counts 1, 2, 3, 5, 6, and 7 withdrawn by the Crown on 13 August 4: 1) sexual assault (s. 271); 2) did with part of his body, for sexual purpose, directly or indirectly touched the body of a person	Count 4: one day in jail (seventy days pre-trial custody), twelve months' probation

		under the age of sixteen (s. 151); 3) procured a person to become a prostitute (s. 212[1]); 5) made child porn in the form of photograph (s. 163.1[2]); 6) possessed child porn (s. 163.1[4]); 7) failed to comply with probation order (s. 733.1[1])	
89. Shanicka Providence	2014	Trafficking for the purpose of sexual exploitation *Trafficking of a person under eighteen years	Outstanding
90. Aloma Shermin Providence	2014	Trafficking for the purpose of sexual exploitation	Outstanding
91. Markus Cole	2014	Trafficking for the purpose of sexual exploitation	Charges withdrawn by Crown
92. Alia Alexandria Abdellatif	2014	Trafficking for the purpose of sexual exploitation *Trafficking of a person under eighteen years	Charges stayed

(continued)

Appendix B: Human Trafficking Charges and Outcomes (*continued*)

Name	Year Charged	Type of Human Trafficking	Outcome	Sentence
93. Natasha Robitaille	2015	Trafficking for the purpose of sexual exploitation *Trafficking of a person under eighteen years	Ms. Robitaille has entered a plea of guilty to two counts of receiving a material benefit from the sexual services of two minors pursuant to s. 286(2) of CCC	Sentence: eight months' incarceration, concurrent on both counts. Ms. Robitaille spent one month in pre-trial custody; properly credited for this time, at 1.5:1, six and a half months are left remaining in her sentence
94. Sage Finestone	2015	Trafficking for the purpose of sexual exploitation *Trafficking of a person under eighteen years	On 30 June 2016, Mr. Finestone pled guilty to one offence of trafficking of a person under the age of eighteen contrary to section 279.011(1) of the Criminal Code	Sentence of four years is imposed; taking into account the three and a half weeks spent in pre-trial custody, calculated at 1.5:1 for a total of thirty-six days, Mr. Finestone is sentenced to three years, ten months, and twenty-four days
95. Nicolas Faria	2015	Trafficking for the purpose of sexual exploitation *Trafficking of a person under eighteen years	Outstanding	
96. Nadine Brown	2015	Trafficking for the purpose of sexual exploitation	Outstanding	
97. Yolanda Mohabeer	2015	Trafficking for the purpose of sexual exploitation	Outstanding	

98. Rory Thomas Mitchell	2015	Trafficking for the purpose of sexual exploitation	Outstanding
99. Kelvin Earl McPherson	2009	Trafficking for the purpose of sexual exploitation *Living on the avails of a person under eighteen	He was found guilty by a jury of two prostitution-related offences under s. 212 of CCC. The convictions were for a) procuring a person to become a prostitute (s. 212[1][d]) and b) controlling her movements with a view to aiding or compelling her to engage in prostitution (s. 212[1][h]); he also pled guilty to one charge of uttering threats against another female complainant	Sentenced to three years for offences under s. 212 and six months for uttering threats (s. 264), to run concurrently
100. Courtney Salmon	2013	Trafficking for the purpose of sexual exploitation *Living on the avails of a person under eighteen	All charges stayed because police fabricated evidence: 1) did unlawfully recruit, transport, receive, hold conceal or harbour or exercise control, direction or influence over the movements of a person for the purpose of exploiting or facilitating the exploitation of that person (s. 279.01[1]); 2) procurement (s. 212[1][d]); 3) did unlawfully receive financial benefit or other material benefit knowing that it resulted from the commission of an offence (s. 279.01(1), contrary to s. 279.02; 4) did live partly on the avails of prostitution of anunderage person (s. 212[2]); 5) did live partly on the avails of prostitution of a person under the age of eighteen and the purpose of profit did aid, abet or counsel her to engage in or carry on prostitution and threaten to use or attempt to use violence, intimidation or coercion (s. 212[2.1]); 6) for the purpose of gain, did exercise control,	

(continued)

Appendix B: Human Trafficking Charges and Outcomes (*continued*)

Name	Year Charged	Type of Human Trafficking	Outcome	Sentence
			direction or influence over the movements of a person in such a manner as to show that he was aiding or abetting that person to engage in prostitution (s. 212[1][h]); 7) did in person knowingly utter a threat to a person to cause death or bodily harm to them (s 264.1[1][a]); 8) did unlawfully commit an assault with a weapon, to wit a hanger, to a person (s. 267[a]); 9) did possess a counterfeit mark, to wit Ontario Drivers' License in the name of the victim (s. 376[2]); 10) did possess a counterfeit mark, to wit a Canadian citizenship card in the name of the victim (s. 367[2]); 11) did cause or attempt to cause a person to use, deal with or act on a forged document as if it were genuine (s. 368[1][b]); 12) did cause or attempt to cause a person to use, deal with or act on a forged document as if it were genuine (s. 368[1][b]); 13) did have in his possession property obtained by or derived from crime, the value of which did not exceed $5,000 (s. 354); 14) did have in his possession property obtained by or derived from crime, the value of which did not exceed $5,000 (s. 354); 15) did have in his possession stolen property the value of which did not exceed $5,000 (s. 354); 16) did commit theft of property of the victim, the value of which did not exceed $5,000 (s. 334[b]); 17) theft not exceeding $5,000 (s. 334[b])	

101. Enoch Johnson	2009	Trafficking for the purpose of sexual exploitation	The accused was found not guilty on all counts in the indictment: 1) did unlawfully recruit, exercise control, direction or influence over the movements of a person for the purpose of exploiting them (s. 279.01); 2) did unlawfully receive a financial benefit knowing that it resulted from the commission of an offence under s. 279.01(1) contrary to s. 279.02; 3) did unlawfully recruit, exercise control, direction or influence over the movements of a person for the purpose of exploiting or facilitating the exploitation of that person (s. 279.01); 4) procurement (s. 212[1][d]); 5) did unlawfully receive financial benefit knowing that it resulted from the commission of an offence (s. 279.01(1), contrary to s. 279.02); 6) did for the purpose of gain, exercise control over the movements of a person in such a manner as to show that he was compelling, aiding or abetting her to engage in prostitution (s. 212[1][h]); 7) did live partly on the avails of prostitution (s. 212[1][j])	
102. Jah-Tyius Joshua Williams	2012	Trafficking for the purpose of sexual exploitation *Living on the avails of a person under eighteen	Pled guilty to count 1 on first day of a ten-day trial: 1) exercise control over the movements of a person for the purpose of exploiting or facilitating the exploitation of that person (s. 279.01) Counts 2–12 withdrawn by the Crown: 2) lived wholly or in part on the avails of prostitution of another person who was under the age of	Sentenced to imprisonment for 1,031 days; DNA primary ordered for 20 years; 529 days pre-trial custody considered at 1.5 = 794 days; has to register with Sex Offender Registry

(continued)

Appendix B: Human Trafficking Charges and Outcomes (*continued*)

Name	Year Charged	Type of Human Trafficking	Outcome	Sentence
			eighteen (s. 212[2]); 3) received a financial or other material benefit, namely money, knowing that it resulted from the commission of an offence (s. 279.01); 4) procured a person to have illicit sex with another (s. 212[1][a]); 5) by threats, without reasonable justification or excuse and with intent to obtain money included a person to engage in sexual act (s. 346[1.1]); 6) without lawful authority confined a person (s. 279.2); 7) with a part of his body, for a sexual purpose, directly touched the body of a person under the age of sixteen (s. 151); 8) for sexual purposes, invited a person under the age of sixteen to directly touch with a part of her body the body of a male (s. 152); 9) with a part of his body, for a sexual purpose, directly touched the body of another person under the age of sixteen (s. 151); 10) committed assault (s. 266); 11) by word of mouth, knowingly uttered a threat to cause death to a person (s. 264.1[2]); 12) wilfully damaged personal effects of a person of value not exceeding $5,000, and thereby committed mischief (s. 430[4])	
103. Renardo Cole	2014	Trafficking for the purpose of sexual exploitation	Outstanding	

104. Nathan Turnbull	2016	Trafficking for the purpose of sexual exploitation	Charges withdrawn
		*Trafficking of a person under eighteen	
105. Deshawn Holmes	2016	Trafficking for the purpose of sexual exploitation	Outstanding
		*Trafficking of a person under eighteen	
106. Camille Beausejour	2016	Trafficking for the purpose of sexual exploitation	Charges withdrawn
		*Trafficking of a person under eighteen	
107. Maziar Masoudi	2015	Trafficking for the purpose of sexual exploitation	Outstanding

(continued)

Appendix B: Human Trafficking Charges and Outcomes (continued)

Name	Year Charged	Type of Human Trafficking	Outcome	Sentence
108. Michael Hazel	2014	Trafficking for the purpose of sexual exploitation *Trafficking of a person under eighteen	Charges withdrawn	
109. Isaiah Omoro	2013	Trafficking for the purpose of sexual exploitation	Counts 1–5 withdrawn by the Crown: 1) assault; 2) confinement (279[2]); 3) exercise control for the purpose of sexual exploitation (279.01); 4) received financial benefit knowing it resulted from the commission of an offence under 279.01, to wit: sexual services (279.02); 5) exploited, to wit by threatening physical harm if she failed to engage in prostitution contrary to s. 279.04 Convicted on counts 6–7: 6) procure a victim to become a prostitute contrary to s. 212 (1)(d); 7) procure a victim, to wit by being habitually in her company while engaging in prostitution contrary to section 212(i)(j)	Count 6: six months' conditional sentence; twelve months' probation; DNA primary for five years; Count 7: six months' conditional sentence concurrent; twelve months' probation concurrent
110. Chanelle Espinosa	2015	Trafficking for the purpose of sexual exploitation	Outstanding	

#	Name	Year	Offence	Status	Details
111.	Alexander Levi	2015	Trafficking for the purpose of sexual exploitation *Trafficking of a person under eighteen	Outstanding	
112.	Jerome Tyrele Belle	2015	Trafficking for the purpose of sexual exploitation	Outstanding	
113.	Hayley McBride	2015	Trafficking for the purpose of sexual exploitation *Trafficking of a person under eighteen	Outstanding	
114.	Marcus Cumsille	2015	Trafficking for the purpose of sexual exploitation	Outstanding	
115.	Joel Edwards	2015	Trafficking for the purpose of sexual exploitation	Outstanding	
116.	R. v. A.A. (3)	2012	Trafficking for the purpose of sexual exploitation	Convicted of two counts of trafficking in persons. Pled guilty to two counts of breach of court orders, one failure to comply with recognizance. Acquitted of two counts of procuring under section 212.	Total sentence twenty-seven months; count 1: two years less a day; count 2: three months consecutive to count 1 *Deportation order under appeal

(continued)

Appendix B: Human Trafficking Charges and Outcomes (*continued*)

Name	Year Charged	Type of Human Trafficking	Outcome	Sentence
117. R. v. A.A. (4)	2011	Trafficking for the purpose of sexual exploitation *Trafficking of a person under eighteen	Outstanding	
118. Sahilan Surenddran	2015	Trafficking for the purpose of sexual exploitation	Outstanding	
119. Taylor Laughlin	2015	Trafficking for the purpose of sexual exploitation *Communicating with a person under eighteen for the purpose of committing an offence under section 212(1)(i)	Guilty of count 6: 6) uttering a threat All other counts withdrawn: 1) did live wholly or in part on the avails of prostitution (s. 212[1][j]); 2) same as count 1; 3) did by means of telecommunication, communicate with a person under eighteen, for the purpose of facilitating the commission of an offence under s. 212(1), contrary to s. 172.1(2); 4) possession of child porn (s. 163.1); 5) distribution of child porn (s. 163.1)	Conditional sentence order twelve months; twelve months probation; DNA secondary order; Section 490 Order of Return; victim surcharge $200

| 120. Matthew Cosmo Deiaco | 2015 | Trafficking for the purpose of sexual exploitation | Pled guilty to counts 2, 3, 7, 10, and 11:
2) did transport or conceal or exercise control, direction or influence over the movements of the victim for the purposes of exploiting or facilitating the exploitation of the victim contrary to s. 279.01;
3) did receive financial or other material benefit, namely a sum of money, knowing that it resulted from the commission of an offence, contrary to s. 279.02(1); 7) kidnapping with intent to cause the victim to be confined against her will (s. 279[1][a]); 10) assault causing bodily harm (s. 267[b]); 11) using an imitation firearm to commit an indictable offence (s. 85[2][a])

Counts 1, 4, 5, 6, 8, 9, 12, 13, and 14 withdrawn:
1) did for the purpose of facilitating an offence under s. 286.1(1) recruit, hold, conceal or harbour the victim who offers or provides sexual services for consideration, contrary to s. 286.3(1);
4) assault (s. 267); 5) did by word of mouth utter death threat (s. 264.1[1][a]); 6) robbery with a weapon (s. 343[d]); 8) confinement (s. 279[2]); 9) confinement (s. 279[2]); 12) did knowingly advertise an offer to provide sexual services for consideration by posting advertisements for sexual services to be provided by victim (s. 286.4); 13) receive financial or other material benefit, namely money, knowing that it was obtained by the commission of an offence (s. 286.2[1]); 14) sexual assault (s. 271) | Global sentence of eight years, less credit for presentence custody;
count 2: five years concurrent to count 7;
count 3: three years concurrent to count 7;
count 7: seven years in custody, less three years, seven months, fourteen days for a remaining sentence of three years, four and a half months to be served;
count 10: three years concurrent to count 7;
count 11: one year consecutive to count 7 |

(continued)

Appendix B: Human Trafficking Charges and Outcomes (continued)

Name	Year Charged	Type of Human Trafficking	Outcome	Sentence
121. Ricardo Spence	2013	Trafficking for the purpose of sexual exploitation	Guilty of counts 1, 3, 4, 8, and 9: 1) exercise control over the movements of a person for the purpose of exploiting them s. 279.01(1); 3) received financial or other material benefit knowing that it resulted from the commission of an offence s. 279.01, contrary to s. 279.02; 4) withheld the documents of a person for the purpose of committing an offence under s. 279.011, contrary to s. 279.03; 6) assault s. 266; 8) utter death threat s. 264.0(2); 9) fail to keep the peace in accordance with peace bond s. 145(5.1) Not guilty of counts 5 and 7: 5) confinement s. 279(2); 7) assault with a weapon s. 267(a) Count 2 stayed: 2) live wholly or in part on the avails of prostitution of another s. 212(1)(j)	Global sentence five years; concurrent sentences as follows: count 1: five years; count 3: three years; count 4: six months; count 6: one year; count 8: six months; count 9: six months
122. Brandon Fraser	2014	Trafficking for the purpose of sexual exploitation	Pled guilty to counts 2, 7, 10, 11, and 13: 2) receive a financial or other material benefit, namely a sum of money, knowing that it resulted from the commission of an offence under section 279.01 (1), or s. 279.011(1), contrary to s. 279.02; 8) procured another person to become a prostitute (s. 212[1][d]); 10) wilfully damaged clothing and electronics, the value of which did not exceed $5,000, and thereby committed mischief (s. 430[4]); 11) attempted to dissuade a person by threats from giving evidence in a judicial proceeding (s. 139[2]); 13) compelled another person to recant her police statement by use of threats of violence (s. 423[1][a]); 14) failed to comply with restraining order	Sentenced to four years; count 2: 2 years plus 118 days of jail; count 7: 1 year concurrent; count 10: 2 years concurrent; count 11: 2 years concurrent; count 13: concurrent; DNA order for life; No contact with victim; Pre-trial custody = 408 days –credited at 1.5 days = 612 days served

123. Jordan Kimmerly	2013	Trafficking for the purpose of sexual exploitation	Counts 1, 3, 4, 5, 6, 7, 9, and 12 withdrawn by the Crown: 1) confine a person (s. 279[2]); 3) exercise control over the movements of a person for the purpose of exploiting or facilitating the exploitation of that person (s. 279.01[1]); 4) for the purpose of gain, exercise control, direction or influence over the movements of a person in such a manner as to show that he was aiding, abetting or compelling that person to engage in prostitution (s. 212[1] [h]); 5) knowingly uttered threats to cause bodily harm (s. 264.1[1][a]); 6) committed an assault (s. 266); 7) lived wholly or in part on the avails of prostitution of another person (s. 212[1][j]); 9) for the purpose of committing or facilitating an offence under s. 279.01(1) or s. 279.011(1), withheld documents, namely a driver's license, birth certificate and health card belonging to another person, which established that person's identity or immigration status (s. 279.03); 12) by telephone knowingly uttered a threat to cause bodily harm (s. 264.1[1][a]) Pled guilty to count 8: 8) procurement s. 212(1) Charges 1–7 and 9–1 withdrawn: 1) exercised control over the movements of a person for the purpose of exploiting them s. 279.01; 2) received financial and	Count 8: twenty-eight months in jail, less ten months for pre-trial custody

(continued)

Appendix B: Human Trafficking Charges and Outcomes (*continued*)

Name	Year Charged	Type of Human Trafficking	Outcome	Sentence
		*Living on the avails of a person under eighteen	other material benefit from the commission of an offence under s. 279.01, contrary to s. 279.02; 3) communicated with a person under eighteen for the purpose of facilitating the commission of an offence under s. 163.1 contrary to s. 172.1(2); 4) possessed child porn s. 163.1(2); 5) made child porn s. 163.1(3); 6) was in a relationship with a young person that was exploitative of that young person with a part of his body, for a sexual purpose, directly or indirectly touched the young person s. 153(1.1); 7) communicated with a person under eighteen for the purpose of facilitating the commission of an offence under s. 212(2.1), contrary to s. 172.1(2)a; 9) procurement s. 212(1)(d); 10) did for the purpose of gain exercise control, direction or influence over the movements of a person in such a manner as to show that he was aiding, abetting or compelling that person to engage in prostitution s. 212(1)(h); 11) did apply or administer or cause a person to take a drug with intent to stupefy or overpower that person in order thereby to enable a person to have illicit sexual intercourse with that person s. 212(1)(i); 12) lived on the avails of prostitution of a person under eighteen s. 212(2.1); 13) sexual assault s. 271	

Summary of Data

Charges According to Year

2016: 3 (2.4 per cent)
2015: 24 (20 per cent)
2014: 41 (33 per cent)
2013: 10 (8 per cent)
2012: 18 (15 per cent)
2011: 4 (3 per cent)
2010: 15 (12 per cent)
2009: 2 (1.6 per cent)
2008: 4 (3 per cent)
2007: 2 (1.6 per cent)
Total: 123 charges

Outcome of Cases

Outstanding: 39 (32 per cent)

The percentage of remaining outcome is calculated from 84 cases where the case results are known.

Stayed: 9 (11 per cent)
Withdrawn: 23 (27 per cent)
Convicted of human trafficking: 7 (8 per cent)
Convicted of other offences but not trafficking: 13 (15 per cent)
Pled guilty to trafficking: 21 (25 per cent)
Pled guilty to other offences but not trafficking: 7 (8 per cent)
Acquitted: 3 (4 per cent)
Miscellaneous: 1 (1 per cent)
Total: 123

Type of Trafficking

Labour trafficking: 17 (14 per cent)
Sex-Trafficking: 106 (87 per cent)
    Trafficking of a person under eighteen: 26 (21 per cent)
    Underage sex work–related charges: 10 (8 per cent)
Total: 123

Interview Participants

Participant 1 – Police officer (anti-trafficking policing unit)
Participant 2 – Police officer (anti-trafficking policing unit)
Participant 3 – Police officer (anti-trafficking policing unit)
Participant 4 – Police officer (anti-trafficking policing unit)
Participant 5 – Police officer (anti-trafficking policing unit)
Participant 6 – Crown attorney
Participant 7 – Crown attorney
Participant 8 – Crown attorney
Participant 9 – Superior Court Judge
Participant 10 – Defence attorney
Participant 11 – Defence attorney
Participant 12 – Defence attorney
Participant 13 – Defence attorney
Participant 14 – Defence attorney
Participant 15 – Crown attorney

Interview Questions

Crown Attorney Questions

Your Experience:

How long have you worked as a Crown attorney?

What, if any, training have you received on human trafficking? What does that entail?

Do Crowns receive any mandates when it comes to prosecuting trafficking cases? If so, what are they?

Understanding Human Trafficking:

Many people assume human trafficking is about migration, is that a misunderstanding? What do you understand human trafficking to mean?

How extensive is the problem and why?

In your opinion, what is the most troubling aspect of the problem of trafficking? Why is it such a pressing problem?

To what extent is the work that you do related to international developments/human rights regimes relating to trafficking?

Why is this issue important to you?

Legal Framework:

What are the elements the Crown must prove to secure a conviction for trafficking? What challenges may arise in proving these elements?

What role does exploitation play in human trafficking? What do you understand exploitation to mean?

Charter issues?

What might explain the recent law enforcement successes with human trafficking offences? i.e. Legal changes? Development of specialized units? Better intelligence gathering? Targeted enforcement?

Prosecutions:

Are there any cases that you have worked on that were
particularly meaningful, challenging? Can you tell me about it?

Is there anything that surprises you about this domain of
criminality?

What kinds of evidence are required before proceeding with trafficking charges?

What, if any, interaction takes place between the Crown and the
police in prosecuting trafficking cases?

What are some of the challenges of prosecuting trafficking?

Victims/Offenders:

Who are the victims of trafficking?

Are there common patterns, demographics, characteristics,
situations?

What dynamics, situations, characteristics make some victims
more vulnerable than others?

Do victims struggle with talking about their experiences?

In the context of domestic violence, dealing with victims can be
difficult. Are there similar challenges that arise in trafficking
cases? If so, how do you deal with them?

Who are the offenders in trafficking cases?

Are there common patterns, demographics, characteristics, situations when it comes to offender types?

Likes/Dislikes/Wishlist

What is the most difficult part of your job?

What is the most satisfying part of your job?

If you could wish for anything relating to human trafficking prosecutions, what would it be?

Defence Attorney Questions

What is your understanding of human trafficking? What, in your
understanding, are the key elements of trafficking? What do you
understand to be the "means" by which one is trafficked?

What are the elements the Crown must prove to secure a conviction
for trafficking? What kind of defence would you mount for these
elements and/or the charge of trafficking? What are the challenges that may arise in these defence strategies?

In Canadian law, exploitation is defined as a central component
of trafficking. Section 279.04 (1) of the Criminal Code defines

exploitation as causing another person to "provide or offer to provide, labour or a service by engaging in conduct that in all circumstances, could reasonably be expected to cause the other person to believe that their safety or the safety of a person known to them would be threatened if they failed to provide, or offer to provide, the labour or service," What role do you see this concept of exploitation playing in Canada's human trafficking cases?

"Pimping" has also been established in legal cases as an exploitive activity that often leads victims to fear for their safety. How, if at all, do you understand this offence as being different from trafficking?

In your experience, who are the victims of human trafficking?

How often, if ever, is your legal strategy informed by the goals of the Palermo Protocol?

Human trafficking has been deemed a violation of the victims' most basic human rights. What role do you see this concept of human rights playing in Canada's trafficking cases?

In your opinion, are human trafficking laws in Canada necessary? Are they doing what they should be doing? If so, why/how? If not, what changes would you suggest?

Questions for Judiciary

Does the judiciary receive training on the offence of human trafficking? If so, what does that entail?

What is your understanding of human trafficking? What, in your understanding are the key elements of trafficking?

What are the elements the Crown must prove to secure a conviction for trafficking?

In Canada's human trafficking law, exploitation is defined as a central component of trafficking. What role do you see this concept of exploitation (both physical and emotional) playing in Canada's human trafficking cases?
How does exploitation in the case of trafficking differ from exploitation in other such situations, including labour exploitation or abusive intimate relationship?

What is the role of consent in human trafficking cases? In your understanding, are there situations where the elements of trafficking are indeed present but the consent asserted by the "victim" is so meaningful that it should not be disregarded?

"Pimping" has also been established in legal cases as an exploitive activity that often leads victims to fear for their safety. How, if at all, do you understand this offence as being different from trafficking?

Human trafficking has been deemed a violation of the victims' most basic human rights. What role do you see this concept of human rights playing in Canada's trafficking cases?

In your experience, who are the victims/accused in human trafficking cases? Do you recall a case where the victim/accused did not fall in line with your understanding of a trafficking victim/trafficker?

Have you seen a rise in the number of trafficking cases coming through Canadian courts in recent years? If so, what might explain this rise?

In your experience, what types of cases are prosecuted under human trafficking legislation? Are these cases consistent with your understanding of human trafficking? Why or why not?

Has your understanding of human trafficking changed since the enactment of Canada's human trafficking laws in 2005? If so, how?

Do international anti-trafficking laws, such as the Palermo Protocol, inform your understanding of and decision-making in human trafficking cases? If so, how?

In your opinion, are human trafficking laws in Canada necessary? Are they doing what they should be doing? If so, why/how? If not, what changes would you suggest?

Police Interview Questions

Your Experience
  How long have you worked in the human trafficking unit?
  What did you do before this?
  How does this work differ from what you did before?
  Did you have to apply to the unit, or were you selected for it?
  What kind of training or professional development have you
    received in this unit?
  How is your job performance evaluated?

Human Trafficking
  Many people assume human trafficking is about migration. Is
    that a misunderstanding? What do you understand human
    trafficking to mean?
  How extensive is the problem, and why?
  In your opinion, what is the most troubling aspect of the problem
    of trafficking? Why is it such a pressing problem?
  To what extent is the work that you do related to international
    developments/human rights regimes relating to trafficking?
  Why is this issue important to you?

The Unit
  Does the unit have a mandate? What does that look like?
  Why was the unit created? Is it one of many? Do all police depart-
    ments have one?
  How many people are in the unit? Are there different tasks/
    positions/duties within the unit?
  Are there male and female officers on the unit? Do you think gen-
    der makes a difference in your field of work?
  Resources? Staffing? Personnel? Other?
  Are there geographic boundaries that restrict your work? Are
    their jurisdictional limits?
  Are there other limits?
  Does the work of the different units vary in relation to their geo-
    graphic location?
  Does the problem of trafficking vary across the country?

The Legal Framework
  To what extent is your work shaped by legal developments?
    What are the specific laws that are relevant to your work?
    Have the amendments to the human trafficking law since its
    initial enactment had any impact on your job? Are their bits of
    the legal provisions that complicate enforcement?
  What role does exploitation play in human trafficking? What do
    you understand exploitation to mean?
  Charter issues?
  What might explain the recent law enforcement successes with
    human trafficking offences? i.e. Development of specialized
    units? Better intelligence gathering? Targeted enforcement?
    Community cooperation?

Day-to-Day Enforcement
  What does your typical day at work look like?

Where does your intelligence on human trafficking come from?
What resources do you use?
Who do you connect with on a daily basis?
  Other police units? Departments?
  What other Canadian and/or international authorities and
    agencies do you interact with in the course of doing your job?
  Is information shared by provincial and national security
    agencies?
  Interactions between national, regional, and district authorities?
  Other countries? Transnational policing agencies? The United
    States?
  Community-based advocates and agencies?
What kinds of networks are most important to you?
To what extent do you rely on information that comes from
  communities?
Do you interact with Crown attorneys in your daily work?
What changes would enhance enforcement? What resources?

Technology and Information Sharing
  How important is technology in your job?
  To what extent does technology make your job easier, more
    difficult?
  To what extent has technology improved information sharing?
  What other forms of information sharing do you use? Informants?
    Undercover officers? Surveillance technologies?
  What kinds of information, information systems, would make
    your job easier? What are the gaps, what are the missing links?

Case Discovery
  What are the ways in which human trafficking cases get
    discovered?
  Are there any cases that you have worked on that were particu-
    larly meaningful, challenging? Can you tell me about it?
  Is there anything that surprises you about this domain of
    criminality?
  What kinds of evidence do you have to have before laying human
    trafficking charges?
  Do you consult with Crown attorneys before laying charges?

Victims/Offenders
  Who are the victims of trafficking?
    Are there common patterns, demographics, characteristics,
      situations?

What dynamics, situations, characteristics make some victims more vulnerable than others?

Do victims struggle with talking about their experiences?

In the context of domestic violence, dealing with victims can be difficult. Are there similar challenges that arise in trafficking cases? If so, how do you deal with them?

Who are the offenders in trafficking cases?

Are there common patterns, demographics, characteristics, situations when it comes to offender types?

Decision-Making

How wide is your capacity to choose between different courses of action in individual cases?

What kinds of decisions do you make on a day-to-day basis in your job?

What other factors influence the choices you make and the decisions you take?

Are there any situations where you have no choice at all over the decision that you must make?

What kinds of considerations inform your decisions?

Are there limitations to this discretion? If so, what are they?

Does politics play a role and/or interfere with your work? Municipal? Provincial? National?

What is the impact of the media? Visibility of your work? Impact of advocacy? Public attention?

Likes/Dislikes/Wishlist

What is the most difficult part of your job?

What is the most satisfying part of your job?

If you could wish for anything relating to human trafficking enforcement and regulation, what would it be?

What changes would make your job easier?

Is there anything that you require in the course of your work that you do not have?

Case Summaries

R. v. Aldain Beckford (2013)

The accused was charged with human trafficking after allegations that he (along with his co-accused Pete Stone) had drugged a sixteen-year-old girl and forced her into prostitution. The complainant was described in court as "troubled," a habitual runaway, and experiencing a number of mental health issues (including bipolar disorder, ADHD, OCD, depression and anxiety, and panic disorders) for which she had been prescribed a number of medications. In addition to this, the complainant was using a number of street drugs and had been in trouble with the law. During the jury trial of the two accused, the complainant made continued inappropriate remarks about the accused, calling them "pervs" and "murderers." In response to this, the defence filed for an application for mistrial, which the judge granted.

R. v. Tyrone Burton (2016)

Tyrone Burton was convicted of numerous counts of human trafficking and sex work–related offences in relation to two complainants over a period of several weeks. Burton entered into a relationship with one of the complainants who fell in love with him, and he began managing her work in the sex trade industry. Out of concern for her friend, the second complainant decided to stay in the situation. The women spent several weeks working out of various Toronto-area hotel rooms servicing numerous clients. Burton was found by the court to have exercised control over the movements and actions of the complainants through veiled threats of violence and living off the avails of their sex work. The situation came to the attention of the police when one of their clients helped them go to the police to report sexual and physical abuse by another client.

R. v. Jaimie Byron (2013)

Byron is a young, first-generation Black Canadian man from Jamaica. He was convicted of luring a young woman with lower cognitive function from her home in Windsor to Montreal. He paid for her trip from Windsor to Montreal. She was under the impression this was for a romantic relationship. Once she is in Montreal, the judge finds that he forces her into sex work and keeps her compliant with violence and threats. She starts travelling on a circuit with other sex workers. He takes the vast majority of her money. The case came to the attention of the police when the complainant locked herself out of the room and needed her room key re-activated. The hotel staff asked for her ID, but she didn't have any to present. The hotel staff found out she was seventeen and called the police since she was not of age to be in the room alone. Byron is convicted of a number of procuring and trafficking offences. He is sentenced to 1,341 days in jail.

R. v. Taylor Dagg (2015)

Taylor Dagg was accused of human trafficking after the complainant, who was addicted to crack cocaine, agreed to engage in sex work and share her income in exchange for drugs for her use and being able to work from a hotel room (instead of the streets). The accused took out Backpage ads for her and set the pricing. The complainant was high and/or drunk for much of the investigated time, and thus her testimony could not be taken entirely for face value. The judge dismissed human trafficking charges, noting that the complainant had free reign to move around as she pleased and that the accused did not intimidate or threaten her into compliance. The judge found that the complainant was a willing sex worker and shared her income in order to obtain alcohol and drugs.

R. v. Greenham (2014)

Anthony Greenham is a young, racialized man who was dating a sex worker. She had a friend (the complainant) who was also interested in becoming involved in sex work. Greenham and his girlfriend gave the complainant information, advice, and tips on escorting. Greenham acted in the role of a manager for the two women, arranging travel plans, hotel rooms, burner phones, etc. in exchange for a cut of her earnings. He was accused of controlling her movements and charged with pimping and human trafficking offences. This is despite the complainant admitting that she was engaging in sex work voluntarily and that she made her own decisions about which clients to accept and which ones to reject, how much to charge, when to work, etc. Greenham was convicted of destruction of personal property for breaking the complainant's phone. All other charges were dismissed.

R. v. Kailey Oliver-Machado (2014)

The case involves three female youths who were found by the court to have trafficked five of their peers, one as young as thirteen, for the purpose of sexual exploitation. Kailey Oliver-Machado was fifteen years old when she was, as the judge described it, "the leader of a highly organized and vicious human trafficking enterprise which found young, underage girls being lured through deception into a web of organized prostitution." Oliver-Machado and her co-accused befriended a total of five girls on Facebook and through other means, inviting them to parties, hangouts, and sleepovers. Once there, the girls were given drugs and alcohol, photographed nude or semi-nude and in various compromising positions, and made to engage in sexual acts with male customers for money, which the accused kept for themselves. Oliver-Machado was found guilty of twenty-seven counts related to the incident, including various counts of human trafficking, and sentenced as an adult to a term of six and a half years in prison, a very high sentence for a crime committed at the age of fifteen.[1] Her co-accused pled guilty to trafficking-related charges and received reduced sentences.

R. v. Zainab Rasool (2015)

Zainab Rasool was accused of trafficking after her housekeeper, who was a migrant worker from Indonesia, contacted the police claiming that her documents were taken, she was living in subpar living conditions, she had no contact with family and friends, she was not allowed to leave the house by herself, and that she did not get paid for her work

---

1 Oliver-Machado was the first minor to be convicted of human trafficking in Canada and received one of the longest sentences for human trafficking for sexual exploitation (https://sherloc.unodc.org/cld/case-law-doc/traffickingpersonscrimetype /can/oliver-machado.html).

in the two years she was working for Ms. Rasool. She also noted that she was too afraid to ask for her money because Ms. Rasool was often angry. The Crown withdrew the charges after one day of trial because the complainant's testimony on trial undermined the charges.

R. v. Gregory Salmon (2014)

Gregory Salmon is a young man who was charged with human trafficking in Ontario in 2014. According to the evidence at trial, Salmon developed an online friendship with the complainant – a young woman[2] from Manitoba. After several months of communicating online, the complainant travelled to visit Salmon in Ontario. The two began a romantic relationship, and she stayed to live with him. Soon after her arrival, however, Salmon lost his job, and the young woman started working in the sex trade to provide financial support. The relationship was a troubled one, and Salmon was frequently violent and abusive, escalating to the point that the complainant called the police. Because she was working in the sex trade and shared her income with him, the police charged Salmon with human trafficking, in addition to domestic violence–related offences (R. v. [Gregory] Salmon 2014). Despite the complainant's testimony in court that she freely chose to enter the sex trade, the Crown attorney argued that Salmon had coerced her into it and that she was therefore a victim of trafficking. While there was no question that Salmon physically abused the complainant during their relationship, the Crown provided no evidence to demonstrate that the violence was used to force her into the sex trade. In the end, the judge rejected this argument and acquitted the accused of trafficking charges.

Other Cases of Interest

R. v. A.A. (2015) (court documents; Court of Appeal transcript; CanLii)

This is a precedent-setting case, as a panel of judges in the Ontario Court of Appeal determined that in the context of human trafficking, exploitation does not actually have to take place in order to establish the offence of human trafficking. As the judges found, the only thing that needs to be established is that the accused had the intent to exploit. This precedent-setting decision is important, as it expands the reach of human trafficking

---

2 The identity of all complainants in the legal cases discussed is protected by a Publication Ban (s. 486) and therefore cannot be disclosed.

laws even further by effectively removing the requirement for exploitation to even take place while setting intent as the key requirement for conviction.

R. v. Cosmo Deiaco (2015) (court documents; media coverage; CanLii)

Cosmo Deiaco is a young, white male who was pimping out a number of women in the Greater Toronto area. In 2015, he was charged with a number of sex work– and human trafficking–related offences. The case is significant since Cosmo Deiaco gave an extensive interview to the *Toronto Star*, describing "the game" – how men lure women into the sex trade.

R. v. D'Souza (2016) (court documents; media coverage; constitutional challenge briefs obtained from defence counsel)

In 2015, David D'Souza was charged with thirteen counts, including human trafficking of a person under the age of eighteen. In 2016, representatives for D'Souza brought a constitutional challenge to human trafficking laws. D'Souza argued that there is international confusion about the term "human trafficking" and that the term is vague. D'Souza argued that the international trafficking laws have been improperly adopted into Canadian legislation and should therefore be deemed unconstitutional. The judge disagreed and dismissed the application.

R. v. Domotor (2011) (court documents; CanLii)

The members of Kolompar and Domotor families were found to have formed a criminal organization and facilitated the migration of other Hungarians to Canada for work in their construction business. Court evidence revealed that upon arrival, the workers' passports were withheld, and they were forced to work long hours at construction sites without pay. When not working, the employees were confined to the family's home basement and fed once a day with scraps. The family also forced the labourers to apply for social assistance, which they subsequently kept for themselves. All accused in the case pled guilty to trafficking-specific or -related offences. All but two of the accused in this case were deported. This case is notable since it is one of very few cases of labour trafficking that has come to the attention of Canadian officials and one of very few transnational trafficking cases prosecuted in Canada.

R. v. Daryn Leung (2015) (court documents; media coverage; participant observation)

Daryn Leung was convicted of human trafficking in connection with his role in the sex work activities of his girlfriend. While it became clear during the trial that Daryn Leung had taken advantage of the complainant, including accepting money she had earned from sex work, she did not appear to be threatened, coerced, or forced into the situation. The circumstances of the case highlight the lack of distinction between procuring and human trafficking.

R. v. Imani Nakpangi (2008) (court documents; media coverage; CanLii)

Imani Nakpangi was Canada's first convicted trafficker. He was charged with human trafficking in 2007 after his involvement in the prostitution of two underage girls was unveiled by an undercover police operation. The first complainant testified against Nakpangi, but the second complainant insisted that she had not feared for her safety. As a result, Nakpangi could only be convicted of one account of trafficking, forcing the court to acquit him of the second trafficking charge. The reluctance of complainants to admit fear and thereby testify against the accused created a problem for the successful prosecution of cases in the courts and led to Criminal Code amendments. The amendments expanded the ability of the Crown to prosecute trafficking offences by changing the legal requirement from subjective to objective fear when it came to the complainants' safety.

R. v. Courtney Salmon (2011) (court documents; Court of Appeal transcripts and exhibits; CanLii; media coverage)

Courtney Salmon entered into a romantic relationship with a seventeen-year-old woman. He convinced her to start working in the sex trade industry and took most of her earnings. Salmon was acquitted of all charges after it was revealed at trial that police fabricated evidence in the case. In particular, the police alleged that the complainant's false ID was in possession of Mr. Salmon at the time of his arrest. It was later revealed that the complainant had turned over her ID to the police at an earlier date.

Note: Courtney Salmon was convicted of human trafficking in 2019 for incidents that took place in 2016. It is unknown whether the case he was convicted for is related to the previous incident for which charges were stayed. He was sentenced to six years in prison on 28 March 2019 (Zangouei, 2019).

R. v. Richard Spence *(2015) (CanLii;*
media coverage; court documents)

Richard Spence was convicted of human trafficking and related offences pertaining to Spence's role in managing, directing, and controlling the sex work activities of his girlfriend. The court established that Spence was intellectually low functioning and was not running a sophisticated pimping operation, consisting only of his girlfriend. She was found by the court to be vulnerable due to her young age (nineteen) and the estranged relationship she had with her family. However, the court also found that she was able to physically leave and therefore was not confined to the situation, at least not in the physical sense. The majority of the court's focus in this case was on Spence's extensive record of violence towards women.

Expanded Research Methods

This study investigates the frontline, on-the-ground anti-trafficking enforcement and prosecution efforts of state and non-state agents in Canada's anti-trafficking agenda. The study investigates Canada's human trafficking laws and legal efforts and examines how relatively new domestic laws against trafficking have been shaped, interpreted, and applied by politicians, police, Crown and defence attorneys, and judges. Focusing on Canada's province of Ontario, the province with the highest number of trafficking charges and convictions, I conducted a qualitative research study using multiple methods of data collection, which included court documents, trial transcripts and audio recordings (which I then transcribed), sentencing decisions, and interviews with criminal justice actors. The multiple methods of data collection were employed in order to learn how human trafficking is understood in Canada's legal context and how this knowledge is formed. By examining data obtained from these different settings, I was able to see how this process takes place, how it varies between settings and actors, what extra-legal information is employed to formulate this knowledge, what discourses are operating within and shaping the knowledge on trafficking, and how the broader discourses around human trafficking are fitting with or diverging from front-line perceptions and approaches to the issue. To explore my broader research questions, I asked a series of more specific questions, including (1) what do human trafficking cases in Canada look like, and what types of activities are characterized as human trafficking? (2) How do police understand trafficking, and how do Crown attorneys, judges, and defence attorneys support, reject, or restructure these definitions? (3) How do the decisions of criminal justice actors contribute to the knowledge around what constitutes human trafficking, the trafficker, and the victim? (4) How are these local practices influenced by and/or influencing broader discourses around trafficking?

To begin answering these questions I conducted extensive research on the secondary scholarship concerning trafficking. This scholarship is now vast and has been generated in a variety of fields, including human rights, migration and border security, criminology, socio-legal studies, and feminist perspectives. To examine the way in which dominant discourses, laws, policies, and enforcement practices shape the prevailing understandings of trafficking, I collected a wide range of primary documentary sources during the period 2005–16. These included international and Canadian government and non-government reports, media reports, and legal documents, including House of Commons debates on various legal bills to create and amend trafficking laws, case law, court documents, and transcripts. While the government and media reports, debates, and case law were collected from across Canada, my primary research, which included court information/indictments, court transcripts, and interviews, was focused in Ontario.

To get a more complete understanding of the enforcement decisions in trafficking cases, including the types of charges laid alongside trafficking charges, who was charged, and the outcomes, I collected court information/indictments for 123 individuals charged with human trafficking (sections 279.01–.011) between 2005 (the year human trafficking was criminalized by Canada's domestic law) and June 2016 in the province of Ontario in Canada. Because neither the Ministry of the Attorney General (MAG) for Ontario nor Canada has a centralized database of trafficking cases, the data for my case list, which included cases from 2005 to 2016, was collected from media and government reports, NGOs, and police-published information. I used the case list to collect court documents, including information and/or indictments for 123 documented cases. This information provided me with an overview of the types of charges that accompanied trafficking charges, the ages of the accused, and the outcome of the cases. I also learned that very few trafficking cases proceeded to trial. Although these numbers did increase during the period of my research, particularly as Ontario rolled out a new province-wide anti-trafficking strategy in 2016, which included the assignment of six Crown attorneys focusing on human trafficking cases. Furthermore, this information enabled me to narrow down the cases that went to trial in order to obtain trial transcripts.

The very high cost of trial transcripts forced me to opt for audio recordings of trials, which I was able to access as a result of a newly implemented MAG for Ontario policy of access to audio recordings. Specifically, I obtained recordings for and analysed eight trials: six full trials, ranging from one day to thirty-three days (*R. v. Dagg* 2015; *R. v. Byron* 2014; *R. v. Oliver-Machado* 2014; *R. v. Greenham* 2015; *R. v. Salmon*

(Gregory) 2014; *R. v. Burton* 2016), one trial where the Crown withdrew the charges after one day of trial (*R. v. Rasool* 2015), and a case that ended in a mistrial (*R. v. Beckford* 2013). I also obtained the transcript of submissions and the decision in the Ontario Court of Appeal 2015 precedent-setting case *R. v. A.A.* (see chapter one for discussion), and the Ontario Court of Appeal transcript for the hearing and decision of *R. v. Salmon (Courtney)* (2015) (see chapter three for discussion). Finally, I conducted a partial participant observation of one trafficking trial (*R. v. Leung* 2015). In some cases, I was also able to obtain copies of court exhibits, which included police interviews with the accused and complainants, defence attorney summary documents, and factums. In addition to these trial recordings and transcripts, I also examined a number of court decisions in trafficking cases across Canada, which I obtained from legal search engines CanLii and QuickLaw. Analysis of these cases provided significant insights into the way in which legal actors not only understand the law but also how legal strategies and tactics, courtroom rituals, narrative formations, language, and forms of questioning contribute to the construction of situations as human trafficking and how complainants are made into victims of trafficking and accused into dangerous exploiters. The analysis of these cases was greatly aided by similar examinations of courtroom processes conducted by scholars before me (Backhouse 2008; Conley and O'Barr 1998; Craig 2015; Cunliffe 2013; Ehrlich 2012; Gewirtz 1996; Matoesian 1993; Sarat 1993; Sheehy 2014; Umphrey 1999).

Trial recordings provide important insights into the way in which the meaning of human trafficking is produced in legal settings through the interpretation and application of legal provisions but also through the creation of particular narratives which resonate with the broader social context. As Bell and Couture contend, deconstructing law through its application demonstrates that law is not objective but is situated in a particular social context (2000, 53). Reading human trafficking trial transcripts within a context of international and domestic trafficking discourses, the politics of trafficking and the push to combat the issue through police and prosecutorial efforts helps us to understand why certain arguments are being advanced and evidence used, but it also illuminates the reasons for certain silences. As Emma Cunliffe notes, "socio-legal transcript research is largely concerned with unearthing law's 'untold stories' and placing legal decisions back within the context of the legal and social disagreements from which they arise" (2013, 2; see also Umphrey 1999). Cunliffe further explains that "law's stories are also constrained by the requirements of the adversarial legal form – witnesses are required to respond to questions rather than speaking freely" (2013, 13). These observations importantly help us understand the way in which courtroom rules and decorum play an important role in helping Crown and defence attorneys shape their perspective narratives of the story while silencing complainants, witnesses, and the accused. Analysis of trial recordings enabled me to observe how carefully scripted examinations, specific use of language, courtroom rituals, and power dynamics of legal actors all played a part in shaping the story, the legal meaning of trafficking, and understandings around who is a trafficker and a victim. At the same time, however, trial recordings provided insights into how these constructions were resisted and challenged by other legal actors, but also complainants, witnesses, and accused persons themselves.

In addition to information/indictments and trial recordings, I also conducted interviews with different criminal justice actors, including police in anti-trafficking policing units, Crown and defence attorneys, and judges. I interviewed fifteen criminal justice actors who had first-hand knowledge of and experience with human trafficking cases, including four Crown attorneys, five defence attorneys, and five members of various police departments with specialized human trafficking units. Although I spoke to three judges, only one of them had first-hand experience with trafficking cases and therefore only one judicial interview was used in this study. Participants for this study were recruited through various methods. Defence attorneys with knowledge of human trafficking were identified from cases I examined and were cold emailed inviting them to participate in the study. While defence attorneys were fairly receptive to partaking in the study, several of them were too busy and in the end were unable to participate due to scheduling conflicts. One defence counsel I met while conducting a participant observation of a trafficking case.

While I initially used the same method of recruitment for Crown attorneys, it was not as effective in securing Crown interviews. Many of the emails sent to Crown attorneys did not receive a response. Of the Crowns that did respond, many declined to be interviewed. Some agreed initially but subsequent attempts at contact went unaddressed. Of those Crowns who agreed at the outset, some had to seek permission from superiors, and most were unable to participate as a result of the Ministry of the Attorney General policy that prohibits Crown attorneys from partaking in academic interviews on the issue of human trafficking. Of the four Crown attorneys whom I ended up interviewing, all but one agreed to participate as a result of personal introductions.

To recruit police officers, I employed several methods, including submitting formal email requests to all anti-trafficking policing units in Ontario. To follow up on these requests, I called all the departments that did not respond to my email request within a specific time period. Yet, these follow-up calls did not prove to be fruitful. In one case, I spoke to anti-trafficking police officers attending a human trafficking trial about the possibility of interviewing them. While the officers were extremely enthusiastic and optimistic about this possibility at the outset, my attempts to contact them subsequently via email and phone were not successful. In the end, I was able to interview five police officers from two different anti-trafficking units in southern Ontario. In one case, my request was approved by the chief of police but required that I enter into a contractual agreement with the police force.

The interviews were conducted between January and July 2016. The recorded interviews ranged from forty-five minutes to two and a half hours in length. Although a set of questions was provided to participants ahead of time, the interviews were semi-structured to allow participants to provide information based on their own front-line experiences and to allow the emergence of unanticipated issues and questions. This approach allowed me to remain flexible and responsive to the participant's area of knowledge. For instance, while direct questions about the legal understanding of trafficking often failed to elicit much response, these questions were often answered through stories told by participants or through various other questions, allowing me to gain insights from related stories and sustained discussion.

These interviews were conducted after the court documents had been collected and analysed. While it was my intention to conduct interviews after also analysing audio recordings of trafficking trials, in order to base the questions on what I had learned from trial hearings, delays with obtaining data from courts forced me to conduct the interviews at the same time as working to obtain access to audio recordings and analysing them. The purpose of the interviews was to supplement and verify the information I had obtained from other sources and learn about the ways in which the crime of trafficking is understood by front-line police and legal actors who operationalize the law and how dominant narratives and international norms shape these understandings.

The data was analysed through a manual method of coding. Although I considered the use of data analysis software, such as NVIVO, I decided that the richness of the data would be best analysed through careful reading of it in the context of themes from existing literature, allowing the discovery of patterns and inconsistencies. I analysed international and state government reports as well as non-government reports, court transcripts from trial recordings, and additional documents, such as exhibits and factums, sentencing decisions, transcripts from my interviews, House of Commons debates, and media reports.

During the fifteen-month research period, I also encountered a number of challenges with researching in Ontario courts. These included various structural and non-structural barriers to accessing public court documents; difficulties getting interviews, particularly with Crown attorneys and judges but also to some extent police officers; and various delays caused by the organizational culture of Ontario courts. These challenges have been discussed in some detail in two separate publications (see Millar et al. 2017).

While I was able to gather extensive research material, as with all research projects, this study comes with certain limitations. Firstly, the primary research materials used for this study, including interviews with legal criminal justice agents, court documents, and trial audio recordings were all obtained from the province of Ontario. Although Ontario has the highest number of trafficking cases in all of Canada, similar data from other provinces may have provided interesting comparisons and/or challenged the findings of this study. Secondly, and as outlined in my publications of research challenges, barriers to accessing criminal justice agents, particularly Crown attorneys and judges, for academic interviews restricts the insights researchers are able to gain (Millar et al. 2017). These insights are particularly important given the central role played by legal and criminal justice actors within anti-trafficking efforts in Canada. Finally, while my research maintained a focus on legal and criminal justice systems due to time and scope limitations, there are a number of other agencies and actors that play an important role in Canada's anti-trafficking efforts, including NGOs, victim-services workers, and the immigration system, but also the accused and complainants in trafficking cases.

Notes

Introduction

1 The identity of all complainants in the legal cases discussed is protected by a Publication Ban (s. 486) and therefore cannot be disclosed.

2 In the Canadian legal system, prosecutors are called Crown attorneys. In this book, I use the terms "Crown attorney," "Crown," "prosecutor," and "Crown prosecutor" interchangeably to refer to Crown attorneys.

3 This is in contrast with thirteen signatures for the 1904 International Agreement for the Suppression of the White Slave Trade; thirteen signatures for the 1910 International Convention for the Suppression of the White Slave Traffic; thirty-three signatures for the 1921 International Convention for the Suppression of the Traffic in Women and Children; and eighty-one signatures for the 1949 Convention for the Suppression of Traffic in Persons and the Exploitation of the Prostitution of Others (Gallagher 2010, 57, 59). International white slavery laws were never directly adopted into Canada's domestic criminal laws, yet the impact of international pressures, particularly from Britain, was felt during certain times through increased police focus on sex work and legal changes that expanded the scope of prostitution laws.

4 Since then, there have been four amendments to the law in the form of the Trafficking Victims Protection Reauthorization Act (TVPRA), revised in 2003, 2005, 2008, and 2013.

5 While migrant labour and deportation are not the focus of this study, it is important to note that these discourses also disproportionately affect migrant women, especially if they labour in sex work. For discussion of the links between trafficking, migration, and deportation, see Bernstein (2010), Durisin (2017), Jeffrey (2005), Kaye (2017), Kempadoo (2005), Kempadoo and Doezema (1998), Lam (2018), and Sharma (2005).

6 These included: *R. v. Dagg* 2015; *R. v. Byron* 2014; *R. v. Oliver-Machado* 2014; *R. v. Greenham* 2015; *R. v. Salmon (Gregory)* 2014; *R. v. Burton* 2016; in *R. v. Rasool* 2015, the Crown withdrew the charges after one day of trial.

1. Legal Regimes

1 The act includes recruiting, transporting, transferring, receiving, holding, concealing, or harbouring a person, or exercising control, direction, or influence over the movements of a person (s. 279.01, CCC).

2 Palermo Protocol is another name for the Trafficking Protocol derived from the fact that the protocol was drafted in Palermo, Italy.

3 "The Latin term *actus reus* refers to the actual act of doing the illegal thing, with no reference to the person's mental state. In order for a person to be convicted of having committed a crime, it must be proven that he [*sic*] engaged in some physical act, or took action, to do so" (LegalDictionary.net).

4 *Mens rea* is a Latin term for a "guilty mind" or criminal intent in committing the act (Dictionary.Law.com)

5 This criterion applies only to adults. When it comes to establishing the trafficking of minors, the "mean" component does not have to be established at all; the only thing that has to be established is that the accused "exercises control, direction or influence over the movements of a person (279.011, CCC). This, as I demonstrate in chapter four, has significant impacts on individuals under the age of eighteen who are working in the sex trade.

6 Common bawdy-house was redefined by Bill C-36 as "for the practice of acts of indecency, a place that is kept or occupied or resorted to by one or more persons" (Casavant and Valiquet 2014a; section 2.11).:

7 *R. v. Domotor* (2011)

8 Notably, my database of cases was not exhaustive, as I was only able to identify cases through publicly available sources; therefore, many more individuals were likely charged during this time period (see Appendix F for detailed methodology). However, the difference in the case numbers remains relevant despite this, as many more cases were reported on following the Bedford decision, indicating an increase in charges overall.

9 It is unclear whether the term "violations" is referring to charges laid, convictions, or a different unit of measurement.

10 The repealed section states that "for the purposes of gain, exercises control, direction or influence over the movements of a person in such manner as to show that he is aiding, abetting or compelling that person to engage in or carry on prostitution with any person or generally" (s. 212.1[h], CCC).

11 "Every person who recruits, transports, transfers, receives, holds, conceals or harbours a person under the age of eighteen years, or exercises control, direction or influence over the movements of a person under the age of eighteen years, for the purpose of exploiting them or facilitating their exploitation is guilty of an indictable offence" (s. 279.011, CCC).

12 The same quote is also used in chapter five.

13 Interestingly, despite the fact that transportation is not a necessary component of a trafficking offence, in the majority of the cases I examined any form of travel by the complainant was emphasized by the Crown, whether that be between cities to meet the accused (*R. v. Byron* 2014; *R. v. Burton 2016; R. v. Rasool* 2015; *R. v. Salmon (Gregory)* 2014;), for the purpose of meeting clients (*R. v. Oliver-Machado* 2014; *R. v. Greenham* 2015; *R. v. Dagg* 2015), or relocating together with the accused (*R. v. Salmon (Gregory)* 2014).

14 The expert in question was Benjamin Perrin, professor of law at the University of British Columbia and author of a book entitled *Invisible Chains: Canada's Underground World of Human Trafficking* (2010). He is a well-known anti–sex work advocate criticized for his biased research, which he claims is "evidence-based research" (see chapter three for discussion). In his rejection of the Crown's request, Justice Baltman noted Mr. Perrin's advocacy as being a part of the reason it would be inappropriate to deem him an expert witness.

15 Exception to section 286.2(3) of CCC comes as follows:
   (a) in the context of a legitimate living arrangement with the person from whose sexual services the benefit is derived;
   (b) as a result of a legal or moral obligation of the person from whose sexual services the benefit is derived;
   (c) in consideration for a service or good that they offer, on the same terms and conditions, to the general public; or
   (d) in consideration for a service or good that they do not offer to the general public but that they offered or provided to the person from whose sexual services the benefit is derived, if they did not counsel or encourage that person to provide sexual services and the benefit is proportionate to the value of the service or good.

16 These include two counts of assault; criminal harassment; possession of cocaine for the purpose of trafficking; possession of marijuana for the purpose of trafficking; careless storage; knowingly possessing a loaded, prohibited firearm; knowingly possessing a firearm with an altered serial number; and breach of a non-communication order (*R. v. A.E.* 2018, para. 109).

17 In *R v. Gladue*, the Supreme Court of Canada (SCC) outlined considerations courts must take into account when sentencing Indigenous offenders under s 718.2(e) of the Criminal Code. In particular, courts were instructed to consider all reasonable forms of sanction other than imprisonment that are available in the circumstances and appropriate given the harm done. Courts were to take into account: "(A) The unique systemic or background factors which may have played a part in bringing the particular aboriginal offender before the courts; and (B) The types of sentencing procedures and sanctions which may be appropriate in the

circumstances for the offender because of his or her particular aboriginal heritage or connection (*R. v. Gladue* 1999, para. 66).

18 The totality principle ensures that sentences applied consecutively do not result in sentences so lengthy as to be out of proportion with the gravity of the offence.

19 This case is currently under appeal as Moazami alleges ineffective assistance of counsel and "abuse of process based on alleged misconduct by James Fisher, a former detective with the Vancouver Police Department" (*R. v. Moazami* 2019, BCCA 226).

20 161 (1) When an offender is convicted, or is discharged on the conditions prescribed in a probation order under section 730 of an offence referred to in subsection (1.1) in respect of a person who is under the age of 16 years, the court that sentences the offender or directs that the accused be discharged, as the case may be, in addition to any other punishment that may be imposed for that offence or any other condition prescribed in the order of discharge, shall consider making and may make, subject to the conditions or exemptions that the court directs, an order prohibiting the offender from

(a) attending a public park or public swimming area where persons under the age of 16 years are present or can reasonably be expected to be present, or a daycare centre, school ground, playground or community centre;

(a.1) being within two kilometres, or any other distance specified in the order, of any dwelling-house where the victim identified in the order ordinarily resides or of any other place specified in the order;

(b) seeking, obtaining or continuing any employment, whether or not the employment is remunerated, or becoming or being a volunteer in a capacity, that involves being in a position of trust or authority towards persons under the age of 16 years;

(c) having any contact – including communicating by any means – with a person who is under the age of 16 years, unless the offender does so under the supervision of a person whom the court considers appropriate; or

(d) using the Internet or other digital networks, unless the offender does so in accordance with conditions set by the court.

21 A DNA order is made by a judge at the sentencing stage. It allows the police to collect a sample of the offender's bodily substance, such as saliva or blood, in order to create a DNA profile. This DNA profile is then stored in a databank maintained by the RCMP and contributes to the surveillance of those whose DNA is in the data bank. The vast majority of these people are marginalized, racialized, and impoverished.

22 The historical and contemporary ways in which sexual norms are governed by notions of dangerousness will be discussed in more detail in subsequent chapters.

23 In cases of dangerous offender designations, courts can impose an "indeterminate detention, a determinate sentence plus a long-term supervision order, or simply a determinate sentence" (Public Safety Canada 2009, 3).

24 The constitutionality of indeterminate sentencing was recently challenged in *R. v. Boutilier* (2017) for being overly broad. The Supreme Court of British Columbia dismissed the argument and found that indeterminate sentencing does not violate the Canadian Charter of Rights and Freedoms since the decisions are made based on individual circumstances of the accused.

2. The Canadian Victim

1 Robert Pickton is a high-profile serial killer who targeted Indigenous sex trade workers and poor women in downtown Eastside of Vancouver, Canada, from 1997 to 2002. While the families and communities of the victims continued to report their loved ones missing, little was done by the police and the justice system to find them. As the Missing Women's Commission of Inquiry found, the response of the police to the missing and murdered Indigenous women was a serious failure. Pickton was arrested in 2002 and confessed to killing forty-nine women. He was charged with the killing of twenty-six women but was convicted of the murder of only six of them (Craig 2014).

2 Christopher's Law is Ontario's sex offender registry, named after eleven-year-old Christopher Stephenson who was kidnapped, sexually assaulted, and killed by a known child sex offender. The registry was launched in 2004.

3 The series of quotes from the *Toronto Star* was used in a previous publication, see Roots 2019, 106.

4 Toronto police use the term "young girls" because they note that "more than half of these victims are under the age of sixteen." See: https://www.youtube.com/watch?v=qcIVytLZ_Bw.

5 2SLGBTQQIA refers to Two-Spirit, lesbian, gay, bisexual, transgender, queer, questioning, intersex, and asexual.

3. Policing Trafficking

1 This quote was also used in a previous publication, see Roots 2019, 102.

2 Participating agencies also include the Immigration, Refugees and Citizenship Canada (IRCC), Indigenous and Northern Affairs Canada

(INAC), Global Affairs Canada (GAC), Status of Women Canada (SWC), Justice Canada (JUS), and Employment and Social Development Canada (ESDC) (Public Safety Canada 2016, 7).

3 This quote was used in a previous publication, see Roots 2019, 102.
4 As above.
5 Backpage was a popular internet forum for sex work ads. The site was shut down by US authorities for conducting online brothel activities. Alternate versions of the site have emerged since the shutdown of Backpage in April 2018.
6 This quote was used in a previous publication, see Roots 2019, 104.
7 This quote was used in a previous publication, see Roots 2019, 102.
8 As above, 103.
9 This quote is also used in chapter five to demonstrate the racialization of knowledge related to trafficking.
10 This includes cases where the accused pled guilty to other offences but not trafficking: seven (8 per cent); was convicted of other offences but not trafficking: thirteen (15 per cent), or where the charges were stayed: nine (11 per cent) or withdrawn: twenty-three (27 per cent) (see Appendix B).
11 Note: Courtney Salmon was arrested in an unrelated case and convicted of human trafficking in 2019 for incidents that took place in 2016. He was sentenced to six years in prison on 28 March 2019 (Zangouei, 2019).
12 In relation to the forged ID she was using.
13 That the Crown decided to pursue trafficking charges despite insistence by the complainant that she had never had a "pimp" and did not feel threatened also demonstrates that Crowns are motivated to pursue charges of human trafficking.
14 "Jonesing" is a term used to describe drug withdrawal symptoms.

4. Trafficking on Trial

1 In the United States, state prosecutors are called prosecutors, while in Canada they are called Crown attorneys.
2 This is likely changing as a result of continued emphasis on prosecuting trafficking offences and the emergence of specialized anti-trafficking prosecutors and guidelines set out by the Department of Justice Canada (2015).
3 Capitalization of texts indicates raised voice and/or yelling.
4 "My friend" is a term used by Crown and defence attorneys in Canadian courts to refer to each other.
5 Capitalization indicates raised voice or yelling.

5. The Villain

1 Taylor Dagg was charged alongside one of his friends. The two men were
   involved in the "pimping" of a number of sex workers.
2 "Every person who knowingly counsels, induces, aids or abets or
   attempts to counsel, induce, aid or abet any person to directly or indirectly
   misrepresent or withhold material facts relating to a relevant matter that
   induces or could induce an error in the administration of this Act is guilty
   of an offence" (s. 126 *IRPA*, SC 2001, c 27).
3 "124 (1) Every person commits an offence who: (a) contravenes a provision
   of this Act for which a penalty is not specifically provided or fails to
   comply with a condition or obligation imposed under this Act; (b) escapes
   or attempts to escape from lawful custody or detention under this Act; or
   (c) employs a foreign national in a capacity in which the foreign national is
   not authorized under this Act to be employed" (IRPA, SC 2001, c 27).
4 CBSA data on section 118 charges and convictions was obtained through a
   Freedom of Information Request.
5 This quote was used in a previous publication, see Roots, 2019, 108.
6 This quote was used in a previous publication, see Roots 2019, 109.
7 This determination was made based on pictures of accused published in
   the news media and/or descriptions of the accused at trial, sentencing
   hearings, or court documents available through CanLii or obtained from
   defence counsel of the accused.
8 I use the term "visibly white" because at the time of the study, police and
   courts did not collect official records on the accused's race. Information
   on the race and/or ethnicity of the accused was gleaned from discussions
   during court processes where the accused and/or their background was
   described and discussed and/or media coverage where the picture of
   the accused accompanied the article. While this method of determining
   race can be undoubtedly inaccurate and even problematic, I suggest that
   the benefits of collecting this information and race analysis outweigh the
   potential harms (see Miller and Owusu-Bempah 20113).
9 As I (with others) have discussed elsewhere, tracking legal cases over
   space and time is a very challenging, time-consuming, and at times
   complicated task (Millar et al. 2017). While only a few academic studies
   have examined trafficking-related legal cases in Canada, their findings,
   like my own, were limited by challenges with data collection (See
   Appendix F; see, too, Ferguson 2012; Millar et al. 2017; Millar et al.
   2015). Nonetheless, the anti-trafficking efforts, on the front line of police
   enforcement and in the courtrooms in Ontario investigated for this study,
   show a disproportionate targeting of young, racialized men as traffickers.

10 This quote was used in a previous publication, see Roots 2019, 105.

11 Out of twenty-four total women who were charged with human trafficking in my study.

12 This includes 8 per cent of cases where the accused pled guilty to other offences but not trafficking, 15 per cent convicted of other offences but not trafficking, 11 per cent where the charges were stayed: 27 per cent withdrawn, 4 per cent acquitted (see Appendix B).

13 An extended version of this quote is also cited in chapter one.

14 Twenty-one out of eighty-four cases where outcome was known by the conclusion of the study.

15 This was likely because the defence attorney himself was a racialized man.

16 We do not find out whether the witnesses' testimony was accepted by the judge, as the case ends in a mistrial due to some inflammatory comments made by the complainant about the accused (see chapter four for discussion)

17 This quote is also seen on p. 118, chapter three, on policing of trafficking and is also used in a previous publication: see Roots, 2019, 102.

18 "Uncle Tom" is a term used to describe "a culturally unconscious, submissive individual who does not identify with any Black community, but instead prefers to see himself as a White-identified, cultureless, raceless, independent American citizen who can achieve the American dream without attaching himself to the Black community as long as he has God" (Jackson 2006, 32).

19 Subjective fear, as noted in chapter one, is no longer a requirement in law. Due to legislative revisions, it is now only necessary that the court finds the presence of objective fear.

20 This quote was used in a previous publication, see Roots 2019, 107.

21 These quotes were used in a previous publication, see Roots 2019, 107.

22 The exception to this is the case of *R. v. Gladue* (1999), a Supreme Court of Canada decision which enabled a set of legal practices that allowed knowledge about offenders' collective and individual experiences of racism and oppression to be integrated into current legal practices. The case also mandated the formation of Gladue courts which focus on Indigenous peoples and integrate specialized Indigenous knowledge into sentencing decisions.

23 Ngoto's sentencing was adjourned pending more information on immigration status, as the judge noted that if Ngoto is sentenced to more than six months in jail she will lose her right to appeal the deportation order (*R. v. Ahmed et al.* 2019, para. 89).

24 N.A. (2017) was sentenced to eighteen months' imprisonment and therefore is subject to a deportation order without the possibility of appeal to the Immigration Appeal Division.

25 I take exception here to cases of non-citizens whose immigration status may and likely will be impacted by the criminal conviction.

References

Literature

Alexander, Michelle. 2012. *The New Jim Crow: Mass Incarceration in the Age of Colourblindness*. New York: The New Press.

Alridge, Derrek P., and James B. Stewart,. 2005. "Hip Hop in History: Past, Present, and Future." *The Journal of African American History* 90, no. 3: 190–5. https://doi.org/10.1086/jaahv90n3p190.

Anderson, Bridget. 2012. "Where's the Harm in That? Immigration Enforcement, Trafficking, and the Protection of Migrants' Rights." *American Behavioral Scientist* 56, no. 9: 1241–57. https://doi.org /10.1177/0002764212443814.

Anderson, Bridget, and Rutvica Andrijasevic. 2008. "Sex, Slaves and Citizens: The Politics of Anti-trafficking." *Soundings* 40: 135–45. https://doi.org /10.3898/136266208820465065.

Andrijasevic, Rutvica. 2007. "Beautiful Dead Bodies: Gender, Migration and Representation in Anti-trafficking Campaigns." *Feminist Review* 86: 24–44. https://doi.org/10.1057/palgrave.fr.9400355.

Aradau, Claudia. 2008. *Rethinking Trafficking in Women: Politics out of Security*. London: Palgrave Macmillan.

Atasu-Topcuoglu, Reyhan. 2015. *Ideology and the Fight against Human Trafficking*. New York: Routledge.

Backhouse, Constance. 2012. "A Feminist Remedy for Sexual Assault: A Quest for Answers." In *Sexual Assault in Canada: Law, Legal Practice and Women's Activism*, edited by Elizabeth Sheehy, 725–40. Ottawa: University of Ottawa Press.

Backhouse, Constance. 2008. *Carnal Crimes: Sexual Assault Law in Canada, 1900–1975*. Toronto: Irwin Law.

Baker, Carrie. 2018. "Racialized Rescue Narratives in Public Discourses on Youth Prostitution and Sex Trafficking in the United States." Study of Women and Gender: Faculty Publications, Smith College, Northampton, MA.

Bakht, Natasha. 2012. "What's in a Face? Demeanour Evidence in the Sexual Assault Context." In *Sexual Assault in Canada: Law, Legal Practice and Women's Activism*, edited by Elizabeth Sheehy591–612. Ottawa: University of Ottawa Press.

Bell, Shannon, and Joseph Couture. 2000. "Justice and Law: Passion, Power, Prejudice, and So-called Pedophilia." In *Law as Gendering Practice*, edited by Dorothy E. Chunn and Dany Lacombe, 40–59. Don Mills, ON: Oxford University Press.

Benedet, Janine, and Isabel Grant. 2007. "Hearing the Sexual Assault Complaints of Women with Mental Disabilities: Evidentiary and Procedural Issues." *McGill Law Journal* 52: 517–51.

Bennett, Lance W., and Martha S. Feldman. 1981. *Reconstructing Reality in the Courtroom*. New Brunswick, NJ: Rutgers University Press.

Bernstein, Elizabeth. 2012a. "Carceral Politics as Gender Justice? The 'Traffic in Women' and Neoliberal Circuits of Crime, Sex and Rights." *Theoretical Sociology* 41: 233–59. https://doi.org/10.1007/s11186-012-9165-9.

Bernstein, Elizabeth. 2010. "Militarized Humanitarianism Meets Carceral Feminism: The Politics of Sex, Rights, and Freedom in Contemporary Antitrafficking Campaigns." *Journal of Women in Culture and Society* 36, no. 1: 45–71. https://doi.org/10.1086/652918. Medline:20827852.

Bernstein, Elizabeth. 2012b. "Sex Trafficking and the Politics of Freedom." Unpublished. https://www.ias.edu/sites/default/files/sss/papers/paper45.pdf.

Bigo, Didier. 2000. "When Two Become One: Internal and External Securitisations in Europe." In *International Relations Theory and the Politics of European Integration: Power, Security and Community*, edited by M. Kelstrup and M. Williams, 171–204. London: Routledge.

Bittle, Steven. 2006. "From Villan to Victim: Secure Care and Young Women in Prostitution." In *Criminalizing Women: Gender and (In)Justice in Neo-Liberal Times*, edited by Gillian Balfour and Elizabeth Comack, 195–213. Halifax, NS: Fernwood Publishing.

Bittle, Steven. 2013. "Still Punishing to 'Protect': Youth Prostitution Law and Policy Reform." In *Selling Sex: Experience, Advocacy, and Research on Sex Work in Canada*, edited by Emily van der Meulen, Elya M. Durisin, and Victoria Love, 279–96. Vancouver: University of British Columbia Press.

Blunt, Daniel, and Ariel Wolf. 2020. "Erased: The Impact of FOSTA-SESTA and the Removal of Backpage on Sex Workers." *Ant-Trafficking Review* 14: 117–21. https://doi.org/10.14197/atr.201220148.

Bonnycastle, Kevin. 2000. "Rape Uncodified: Reconsidering Bill C-49 Amendments to Canadian Sexual Assault Laws. In *Law as Gendering Practice*, edited by Dorothy E. Chunn and Dany Lacombe, 60–78. Don Mills, ON: Oxford University Press.

Brock, Deborah. 1998. *Making Work, Making Trouble: Prostitution as a Social Problem*. Toronto: University of Toronto Press.

Brode, Patrick. 2008. "'Pervert's a Menace: The Development of the Criminal Sexual Psychopathy Offence 1948." In *Essays in the History of Canadian Law: Volume X, a Tribute to Peter N. Oliver*, edited by Jim Philips, R. Roy McMurtry, and John T. Saywell, 107–28. The Osgoode Society for Canadian Legal History. Toronto: University of Toronto Press.

Browne, Simone. 2015. *Dark Matters: On the Surveillance of Blackness*. Durham, NC: Duke University Press.

Bruckert, Chris. 2018a. "Introduction: Revisioning Third Parties in the Sex Industry." In *Getting Past the "Pimp": Management in the Sex Industry*, edited by Chris Buckert and Colette Parent, 3–18. Toronto: University of Toronto Press.

Bruckert, Chris. 2018b. "Who Are Third Parties? Pathways in and out of Third Party Work." In *Getting Past the "Pimp": Management in the Sex Industry*, edited by Chris Buckert and Colette Parent, 36–55. Toronto: University of Toronto Press.

Bruckert, Chris and Tuulia Law. 2013. "Beyond Pimps, Procurers and Parasites: Mapping Third Parties in the Incall/Outcall Sex Industry." https://www.nswp.org/ru/node/1460.

Bruckert, Chris, and Colette Parent. 2004. *Organized Crime and Human Trafficking in Canada: Tracing Perceptions and Discourses*. Royal Canadian Mounted Police. http://publications.gc.ca/Collection/PS64-1-2004E.pdf.

Bullough, Bonnie, and Vern Bullough. 1987. *Women and Prostitution: A Social History*. Buffalo, NY: Crown Publishers.

Bumiller, Kristin. 2008. *In an Abusive State: How Neoliberalism Appropriated the Feminist Movement against Sexual Violence*. Durham, NC: Duke University Press.

Bunting, Annie, and Joel Quirk. 2017. "Contemporary Slavery as More Than Rhetorical Strategy? The Politics and Ideology of a New Political Cause." In *Contemporary Slavery: Popular Rhetoric and Political Practice*, edited by Annie Bunting and Joel Quirk, 5–35. Vancouver: University of British Columbia Press.

Burt, Geoff, Mark Sedra, Bernard Headley, Camille Hernandez-Ramdwar, Randy Seepersad, and Scot Wortley. 2016. *Deportation, Circular Migration and Organized Crime: Jamaican Case Study*. Research Report 2016-R007. Ottawa: Government of Canada. Public Safety Canada. https://www.publicsafety.gc.ca/cnt/rsrcs/pblctns/2016-r007/2016-r007-en.pdf.

Cameron, Sally. 2008. "Trafficking of Women for Prostitution." In *Trafficking in Humans: Social, Cultural and Political Dimensions*, edited by Sally Cameron and Edward Newman, 80–110. New York: United Nations University Press.

Chan, Wendy, and Dorothy Chunn. 2014. *Racialization, Crime, and Criminal Justice in Canada*. Toronto: University of Toronto Press.

Chapkins, Wendy. 1997. *Live Sex Acts: Women Performing Erotic Labour*. London: Cassell Wellington House.

Chermak, Steven, and Alexander Weiss. 2005. "Maintaining Legitimacy Using External Communication Strategies: An Analysis of Police–Media Relations." *Journal of Criminal Justice* 33: 501–12. https://doi.org/10.1016/j.jcrimjus.2005.06.001.

Chuang, Janie. A. 2014. "Exploitation Creep and the Unmaking of Human Trafficking Law." *The American Journal of International Law* 108, no. 4: 609–49. https://doi.org/10.5305/amerjintelaw.108.4.0609.

Cole, Teju. 2012. "The White-Saviour Industrial Complex." *The Atlantic* (21 March), https://www.theatlantic.com/international/archive/2012/03/the-white-savior-industrial-complex/254843/.

Collacott, Martin. 2006. *Canada's Inadequate Response to Terrorism: The Need for Policy Reform*. Fraser Institute Digital Publications. https://www.fraserinstitute.org/sites/default/files/InadequateResponsetoTerrorism.pdf.

Comack, Elizabeth, and Gillian Balfour. 2004. *The Power to Criminalize: Violence, Inequality and the Law*. Halifax, NS: Fernwood Publishing.

Comack, Elizabeth, and Gillian Balfour. 2004. *The Power to Criminalize: Violence, Inequality and the Law*. Halifax, NS: Fernwood Publishing.

Comack, Elizabeth, and Tracy Peter. 2005. "How the Criminal Justice System Responds to Sexual Assault Survivors: The Slippage Between Responsibilization and Blaming the Victim." *Canadian Journal of Women and the Law* 17, no. 2: 283–309.

Conley, John M., and William M. O'Barr. 1998. *Just Words: Law, Language and Power*. Chicago: University of Chicago Press.

Conty, Sheridan. 2019. *The National Inquiry into Missing and Murdered Indigenous Women and Girls: A Counter-Archive*. MA thesis, Carleton University, Ottawa.

Cordasco, Francesco. 1981. *The White Slave Trade and the Immigrants: A Chapter in American Social History*. Detroit: Blaine Ethridge Books.

Craig, Elaine. 2015. "The Inhospitable Court." *University of Toronto Law Journal* 66, no. 2: 197–207. https://doi.org/10.3138/utlj.3398.

Craig, Elaine. 2014. "Person(s) of Interest and Missing Women: Legal Abandonment in the Downtown Eastside." *McGill Law Journal* 60, no. 1: 1–42. https://doi.org/10.7202/1027718ar.

Craig, Elaine. 2018. *Putting Trials on Trial: Sexual Assault and the Failure of the Legal Profession*. Montreal: McGill-Queen's University Press.

Cunliffe, Emma. 2013. "Untold Stories or Miraculous Mirrors? The Possibilities of a Text-Based Understanding of Socio-Legal Transcript Research." https://ssrn.com/abstract=2227069.

Dauda, Carol. 2010a. "Childhood, Age of Consent and Moral Regulation in Canada and the UK." *Contemporary Politics* 16, no. 3: 227–47. https://doi.org/10.1080/13569775.2010.501634.

Dauda, Carol. 2010b. "Sex, Gender and Generation: Age of Consent and Moral Regulation in Canada." *Politics & Policy* 38, no. 6: 1159–85. https://doi.org/10.1111/j.1747-1346.2010.00273.x.

Davis, Angela. 2017a. "Introduction." In *Policing the Black Man*, edited by Angela Davis, xi–2. New York: Pantheon Books.

Davis, Angela. 2017b. "The Prosecution of Black Men." In *Policing the Black Man*, edited by Angela Davis, 178–208. New York: Pantheon Books.

Davis, Angela. 1983. *Women, Race and Class*. New York: Random House

De Shalit, Ann. 2021. *Neoliberal Paternalism and Displaced Culpability: Examining the Governing Relations of the Human Trafficking Problem*. PhD diss., Ryerson University.

De Shalit, Ann, Robert Heynen, and Emily van der Meulen. 2014. "Human Trafficking and Media Myths: Federal Funding, Communication Strategies, and Canadian Anti-Trafficking Programs." *Canadian Journal of Communication* 39, no. 3: 385–412. https://doi.org/10.32920/ryerson.14636976.v1.

De Shalit, Ann, Katrin Roots, and Emily van der Meulen. 2021. "Knowledge Mobilization by Provincial Politicians: The United Front against Trafficking in Ontario, Canada." *Journal of Human Trafficking*. https://doi.org/10.1080/23322705.2021.1934370.

Doe, Jane. 2003. *The Story of Jane Doe: A Book about Rape*. Toronto: Vintage Canada.

Doezema, Jo. 2000. "Loose Women or Lost Women? The Re-emergence of the Myth of 'White Slavery' in Contemporary Discourses of 'Trafficking in Women.'" *Gender Issues* 18: 23–50. https://doi.org/10.1007/s12147-999-0021-9. Medline:12296110.

Doezema Jo. 2001. "Ouch! Western Feminists' 'Wounded Attachment' to the 'Third World Prostitute.'" *Feminist Review* 67, no. 1: 16–38. https://doi.org/10.1080/01417780150514484.

Doezema, Jo. 2010. *Sex Slaves and Discourse Masters: The Construction of Trafficking*. London: Zed Books.

Doezema, Jo. 2007. "Who Gets to Choose? Coercion, Consent and the UN Trafficking Protocol." In *Gender Trafficking and Slavery*, edited by R. Masika, 20–7. London: Oxfam Focus on Gender.

Donovan, Brian. 2006. *White Slave Crusades: Race, Gender, and Activism 1887–1918*. Chicago: University of Illinois Press.

Dorais, Michel, and Patrice Corriveau. 2002. *Gangs and Girls: Understanding Juvenile Prostitution*. Montreal: McGill-Queen's University Press.

Drew, Paul. 1992. "Contested Evidence in Courtroom Cross Examination: The Case of a Trial for Rape." In *Talk at Work: Interaction in Institutional Settings*, edited by Paul Drew and John Heritage, 470–517. Cambridge: Cambridge University Press.

DuBois, Teresa. 2012. "Police Investigation of Sexual Assault Complainants: How Far Have We Come Since Jane Doe?" In *Sexual Assault in Canada: Law, Legal Practice and Women's Activism*, edited by Elizabeth Sheehy, 191–210. Ottawa: University of Ottawa Press.

Durisin, Elya. 2017. *White Slavery Reconfigured: The "Natasha Trade" and Sexualized Nationalism in Canada*. PhD diss., York University. https://yorkspace.library.yorku.ca/xmlui/handle/10315/34522?show=full.

Durisin, Elya, and Emily van der Meulen. 2021. "The Perfect Victim: 'Young Girls,' Domestic Trafficking, and Anti-prostitution Politics in Canada." *Anti-Trafficking Review* 16: 145–9. https://doi.org/10.14197/atr.201221169.

Durisin, Elya, and Emily van der Meulen. 2020. "Sexualized Nationalism and Federal Human Trafficking Consultations: Shifting Discourses of Sex Trafficking in Canada." *Journal of Human Trafficking*. https://doi.org/10.1080/23322705.2020.1743604.

Ehrlich, Susan. 2012. "Perpetuating – and Resisting – Rape Myths in Trial Discourse." In *Sexual Assault in Canada: Law, Legal Practice and Women's Activism*, edited by Elizabeth Sheehy, 389–408. Ottawa: University of Ottawa Press.

Ericson, V. Richard. 1983. *Making Crime: A Study of Detective Work*. Toronto: Butterworths.

Esser, Luuk B., and Corinne E. Dettmeijer-Vermeulen. 2016. "The Prominent Role of National Judges in Interpreting the International Definition of Human Trafficking." *Anti-Trafficking Review* 6: 91–106. https://doi.org/10.14197/atr.20121666.

Estrich, Susan. 1987. *Real Rape: How the Legal System Victimizes Women Who Say No*. Cambridge, MA: Harvard University Press.

Estrich, Susan. 1987. *Representing Rape: Language and Sexual Consent*. London: Routledge.

Farrell, Amy, Monica DeLateur, Colleen Owens, and Stephanie Fahy. 2016. "The Prosecution of State-Level Human Trafficking Cases in the United States." *Anti-Trafficking Review* 6: 48–70. https://doi.org/10.14197/atr.20121664.

Farrell, Amy, Rebecca Pfeffer, and Katherine Bright. 2015. "Police Perceptions of Human Trafficking," *Journal of Crime and Justice* 38, no. 3: 315–33. https://doi.org/10.1080/0735648x.2014.995412.

Fatsis, Lambros. 2019. "Grime: Criminal Subculture or Public Counterculture? A Critical Investigation into the Criminalization of Black Musical

Subcultures in the UK." *Crime Media Culture* 15, no. 3: 447–61.
https://doi.org/10.1177/1741659018784111.

Feingold, David. 2005. "Human Trafficking." *Foreign Policy* 150: 26–32.

Feldstein, Ruth. 1998. "Antiracism and Maternal Failure in the 1940s and
1950s." In *Bad Mothers: The Politics of Blame in the Twentieth-Century America*,
edited by Molly Ladd-Taylor and Lauri Umansky, 145. New York: New York
University Press.

Ferguson, John A. 2012. *International Human Trafficking in Canada: Why so Few
Prosecutions?* PhD diss., University of British Columbia, Faculty of Graduate
Studies (Law).

Finn, Jonathan. 2009. *Capturing the Criminal Image: From Mug Shot to
Surveillance Society*. Minneapolis: University of Minnesota Press.

Fiske, John. 2000. "White Watch." In *Ethnic Minorities and the Media: Changing
Cultural Boundaries*, edited by Simon Cottle, 50–66. Buckingham, UK: Open
University Press.

Gallagher, Anne. 2006. "Human Rights and Human Trafficking in Thailand:
A Shadow TIP Report." In *Trafficking and the Global Sex Industry*, edited by
K. Beeks and D. Amir, 139–63. Oxford: Lexington Books.

Gallagher, Anne. 2010. *The International Law of Human Trafficking*. Cambridge:
Cambridge University Press.

Gallagher, Anne. 2016. "The Problems and Prospects of Trafficking
Prosecutions: Ending Impunity and Securing Justice." *Anti-Trafficking
Review* 6: 1–12. https://doi.org/10.14197/atr.20121661.

Gallagher, Anne, and Rebecca Surtees. 2012. "Measuring the Success of
Counter-Trafficking Interventions in the Criminal Justice Sector: Who
Decides – and How?" *Anti-Trafficking Review* 1: 10–30. https://doi.org
/10.14197/atr.201211.

Garland, David. 2001. *The Culture of Control: Crime and Social Order in
Contemporary Society*. Chicago: University of Chicago Press.

Gewirtz, Paul. 1996. "Narrative and Rhetoric in Law." In *Law's Stories:
Narrative and Rhetoric in the Law*, edited by Peter Brooks and Paul Gewitrtz,
2–13. New Haven, CT: Yale University Press.

Giles, Melinda V. 2012. "From 'Need' to 'Risk': The Neoliberal Construction of
the 'Bad' Mother." *Journal of the Motherhood Initiative* 3, no. 1: 112–33.

Gilles, Kara, and Chris Bruckert. 2018. "Pimps, Partners and Procurers:
Criminalizing Street-Based Sex Workers' Relationship with Partners
and Third Parties." In *Red Light Labour: Sex Work Regulation, Agency and
Resistance*, edited by Elya M. Durisin, Emily van der Meulen, and Chris
Bruckert, 82–93. Vancouver: University of British Columbia Press.

Glasbeek, Amanda. 2006. "'My Wife Has Endured a Torrent of Abuse':
Gender, Safety, and Anti-Squeegee Discourses in Toronto, 1998–2000."
Windsor Year Book Access to Justice 24, no. 1: 55–75.

Gotell, Lise. 2008. "Rethinking Affirmative Consent in Canadian Sexual Assault Law: Neoliberal Sexual Subject and Risky Women." *Akron Law Review* 41, no. 4: 865–98.

Gotell, Lise. 2012. "Third-Wave Anti-rape Activism on Neoliberal Terrain: The Garneau Sisterhood." In *Sexual Assault in Canada: Law, Legal Practice and Women's Activism*, edited by Elizabeth Sheehy, 243–66. Ottawa: University of Ottawa Press.

Gruber, Aya. 2020. *The Feminist War on Crime: The Unexpected Role of Women's Liberation in Mass Incarceration*. Oakland: University of California Press.

Hall, Rachel. 2004. "'It Can Happen to You': Rape Prevention in the Age of Risk Management." *Hypatia* 19, no. 3: 1–19. https://doi.org/10.1353/hyp.2004.0054.

Hannah-Moffat, Kelly. 2006. "Empowering Risk: The Nature of Gender-Responsive Strategies." In *Criminalizing Women: Gender and (In)Justice in Neoliberal Times*, edited by Gillian Balfour and Elizabeth Comack, 250–66. Halifax, NS: Fernwood Publishing.

Hastie, Bethanie, and Alison Yule. 2014. "Milestone or Missed Opportunity? A Critical Analysis of the Impact of Domotor on the Future of Human Trafficking Cases in Canada." *Appeal: Review of Current Law and Law Reform* 19: 83–93.

Hill Collins, Patricia. 2004. *Black Sexual Politics: African American Gender and the New Racism*. New York: Routledge.

hooks, bell. 2003. *We Real Cool: Black Men and Masculinity*. Milton Park, UK: Routledge.

Horning, Amber, and Anthony Marcus. 2017. "Introduction: In Search of Pimps and Other Varieties." In *Third Party Sex Work and Pimps in the Age of Anti-Trafficking*, edited by Amber Horning and Anthony Marcus. New York: Springer International Publishings.

Hua, Julietta. 2011. *Trafficking Women's Human Rights*. Minneapolis: University of Minnesota Press.

Hua, Julietta, and Holly Nigorizawa. 2010. "US Sex Trafficking, Women's Human Rights and the Politics of Representation." *International Feminist Journal of Politics* 12, nos. 3–4: 401–23. https://doi.org/10.1080/14616742.2010.513109.

Hunt, Sarah. 2010. "Colonial Roots, Contemporary Risk Factors: A Cautionary Exploration of the Domestic Trafficking of Aboriginal Women and Girls in British Columbia, Canada." *Alliance News* 33: 27–31.

Hunt, Sarah. 2013. "Decolonizing Sex Work: Developing an Intersectional Indigenous Approach." In *Selling Sex: Experience, Advocacy, and Research on Sex Work in Canada*, edited by Emily van der Meulen, Elya M. Durisin, and Victoria Love, 82–100. Vancouver: University of British Columbia Press.

Hunt, Sarah. 2017. "Foreword." In *Responding to Human Trafficking: Dispossession, Colonial Violence, and Resistance among Indigenous and Racialized Women* by Julie Kaye. Toronto: University of Toronto Press.

Hunt, Sarah. 2015. "Representing Colonial Violence: Trafficking, Sex Work and the Violence of Law." *Atlantis: Critical Studies in Gender, Culture & Social* 37.2, no. 1: 25–39.

Jackson, Ronald. 2006. *Scripting the Black Masculine Body: Identity, Discourse, and Racial Politics in Popular Media*. New York: State University of New York Press.

James, Carl E. 2012. "Troubling Role Models: Seeing Racialization in the Discourse Relating to 'Corrective Agents' for Black Males." In *Troubled Masculinities: Reimagining Urban Men*, edited by Kenneth James Moffatt, 77–93. Toronto: University of Toronto Press.

Jefferess, David. 2021. "On Saviours and Saviourism: Lessons from the #WEscandal." *Globalisation, Societies and Education* 19, no. 4: 420–31. https://doi.org/10.1080/14767724.2021.1892478.

Jeffrey, Leslie Ann. 2005. "Canada and Migrant Sex Work: Challenging the 'Foreign' in Foreign Policy." *Canadian Foreign Policy* 12, no. 1: 33–48. https://doi.org/10.1080/11926422.2005.9673387.

Jeffrey, Leslie Ann, and Gayle MacDonald. 2006. *Sex Workers in the Maritimes Talk Back*. Vancouver: University of British Columbia Press.

Jeffries, Michael. 2011. "Thug Life and Social Death." In *Thug Life: Race, Gender, and the Meaning of Hip-Hop*, edited by Michael Jeffries, 77–111. Chicago: University of Chicago Press.

Jessome, Phonse. 1996. *Somebody's Daughter: Inside the Toronto/Halifax Pimping Ring*. Halifax, NS: Nimbus Publishings.

Jiwani, Yasmin, and Mary Lynn Young. 2007. "Missing and Murdered Women: Reproducing Marginality in News Discourse." *Canadian Journal of Communication* 31: 895–917. https://doi.org/10.22230/cjc.2006v31n4a1825.

JJ. 2013. "We Speak for Ourselves: Anti-Colonial and Self-Determined Responses to Young People Involved in the Sex Trade." In *Selling Sex: Experience, Advocacy, and Research on Sex Work in Canada*, edited by Emily van der Meulen, Elya M. Durisin, and Victoria Love, 74–81. Vancouver: University of British Columbia Press.

Johnson, Meagan. 2012. "Sisterhood Will Get Ya: Anti-Rape Activism and the Criminal Justice System." In *Sexual Assault in Canada: Law, Legal Practice and Women's Activism*, edited by Elizabeth Sheehy, 267–300. Ottawa: University of Ottawa Press.

Jun-Rong Ting, David Allan, and Carisa R. Showden. 2019. "Structural Intersectionality and Indigenous Canadian Youth Who Trade Sex: Understanding Mobility beyond the Trafficking Model." *AlterNative* 15, no. 3: 261–70. https://doi.org/10.1177/1177180119876679.

Kalunta-Crumpton, Anita. 1998. "The Prosecution and Defence of Black Defendants in Drug Trials." *British Journal of Criminology* 38, no. 4: 561–91. https://doi.org/10.1093/bjc/38.4.561.

Kapur, Ratna. 2005. "Cross Border Movements and the Law: Negotiating the Boundaries of Difference." In *Trafficking and Prostitution Reconsidered: Perspectives on Migration, Sex Work and Human Rights,* edited by K. Kempadoo, J. Sanghera, and B. Pattanaik, 25–41. Boulder, CO: Paradigm Publishers.

Kaye, Julie. 2017. *Responding to Human Trafficking: Dispossession, Colonial Violence, and Resistance among Indigenous and Racialized Women.* Toronto: University of Toronto Press.

Kaye, Julie, and Bethany Hastie. 2015. "The Canadian Criminal Code Offence of Trafficking in Persons: Challenges from the Field and within the Law." *Social Inclusion* 3, no. 1: 88–102. https://doi.org/10.17645/si.v3i1.178.

Kempadoo, Kamala. 2005. "Introduction: From Moral Panic to Global Justice: Changing Perspectives on Trafficking." In *Trafficking and Prostitution Reconsidered: New Perspectives on Migration, Sex Work and Human Rights,* edited by K. Kempadoo, J. Sanghera, and B. Pattanaik, vii–xxxiv. Boulder, CO: Paradigm Publishers.

Kempadoo, Kamala. 2015. "The Modern-Day White (Wo)Man's Burden: Trends in Anti-Trafficking and Anti-Slavery Campaigns." *Journal of Human Trafficking* 1: 8–20. https://doi.org/10.1080/23322705.2015.1006120.

Kempadoo, Kamala, and Jo Doezema, eds. 1998. *Global Sex Workers Rights, Resistance, and Redefinition.* Milton Park, UK: Routledge.

Khan, Ummni. 2022. "A Guilty Pleasure: The Legal, Social Scientific and Feminist Verdict against Rap," *Theoretical Criminology* 26, no. 2: 245–63. https://doi.org/10.1177/13624806211028274.

Ladd-Taylor, Molly, and Lauri Umansky. 1998. "Introduction." In *'Bad' Mothers: The Politics of Blame in the Twentieth Century America,* edited by Molly Ladd-Taylor and Lauri Umansky, 1–30. New York: New York University Press.

Lam, Elaine, and Annalee Lepp. 2019. "Butterfly: Resisting the Harms of Anti-trafficking Policies and Fostering Peer-Based Organizing in Canada." *Anti-Trafficking Review* 12, no. 12: 91–107. https://doi.org/10.14197/atr.201219126.

Lawrence, W. Levine. 1977. *Black Culture and Black Consciousness: Afro-American Folk Thought from Slavery to Freedom.* Oxford: Oxford University Press.

Lester, Julia, Rebecca Pates, and Anne Dolemeyer. 2017. "The Emotional Leviathan – How Street-Level Bureaucrats Govern Human Trafficking Victims." *Digithum* 19: 19–36. https://doi.org/10.7238/d.v0i19.3088.

Lindberg, Tracey, Priscilla Campeau, and Maria Campbell. 2012. "Indigenous Women and Sexual Assault in Canada," In *Sexual Assault in Canada: Law,*

Legal Activism and Women's Activism, edited by Elizabeth Sheehy, 87–110. Ottawa: University of Ottawa Press.

Lowman, John. 2013. "Crown Expert-Witness Testimony in Bedford v. Canada: Evidence-Based Argument or Victim-Paradigm Hyperbole?" In *Selling Sex: Experience, Advocacy, and Research on Sex Work in Canada*, edited by Emily van der Meulen, Elya Durisin, and Victoria Love, 230–50. Vancouver: University of British Columbia Press.

Matoesian, Gregory M. 1993. *Reproducing Rape: Domination through Talk in the Courtroom*. Cambridge: Polity Press.

Maynard, Robyn. 2015. "Fighting Wrongs with Wrongs? How Canadian Anti-trafficking Crusades Have Failed Sex Workers, Migrants, and Indigenous Communities." *Atlantis: Critical Studies in Gender, Culture & Social Justice* 37.2: 40–56.

Maynard, Robyn. 2017. *Policing Black Lives: State Violence in Canada from Slavery to the Present*. Halifax, NS: Fernwood Publishing.

McGillivray, Anne. 1998. "'A Moral Vacuity in Her Which Is Difficult If Not Impossible to Explain': Law, Psychiatry and the Remaking of Karla Homolka." *International Journal of the Legal Profession* 5, nos. 2–3: 255–88. https://doi.org/10.1080/09695958.1998.9960450.

McLaren, John. 1986a. "Chasing the Social Evil: The Evolution of Canada's Prostitution Laws 1867–1917." *Canadian Journal of Law and Society* 1, no. 1: 125–66. https://doi.org/10.1017/s0829320100001034.

McLaren, John. 1990. "Recalculating the Wages of Sin: The Social and Legal Construction of Vice, 1850–1920." Lecture given at the Fourth Annual Gibson-Armstrong Lecture in Law and History. Osgoode Hall Law School, 28 February.

McLaren, John. 1986b. "'White Slavers': The Reform of Canada's Prostitution Laws and Patterns of Enforcement, 1900–1920." Paper presented at American Society for Legal History Faculty of Law, University of Toronto, 23–5 October.

Mensah, Nengeh Maria. 2018. "The Representation of the 'Pimp': A Barrier to Understanding the Work of Third Parties in the Adult Canadian Sex Industry." In *Getting Past the "Pimp": Management in the Sex Industry*, edited by Chris Bruckert and Colette Parent, 19–35. Toronto: University of Toronto Press.

Meshkovska, Biljana, Nikola Mickovski, Arjan E. R. Bos, and Melissa Siegel. 2016. "Trafficking of Women for Sexual Exploitation in Europe: Prosecution, Trials and Their Impact." *Anti-Trafficking Review* 6: 71–90. https://doi.org/10.14197/atr.20121665.

Millar, Hayli, and Tamara O'Doherty. 2020. "Racialized, Gendered, and Sensationalized: An Examination of Canadian Anti-trafficking Laws, Their Enforcement and Their (Re)presentation." *Canadian Journal of Law and Society* 35, no. 1: 23–44. https://doi.org/10.1017/cls.2020.2.

Millar, Hayli, Tamara O'Doherty, and Katrin Roots. 2017. "A Formidable Task: Reflections on Obtaining Legal Empirical Evidence on Human Trafficking in Canada." *Anti-Trafficking Review* 8: 34–49. https://doi.org/10.14197/atr.20121783.

Millar, Hayli, Tamara O'Doherty, and SWAN Vancouver Society. 2015. *The Palermo Protocol & Canada: The Evolution and Human Rights Impacts of Anti-trafficking Laws in Canada (2002–2015)*. https://icclr.org/publications/the-palermo-protocol-canada-the-evolution-and-human-rights-impacts-of-anti-trafficking-laws-in-canada-2002-2015/

Miller, Paul, and Akwasi Owusu-Bempah. 2011. "Whitewashing Criminal Justice in Canada: Preventing Research through Data Suppression." *Canadian Journal of Law and Society* 26, no. 3: 653–61. https://doi.org/10.3138/cjls.26.3.653.

Milner, Christina, and Richard Milner. 1977. *Black Players: The Secret World of Black Pimps*. Mayfield, KY: Kings Publishing.

Monaghan, Jeffrey. 2014. "Security Traps and Discourses of Radicalization: Examining Surveillance Practices Targeting Muslims in Canada." *Surveillance & Society* 12, no. 4: 485–501. https://doi.org/10.24908/ss.v12i4.4557.

Moore, Dawn, and Mariana Valverde. 2000. "Party Girls and Predators: A Chronotope of Female Risk." *Tessera* 29. https://doi.org/10.25071/1923-9408.25208.

Mullings, Delores, Anthony Morgan, and Heather Kere. 2016. "Canada the Great White North: Where Anti-Black Racism Thrives: Kicking Down the Doors and Exposing the Realities." *Phylon* 53, no. 1: 20–41.

Murdocca, Carmela. 2004. "The Racial Profile: Governing Race through Knowledge Production (Research Note)." *Canadian Journal of Law and Society* 19, no. 2: 153–67.

Musto, Jennifer Lynne. 2010. "The NGO-ification of the Anti-trafficking Movement in the United States: A Case Study of the Coalition to Abolish Slavery and Trafficking." In *Sex Trafficking, Human Rights and Social Justice*, edited by Tiantian Zheng, 23–36. London: Routledge.

Musto, Jennifer Lynne. 2016. *Control and Protect: Collaboration, Carceral Protection, and Domestic Sex Trafficking in the United States*. Oakland: University of California Press.

Musto, Jennifer, Mitali Thakor, and Borislav Gerasimon. 2020. "Editorial: Between Home and Hype: Critical Evaluation of Technology's Role in Anti-trafficking." *Anti-Trafficking Review* 14: 1–12. https://doi.org/10.14197/atr.201220141.

Mutua, Makau. 2002. *Human Rights: A Political and Cultural Critique*. Philadelphia: University of Pennsylvania Press.

Mutua, Makau. 2001. "Savages, Victims, and Saviors: The Metaphor of Human Rights." *Harvard International Law Journal* 42, no. 1: 201–45.

Mutua, Makau. 2007. "Standard Setting in Human Rights: Critique and Prognosis." *Human Rights Quarterly* 29: 547–630. https://doi.org /10.1353/hrq.2007.0030.

Nielson, Erik, and Andrea L. Dennis. 2019. *Rap on Trial: Race, Lyrics, and Guilt in America*. New York: The New Press.

O'Connell Davidson, Julia. 2015a. *Modern Slavery: The Margins of Freedom*. New York: Palgrave Macmillan.

O'Connell Davidson, Julia. 2015b. "Rights Talk, Wrong Comparison: Trafficking and Transatlantic Slavery." *Open Democracy*, https://www .opendemocracy.net/beyondslavery/julia-o%27connell-davidson /rights-talk-wrong-comparison-trafficking-and-transatlantic-sl.

Odette, Fran. 2012. "Sexual Assault and Disabled Women Ten Years after Jane Doe." In *Sexual Assault in Canada: Law, Legal Practice and Women's Activism*, edited by Elizabeth Sheehy, 173–90. Ottawa: University of Ottawa Press.

O'Doherty, Tamara, Hayli Anne Millar, and Kimberly Mackenzie. 2018. "Misrepresentations, Inadequate Evidence, Impediments to Justice: Human Rights Impacts of Canada's Anti-Trafficking Efforts." In *Red Light Labour: Sex Work Regulation, Agency and Resistance*, edited by Elya M. Durisin, Emily van der Meulen, and Chris Bruckert, 104–20. Vancouver: University of British Columbia Press.

Pheterson, Gail. 1993. "The Whore Stigma: Female Dishonor and Male Unworthiness." *Social Text* 37: 39–64. https://doi.org/10.2307/466259.

Pratt, Anna. 2012. "Immigration Penalty and the Crime-Security Nexus: The Case of Tran Trong Nghi Nguyen." In *Canadian Criminal Justice Policy: A Contemporary Reader*, edited by Karim Ismaili, Jane Sprott, and Kim Varma, 273–98. Oxford: Oxford University Press.

Pratt, Anna. 2005. *Securing Borders: Detention and Deportation in Canada*. Vancouver: University British Columbia Press.

Pratt, Anna. 2014. "Wanted by the CBSA." In *Criminalization, Representation and Regulation: Thinking Differently About Crime*, edited by Deborah Brock, Amanda Glasbeek, and Carmela Murdocca, 285–326. Oxford: Oxford University Press.

Pratt, Anna, and Mariana Valverde. 2002. "From Deserving Victims to 'Masters of Confusion': Redefining Refugees in the 1990s." *Canadian Journal of Sociology* 27, no. 2: 135–61. https://doi.org/10.2307/3341708.

Public Safety Canada. 2019. *National Strategy to Combat Human Trafficking 2019-2024*. https://www.publicsafety.gc.ca/cnt/rsrcs/pblctns/2019-ntnl-strtgy -hmnn-trffc/index-en.aspx.

Quinn, Eithne. 2000. "'Who's the Mack?': The Performativity and Politics of the Pimp Figure in Gangsta Rap." *Journal of American Studies* 34, no. 1: 115–36. https://doi.org/10.1017/s0021875899006295.

Rabinow, Paul. 1984. *Foucault: The Reader*. New York: Pantheon Books.

Randall, Melanie. 2010. "Sexual Assault Law, Credibility, and 'Ideal Victim': Consent, Resistance and Victim Blaming." *Canadian Journal of Women and the Law* 22: 397–433. https://doi.org/10.3138/cjwl.22.2.397.

Render, Michael. 2019. "Foreword." In *Rap on Trial: Race, Lyrics and Guilt in America* by Erik Nelson and Andrea L. Dennis. New York: The New Press.

Ringrose, Jessica, Laura Harvey, Rosalind Gill, and Sonia Livingstone. 2013. "Teen Girls, Sexual Double Standards and 'Sexting': Gendered Value in Digital Image Exchange." *Feminist Theory* 14, no. 3: 305–23. https://doi.org/10.1177/1464700113499853.

Rizer, Arthur, and Sheri R. Glaser. 2011. "Breach: The National Security Implications of Human Trafficking." *Widener Law Review* 17: 69.

Robinson, Kerry H. 2012. "'Difficult Citizenship': The Precarious Relationships between Childhood, Sexuality and Access to Knowledge." *Sexualities* 15, nos. 3/4: 257–76. https://doi.org/10.1177/1363460712436469.

Roots, Katrin. 2019. "Human Trafficking in Canada as a Historical Continuation of the 1980s Juvenile Prostitution Panic." In *The Palgrave International Handbook of Human Trafficking*, edited by J. Jones and J. Winterdyk, 97–113. London: Palgrave Macmillan Publishing.

Roots, Katrin. 2011. *Human Trafficking in Canada: "Crisis" or Confusion? An Examination of Canada's Trafficking Legislation and the Development of a "Social Crisis,"* MA thesis, Lakehead University, Thunder Bay, Ontario.

Roots, Katrin. 2013. "Trafficking or Pimping: An Analysis of Canada's Human Trafficking Law and Its Implications." *Canadian Journal of Law and Society* 28: 21–40. https://doi.org/10.1017/cls.2012.4.

Roots, Katrin, and Ann De Shalit. 2015. "Evidence That Evidence Doesn't Matter: The Case of Human Trafficking in Canada." *Atlantis: Critical Studies in Gender, Culture & Social Justice* 37, no. 2: 65–80.

Roots, Katrin, and Emily Lockhart. 2021. "To Protect and Responsibilize: Examining the Narratives of Youth in Human Trafficking Trials." *Canadian Journal of Women and the Law* 3, Vol 33(1): 58–83,

Sanghera, Jyoti. 2005. "Unpacking the Trafficking Discourse." In *Trafficking and Prostitution Reconsidered: Perspectives on Migration, Sex Work, and Human Rights*, edited by K. Kempadoo, J. Sanghera, and B. Pattanaik, 3–24. Boulder, CO: Paradigm Publishers.

Sharapov, Kiril. 2014. "Giving Us the 'Biggest Bang for the Buck' (or Not): Anti-trafficking Government Funding in Ukraine and the United Kingdom." *Anti-Trafficking Review* 3: 16–40. https://doi.org/10.14197/atr.20121432.

Sharma, Nandita. 2005. "Anti-trafficking Rhetoric and the Making of a Global Apartheid." *NWSA Journal* 17, no. 3: 88–111. https://doi.org/10.2979/nws.2005.17.3.88.

Sheehy, Elizabeth. 2014. *Defending Battered Women on Trial: Lessons from the Transcripts*. Vancouver: University of British Columbia Press.

Sheehy, Elizabeth. 2012a. "Introduction." In *Sexual Assault in Canada: Law, Legal Practice and Women's Activism*, edited by Elizabeth Sheehy, 7–22. Ottawa: University of Ottawa Press.

Sheehy, Elizabeth. 2012b. "Judges and the Reasonable Steps Requirement: The Judicial Stance on Perpetration against Unconscious Women." In *Sexual Assault in Canada: Law, Legal Practice and Women's Activism*, edited by Elizabeth Sheehy, 483–540. Ottawa: University of Ottawa Press.

Sibley, Marcus A. 2020. "Attachments to Victimhood: Anti-trafficking Narratives and the Criminalization of the Sex Trade." *Social & Legal Studies* 29, no. 5: 699–717. https://doi.org/10.1177/0964663919897970.

Smart, Carol. 1989. *Feminism and the Power of Law*. London: Routledge.

Smart, Carol. 1995. *Law, Crime and Sexuality: Essays in Feminism*. London: Sage Publications.

Smith, Tanya Dawne. 2000. *Pimping and Prostitution in Halifax in the Early 1990s: The Evolution of a Moral Panic*. MA thesis, Dalhousie University. http://www.collectionscanada.gc.ca/obj/s4/f2/dsk2/ftp01/MQ57327.pdf.

Soderlund, Gretchen. 2005. "Running from the Rescuers: New U.S. Crusades against Sex Trafficking and the Rhetoric of Abolition." *NWSA Journal* 17, no. 3: 64–87. https://doi.org/10.2979/nws.2005.17.3.64.

Stevenson, Bryan. 2017. "A Presumption of Guilt: The Legacy of American's History of Racial Injustice." In *Policing the Black Man: Arrest, Prosecution and Imprisonment*, edited by Angela Davis, 3–30. New York: Pantheon Books.

Suchland, Jennifer. 2015. *Transnational Feminism, Postsocialism, and the Politics of Sex Trafficking*. Durham, NC: Duke University Press.

Swenstein, Abigail, and Kate Mogulescu. 2016 "Resisting the Carceral: The Need to Align Anti-trafficking Efforts with Movements for Criminal Justice Reform." *Anti-Trafficking Review* 6: 118–22. https://doi.org/10.14197/atr.201216610.

Tanovich, M. David. 2006. *The Colour of Justice: Policing Race in Canada*. Toronto: Irwin Law.

Thakor, Mitali, and danah boyd. 2013. "Networked Trafficking: Reflections on Technology and the Anti-trafficking Movement." *Dialect Anthropology* 37: 277–90. https://doi.org/10.1007/s10624-012-9286-6.

Thurer, Shari. 1994. *The Myths of Motherhood: How Culture Reinvents the Good Mother*. Boston: Houghton Mifflin Company.

Tichenor, Erin. 2020. "'I've Never Been So Exploited': The Consequences of FOSTA-SESTA in Aotearoa New Zealand," *Anti-Trafficking Review* 14: 99–115. https://doi.org/10.14197/atr.201220147.

Umphrey, Martha Merrill. 1999. "The Dialogics of Legal Meaning: Spectacular Trials, the Unwritten Law, and Narratives of Criminal Responsibility." *Law and Society Review* 33, no. 2: 393–423. https://doi.org/10.2307/3115169.

Valverde, Mariana. 2008. *The Age of Light, Soap and Water*. Toronto: University of Toronto Press.

Van der Meulen, Emily. 2010. "Ten: Illegal Lives, Loves, and Work: How the Criminalization of Procuring Affects Sex Workers in Canada." *Journal of Transnational Women's and Gender Studies* 8: 217–40.

Wacquant, Loic. 2002. "From Slavery to Mass Incarceration." *New Left Review* 13: n.p.

Wacquant, Loic. 2005. "Race as Civic Felony." *International Social Science Journal* 57, no. 183: 127–42. https://doi.org/10.1111/j.0020-8701.2005.00536.x.

Walker, Barrington. 2010. *Race on Trial: Black Defendants in Ontario's Criminal Courts, 1858–1958*. Toronto: University of Toronto Press.

Walkowitz, Judith R. 1980. *Prostitution and Victorian Society: Women, Class and the State*. Cambridge: Cambridge University Press.

Walsh, Kieran. 2010. "Images of Childhood, Adolescent Sexual Reality and the Age of Consent." In *Sex, Drugs and Rock and Roll: Psychological, Legal and Cultural Examinations of Sex and Sexuality*, edited by Helen Gavin and Jacquelyn Bent, 47–58. Oxford: Inter-Disciplinary Press Oxford.

Wiegman, Robyn. 1993. "The Anatomy of Lynching." *Journal of the History of Sexuality* 3, no. 3: 445–67.

Williamson, Kathleen, and Anthony Marcus. 2017. "Black Pimps Matter: Racially Selective Identification and Prosecution of Sex Trafficking in the United States," In *Third Party Sex Work and Pimps in the Age of Anti-Trafficking*, edited by Amber Horning and Anthony Marcus, 177–96. New York: Springer International Publishings.

Wortley, Scott. 1996. "Justice for All? Race and Perceptions of Bias in the Ontario Criminal Justice System – a Toronto Survey." *Canadian Journal of Criminology* 38, no. 4: 439–67. https://doi.org/10.3138/cjcrim.38.4.439.

Young, Marion Iris. 2003. "Feminist Reactions to the Contemporary Security Regime." *Hypatia* 18, no. 1: 223–32. https://doi.org/10.1111/j.1527-2001.2003.tb00792.x.

Zheng, Tiantian. 2010. "Anti-trafficking Campaign and the Sex Industry in Urban China." In *Sex Trafficking, Human Rights and Social Justice*, edited by Tiantian Zheng, 84–101. New York: Routledge.

Reports and Websites

Barrett, Nicole A. 2010. "An Exploration of Promising Practices in Response to Human Trafficking in Canada." International Centre for Criminal Law Reform & Criminal Justice Policy. https://www.princeedwardisland.ca/sites/default/files/publications/human_trafficking.pdf.

British Columbia (BC) Ministry of Justice. 2013. "BC's Action Plan to Combat
Human Trafficking." https://www2.gov.bc.ca/assets/gov/law-crime-and
-justice/criminal-justice/victims-of-crime/human-trafficking/about-us
/action-plan.pdf.

Canadian Bar Association. 2018. "Submission on Bill C-75 *Criminal Code and
Youth Criminal Justice Act Amendments*." https://www.cba.org/CMSPages
/GetFile.aspx?guid=2058601f-9ae0-4dbb-9e8b-7e829462213b.

Canadian Resource Centre for Victims of Crime. 2012. "Consecutive
Sentencing for Multiple Murderers in Canada." https://crcvc.ca/docs
/consecutive-sentencing-2012.pdf.

Casavant, Lyne, and Dominique Valiquet. 2014. "Legislative Summary of
Bill C-36: An Act to Amend the Criminal Code in Response to the Supreme
Court of Canada Decision in Attorney General of Canada v. Bedford
and to Make Consequential Amendments to Other Acts." Library of
Parliament. https://lop.parl.ca/sites/PublicWebsite/default/en_CA
/ResearchPublications/LegislativeSummaries/412C36E.

Clancey, Alison. 2018. "Realities of the Anti-trafficked: How Canada's
Human Trafficking Response Increases Vulnerability for Im/migrant Sex
Workers." Brief to the Standing Committee on Justice and Human Rights
on Human Trafficking, 19 March. Supporting Women's Alternatives
Network (SWAN) Society (Vancouver). https://www.ourcommons.ca
/Content/Committee/421/JUST/Brief/BR9760992/br-external
/SupportingWomensAlternativesNetworkSociety-e.pdf.

Coleman, Lara. 2015. "Trafficking in Persons." Library of Parliament.
https://lop.parl.ca/sites/PublicWebsite/default/en_CA/Research
Publications/201159E.

Criminal Intelligence Service Canada (CISC). 2008. "Organized Crime and
Domestic Trafficking in Persons in Canada." Strategic Intelligence Brief,
Ottawa. http://www.unicef.ca/sites/default/files/imce_uploads
/DISCOVER/OUR%20WORK/CHILD%20SURVIVAL/sib_web_en.pdf.

Department of Justice. 2017. "An Act to Amend an Act to Amend the Criminal
Code (Exploitation and Trafficking in Persons) - Questions and Answers."
https://www.justice.gc.ca/eng/csj-sjc/pl/shtl/qa.html.

Department of Justice Canada. 2015a. "A Handbook for Criminal Justice
Practitioners on Trafficking in Persons." http://www.justice.gc.ca/eng
/rp-pr/cj-jp/tp/hcjpotp-gtpupjp/hcjpotp-gtpupjp.pdf.

Department of Justice Canada. 2016. "Human Trafficking: Partnerships."
http://www.justice.gc.ca/eng/cj-jp/tp/part.html#rcmp.

Executive Director, Social Development, Finance & Administration. 2013.
"Human Trafficking." City of Toronto (22 January), https://www.toronto
.ca/legdocs/mmis/2013/ex/bgrd/backgroundfile-55437.pdf.

Financial Transactions and Reporting Analysis Centre of Canada (FINTRAC).
2016. "Results in the Fight against Money Laundering and Terrorism

Financing: FINTRAC Annual Report." http://www.fintrac.gc.ca /publications/ar/2016/ar2016-eng.pdf.

Government of British Columbia. (BC). 2014a. "Domestic Sex Trafficking of Aboriginal Girls and Women." https://www2.gov.bc.ca/gov/content /justice/criminal-justice/victims-of-crime/human-trafficking/human -trafficking-training/module-2/aboriginal-women.

Government of British Columbia (BC). 2014b. "What Makes Someone Vulnerable to Human Trafficking?" https://www2.gov.bc.ca/gov/content /justice/criminal-justice/victims-of-crime/human-trafficking/human -trafficking-training/module-1/vulnerabilities.

Government of Canada. 2018. "Opening Remarks by Luc Beaudry, Assistant Director, Collaboration, Development and Research, Financial Transactions and Reports Analysis Centre of Canada at the House of Commons Finance Committee Parliamentary Review of the Proceeds of Crime (Money Laundering) and Terrorist Financing Act." https://www.ourcommons.ca /DocumentViewer/en/42-1/fina/meeting-133/evidence.

Government of Manitoba. 2019. "Tracia's Trust: Manitoba's Strategy to Prevent Sexual Exploitation and Sex Trafficking." Manitoba Government. https://www.gov.mb.ca/fs/traciastrust/pubs/tracias_trust_report_2019.pdf.

Government of Ontario. 2020a. "Human Trafficking." https://www.ontario .ca/page/human-trafficking.

Government of Ontario. 2016. "Ontario Names Director of Anti-trafficking Office." News release, 10 November 2016, https://news.ontario.ca/en /release/42617/ontario-names-director-of-anti-human-trafficking-office

Government of Ontario. 2020b. "Ontario's Anti-human Trafficking Strategy 2020–2025." https://www.ontario.ca/page/ontarios-anti-human -trafficking-strategy-2020-2025.

Hanger, Art, and John Maloney. 2006. "The Challenge of Change: A Study of Canada's Criminal Prostitution Laws." House of Commons Canada, Standing Committee on Justice and Human Rights, Subcommittee on Solicitation Laws.http://www.parl.gc.ca/HousePublications/Publication .aspx?DocId=2599932&Language=E&Mode=1&Parl=39&Ses=1.

Housefather, Anthony. 2018. "Moving Forward in the Fight against Human Trafficking in Canada." House of Commons Canada, Standing Committee on Justice and Human Rights.https://www.ourcommons.ca/Content /Committee/421/JUST/Reports/RP10243099/justrp24/justrp24-e.pdf.

Ibrahim, Dyna. 2018. "Trafficking in Persons in Canada, 2016." Statistics Canada. https://www150.statcan.gc.ca/n1/pub/85-005-x/2018001 /article/54979-eng.htm.

Lam, Elene. "Stop the Harm from Anti-trafficking Policies & Campaigns: Support Sex Workers' Rights, Justice and Dignity." Butterfly – Asian and Migration Sex Workers Support Network. https://www.butterflysw.org /harm-of-anti-trafficking-campaign-.

MacKay, Ryan. 2014. "Bill C-26: An Act to Amend the Criminal Code, the Canada Evidence Act and the Sex Offender Information Registration Act, to Enact the High Risk Child Sex Offender Database Act and to Make Consequential Amendments to Other Acts." Library of Parliament. http://publications.gc.ca/collections/collection_2016/bdp-lop/ls/YM32-3-412-C26-eng.pdf.

Mackenzie, Kimberly, and Alison Clancey. 2020. *Im/Migrant Sex Workers, Myths & Misconceptions: Realities of the Anti-trafficked.* 2nd ed. https://3ef32e5e-964e-4a01-a2dc-2292a5000739.filesusr.com/ugd/3a120f_8cf163d66eb345d385b254eb91d72cd2.pdf.

Maisie, Karam. 2016. "Trafficking in Persons in Canada, 2014." Statistics Canada. http://www.statcan.gc.ca/pub/85-002-x/2016001/article/14641-eng.htm.

Ministry of Community Safety and Social Services. 2018. "Ontario's Strategy to End Human Trafficking: First Year Progress Report." https://www.mcss.gov.on.ca/en/mcss/programs/humantrafficking/firstYearProgress.aspx.

Ministry of Community Safety and Social Services. 2017. "Ontario's Strategy to End Human Trafficking Progress Report." https://news.ontario.ca/en/backgrounder/43810/ontarios-strategy-to-end-human-trafficking-progress-report.

Ministry of the Status of Women. 2016. "Ontario Taking Steps to End Human Trafficking Province Investing in Strategy to Improve Services, Help Survivors." News release (30 June), https://news.ontario.ca/owd/en/2016/06/ontario-taking-steps-to-end-human-trafficking.html?_ga=2.66534702.1614810972.1495978287-1237777190.1495978287.

Moore Kloss, Avery (Host), and Katrin Roots (Executive Producer). (Fall 2022). Human Trafficking: Questioning Canada's Anti-trafficking Framework (Audio podcast episode). In *CRSP Talk*. Wilfrid Laurier University Centre for Research on Security Practices and Folktale Studio. https://crsp-talk.simplecast.com/.

National Inquiry into Missing and Murdered Indigenous Women and Girls. 2019. "Reclaiming Power and Place: The Final Report of the National Inquiry into Missing and Murdered Indigenous Women and Girls." https://www.mmiwg-ffada.ca/final-report/.

Organization for Security and Cooperation in Europe (OSCE). 2017. "The OSCE Special Representative and Co-ordinator for Combating Trafficking in Human Beings: 2016–17 Report." https://www.osce.org/secretariat/360796?download=true.

Oxman-Martinez, Jacqueline, Marie Lacroix, and Jill Hanley. 2005. *Victims of Trafficking in Persons: Perspectives from the Canadian Community Sector.* Department of Justice Canada, Research and Statistics Division. http://www.justice.gc.ca/eng/rp-pr/cj-jp/tp/rr06_3/rr06_3.pdf

Public Safety Canada. 2009. "The Investigation, Prosecution and Correctional Management of High-Risk Offenders: A National Guide." https://www.publicsafety.gc.ca/cnt/rsrcs/pblctns/2009-pcmg/2009-pcmg-eng.pdf.

Public Safety Canada. 2012. "National Action Plan to Combat Human Trafficking." Government of Canada. https://www.publicsafety.gc.ca/cnt/rsrcs/pblctns/ntnl-ctn-pln-cmbt/index-eng.aspx.

Public Safety Canada. 2016. "National Action Plan to Combat Human Trafficking: 2015–2016 Annual Report on Progress." Government of Canada. https://www.publicsafety.gc.ca/cnt/rsrcs/pblctns/ntnl-ctn-pln-cmbt-prgrss-2016/ntnl-ctn-pln-cmbt-prgrss-2016-en.pdf.

Public Safety and Emergency Preparedness Canada. 2005. "Sentence Calculation: A Handbook for Judges and Correctional Officials." http://publications.gc.ca/collections/Collection/PS4-17-2005E.pdf.

Ratansi, Yasmin. 2007. "Turning Outrage into Action to Address Trafficking for the Purpose of Sexual Exploitation in Canada." House of Commons Canada, Standing Committee on the Status of Women. https://www.ourcommons.ca/DocumentViewer/en/39-1/FEWO/report-12/.

Royal Canadian Mounted Police. 2013a. "Domestic Human Trafficking for Sexual Exploitation in Canada." http://publications.gc.ca/collections/collection_2014/grc-rcmp/PS64-114-2014-eng.pdf

Royal Canadian Mounted Police. 2022. "Recognizing Human Trafficking Victims." https://www.rcmp-grc.gc.ca/en/human-trafficking/recognizing-human-trafficking-victims.

Royal Canadian Mounted Police. 2016a. "Human Trafficking in Canada: A Threat Assessment." http://www.rcmp-grc.gc.ca/pubs/ht-tp/htta-tpem-eng.htm.

Royal Canadian Mounted Police. 2012. "I Am Not for Sale." Youth Booklet. http://www.rcmp-grc.gc.ca/ht-tp/publications/booklet-brochure-youth-jeunes-eng.htm.

Statistics Canada. 2016. "Immigration and Ethnocultural Diversity in Canada." http://www12.statcan.gc.ca/nhs-enm/2011/as-sa/99-010-x/99-010-x2011001-eng.cfm#a4.

Swiss Federal Department of Justice and Police 2016. "The joint fight against human trafficking." https://www.ejpd.admin.ch/ejpd/en/home/latest-news/reden---interviews/reden/archiv/reden-simonetta-sommaruga/2016/2016-10-20.html

United Nations Office of Drugs and Crime. 2013. "Abuse of a Position of Vulnerability and Other 'Means' within the Definition of Trafficking in Persons." Issue Paper. https://www.unodc.org/documents/human-trafficking/2012/UNODC_2012_Issue_Paper_-_Abuse_of_a_Position_of_Vulnerability.pdf.

United Nations Office of Drugs and Crime. 2016a. "Global Report on Trafficking in Persons." https://www.unodc.org/documents/data-and-analysis/glotip/2016_Global_Report_on_Trafficking_in_Persons.pdf.

United Nations Office of Drugs and Crime. 2013. "Issue Paper: Abuse of a Position of Vulnerability and Other 'Means' within the Definition of Trafficking in Persons." https://www.unodc.org/documents/human-trafficking/2012/UNODC_2012_Issue_Paper_-_Abuse_of_a_Position_of_Vulnerability.pdf.

United Nations Office of Drugs and Crime. 2015a. "Issue Paper: The Concept of 'Exploitation' in the Trafficking in Persons Protocol." https://www.unodc.org/documents/congress/background-information/Human_Trafficking/UNODC_2015_Issue_Paper_Exploitation.pdf.

United Nations Office of Drugs and Crime. 2014. "Issue Paper: The Role of 'Consent' in the Trafficking in Persons Protocol." http://www.unodc.org/documents/human-trafficking/2014/UNODC_2014_Issue_Paper_Consent.pdf.

United Nations Office of Drugs and Crime. 2008. "Profiling the Traffickers." The Vienna Forum to Fight Human Trafficking, 13–15 February, Austria Center Vienna. Background Paper. https://www.unodc.org/documents/human-trafficking/2008/BP016ProfilingtheTraffickers.pdf.

United Nations Office of Drugs and Crime. 2015b. "Remarks of UNODC Executive Director, Yury Fedotov, at the United Nations Security Council Thematic Debate on 'Trafficking in Persons in Situations of Conflict: ISIL and Beyond.'" https://www.unodc.org/unodc/en/press/releases/2015/December/remarks-of-the-executive-director-un-office-on-drugs-and-crime-at-the-un-security-council-thematic-debate-on-trafficking-in-persons-in-situations-of-conflict_-isil-and-beyond.html.

United States Department of Justice and Government of Canada. 2006. "Bi-national Assessment of Trafficking in Persons." http://publications.gc.ca/collections/collection_2017/sp-ps/PS4-228-2006-eng.pdf.

University College of Fraser Valley, Royal Canadian Mounted Police, UN Office of Drugs and Crime, and the International Centre for Criminal Law Reform and Criminal Justice Policy. 2005. "Human Trafficking: Reference Guide to Canadian Law Enforcement." https://icclr.org/publications/human-trafficking-reference-guide-for-canadian-law-enforcement/.

US Department of State. 2017. "Trafficking in Persons Report." https://www.state.gov/reports/2017-trafficking-in-persons-report/.

US Department of State. 2016. "Trafficking in Persons Report." https://2009-2017.state.gov/documents/organization/258876.pdf.

US Department of State. 2015. "Trafficking in Persons Report." https://2009-2017.state.gov/documents/organization/245365.pdf.

US Department of State. 2014. "Trafficking in Persons Report." https://2009-2017.state.gov/j/tip/rls/tiprpt/2014/index.htm.

US Department of State. 2012. "Trafficking in Persons Report." https://2009-2017.state.gov/j/tip/rls/tiprpt/2012/index.htm.

US Department of State. 2010. "Trafficking in Persons Report." https://2009-2017.state.gov/documents/organization/142979.pdf.

US Department of State. 2003. "Trafficking in Persons Report." https://2001-2009.state.gov/r/pa/ei/rls/21475.htm.

Legal Cases

Canada (Attorney General) v. Bedford. 2013 SCC 72, [2013] 3 S.C.R. 1101

R. v. A.A. 2012 O.J. No. 6256

R. v. A.A. 2015 ONCA 558

R. v. A.E. 2018 ONSC 471

R. v. Ahmed 2019 O.J. No 4808

R. v. Antoine 2020 ONSC 181

R. v. A.S. 2017 ONSC 802

R. v. Beckford 2013 ONSC 653

R. v. Bedford 2013 SCC 72

R. v. Boutilier 2017 SCC 64

R. v. Brighton 2016 ONSC 7641

R. v. Brown 2018 ABQB 469

R. v. Burton 2013 ONSC 2160

R. v . Burton 2016 ONCJ 103

R. v. Burton 2018 ONCJ 153

R. v. Byron 2014 ONSC 990

R. v. Cole 2004 CanLII 58282 QC CM

R. v. D.A. 2017 ONSC 3722

R. v. Dagg 2015 ONSC 2463

R. v. Deiaco 2017 ONSC 3174

R. v. Domotor 2011 ONSC 626

R. v. D'Souza 2016 ONSC 2749

R. v. Finestone 2017 ONCJ 22

R. v. Gladue 1999 1 S.C.R. 688

R. v. Greenham 2015 O.J. No. 2414

R. v. Johnson 2011 ONSC 195

R. v. Leung 2015

R. v. McPherson 2011 ONSC 7717

R. v. Moazami 2015 BCSC 2055

R. v. Moazami 2019 BCCA 226*R. v. N.A.* 2017 ONCJ 665

R. v. Nakpangi 2008 O.J. No. 6022

R. v. Oliver-Machado 2014

R. v. Pham 2013 SCC 15

R. v. Rasool 2015

R. v. Reginald Louis Jean 2020 ONSC 624

R. v. R.R.S. 2015 ONSC 7749

R. v. Salmon (Courtney) 2011 ONSC 3654

R. v. Salmon (Courtney) 2013 ONCA 203

R. v. Salmon (Gregory) 2014 ONSC 1437

Laws and Bills

The Faster Removal of Foreign Criminals Act. S.C. 2013, c. 16

House of Commons Debates. Canadian Parliament. Bill C-36, *The Protection of Communities and Exploited Persons Act* [PCEPA]. 41st Parliament, 2nd Session, 3 October 2014.

House of Commons Debates. Canadian Parliament. Bill C-36, *The Protection of Communities and Exploited Persons Act* [PCEPA]. Justice Committee on Human Rights. 41st Parliament, 2nd Session, 8 July 2014.

House of Commons Debates. Canadian Parliament. Bill C-36, *The Protection of Communities and Exploited Persons Act* [PCEPA]. 41st Parliament, 2nd Session, 11 June 2014.

House of Commons Debates. Canadian Parliament. Bill C-38, *An Act to Amend the Criminal Code (Exploitation and Trafficking in Persons).* 42nd Parliament. 1st Session, 11 December 2017.

House of Commons Debates. Canadian Parliament. Bill C-268, *An Act to Amend the Criminal Code (Minimum Sentence for Offences Involving Trafficking of Persons under the Age of Eighteen Years).* 41st Parliament, 2nd Session, 26 November 2013.

House of Commons Debates. Canadian Parliament. Bill C-268, *An Act to Amend the Criminal Code (Minimum Sentence for Offences Involving Trafficking of Persons under the Age of Eighteen Years).* 40th Parliament, 2nd Session, 1 June 2009.

House of Commons Debates. Canadian Parliament. Bill C-268, *An Act to Amend the Criminal Code (Minimum Sentence for Offences Involving Trafficking of Persons under the Age of Eighteen Years).* 40th Parliament, 2nd Session, 27 February 2009.

House of Commons Debates. Canadian Parliament. Bill C-310, *The Act to Amend the Criminal Code (Trafficking in Persons).* 41st Parliament, 1st Session, 12 December 2011.

House of Commons Debates. Canadian Parliament. Bill C-452, *An Act to Amend the Criminal Code (Exploitation and Trafficking in Persons).* Third Reading, 41st Parliament, 2nd Session, Volume 149, Issue 140, 12 May 2015.

House of Commons Debates. Canadian Parliament. Bill C-452, *An Act to Amend the Criminal Code (Exploitation and Trafficking in Persons)*. 41st Parliament, 2nd Session, 26 November 2013.

House of Commons Debates. Canadian Parliament. Bill C-452, *An Act to Amend the Criminal Code (Exploitation and Trafficking in Persons)*. Justice Committee on Human Rights. 41st Parliament, 1st Session, 1 May 2013.

House of Commons Debates. Canadian Parliament. Bill C-452, *An Act to Amend the Criminal Code (Exploitation and Trafficking in Persons)*. 41st Parliament, 2nd Session, 29 April 2013.

House of Commons Debates. Canadian Parliament. Bill C-452, *An Act to Amend the Criminal Code (Exploitation and Trafficking in Persons)*. 41st Parliament, 1st Session, 29 January 2013.

House of Commons Debates. Canadian Parliament. Bill C-612, *An Act to Amend the Criminal Code (Trafficking in Persons)*. 40th Parliament, 3rd Session, 24 March 2011.

Immigration and Refugee Protection Act (IRPA). SC. 2001. C-27, S. 37(1) and S. 118

Legislative Assembly of Ontario. Private Member's Bill. Human Trafficking. 14 May 2015.

Legislative Assembly of Ontario. Debates. Bill C-17, *The Saving the Girl Next Door Act*. 6 October 2016.

Legislative Assembly of Ontario. Bill C-251, *Anti-Human Trafficking Strategy Act, 2021*.

United Nations. 2000a. "Convention against Transnational Organized Crime and the Protocols Thereto." https://www.unodc.org/documents/treaties/UNTOC/Publications/TOC%20Convention/TOCebook-e.pdf.

United Nations. 2000b. "Protocol to Prevent, Suppress and Punish Trafficking in Persons, Especially Women and Children, Supplementing the United Nations Convention Against Transnational Organized Crime." https://treaties.un.org/pages/viewdetails.aspx?src=ind&mtdsg_no=xviii-12-a&chapter=18pdf

United Nations. 1989. "Convention on the Rights of the Child." http://www.ohchr.org/EN/ProfessionalInterest/Pages/CRC.aspx.

United Nations General Assembly. 1921. "International Convention for the Suppression of the Traffic in Women and Children".

United Nations General Assembly. 1910. "International Convention for the Suppression of the White Slave Traffic."

United Nations General Assembly. 1904. "International Agreement for the Suppression of the White SlaveTraffic." https://www1.umn.edu/humanrts/instree/whiteslavetraffic1910.html.

United States. 2000. *Trafficking Victims' Protection Act*. Washington, DC. https://www.govinfo.gov/content/pkg/PLAW-106publ386/pdf/PLAW-106publ386.pdf.

Media

680 News. 2015. "9 Charged, Another Sought, in Canada-wide Human Trafficking Ring." 22 April, http://www.680news.com/2015/04/22 /9-charged-another-sought-in-canada-wide-human-trafficking-ring/.

Brown, Liz. 2016. "'Animals' Force Victims into Sex Trade: Cop." *Toronto Sun* (12 December), http://torontosun.com/2016/12/12/animals -force-victims-into-sex-trade-cop/wcm/032c15ac-698e-49b7-bd29 -d6ce9ba8461e.

Canadian Alliance for Sex Workers Law Reform. "Sex Worker Human Rights Groups Oppose Police Operation Northern Spotlight." Press release, 9 October 2018. http://sexworklawreform.com/wp-content /uploads/2019/02/ONS-press-release.pdf.

The Canadian Press. 2016. "32 People Charged with 78 Offences in Canada-wide Human Trafficking Investigation." *Global News* (18 October), https://globalnews.ca/news/3010667/32-people-charged-with -78-offences-in-canada-wide-human-trafficking-investigation/.

The Canadian Press. 2018. "Toronto Police Arrest 4 Men in Human Trafficking Probe Involving Teen Victims." *Global News* (12 February), https: //globalnews.ca/news/4020620/toronto-police-human-trafficking/.

Carter, Adam. 2014. "20 Hamilton Human Trafficking Ring Members Deported." CBC News (22 July), http://www.cbc.ca/news/canada /hamilton/news/20-hamilton-human-trafficking-ring-members -deported-1.2714261.

Carville, Olivia. 2015a. "The Game: Living Hell in Hotel Chains." *Toronto Star* (14 December), http://projects.thestar.com/human-sex-trafficking -ontario-canada/.

Carville, Olivia. 2015b. "How a Young Girl Became a Victim of Sex Trafficking." *Toronto Star* 14 December), https://www.thestar.com /news/canada/2015/12/14/how-a-young-girl-became-a-victim-of -sex-trafficking.html.

Carville Olivia. 2015c. "'The Pimps Turn You into a Robot. All You Know Is Money, Drugs and Sex." *Toronto Star* (13 December), https://www .pressreader.com/canada/toronto-star/20151213/281479275359146.

Carville Olivia. 2015d. "They Are Being Beaten, Branded, Bought and Sold along Our Highways and in Our Hotels. A Toronto Star Investigation into Human Sex Trafficking in Ontario." *Toronto Star* (12 December), https://www.pressreader.com/canada/toronto-star/20151212.

Covenant House Toronto. 2020. "Covenant House Toronto Launches Shoppable Girls Campaign to Draw Attention to Sex Trafficking." *PR Newswire* (18 February), https://www.newswire.ca/news-releases /covenant-house-toronto-launches-shoppable-girls-campaign-to-draw -attention-to-sex-trafficking-801337446.html.

CTV News. 2014. "Pickering Man Charged Following Sex Trade Allegations."
The Canadian Press (2 April), https://toronto.ctvnews.ca/pickering-man
-charged-following-sex-trade-allegations-1.1757138.

D'Aliesio, Renata. 2013. "Toronto Police Chief Bill Blair Weighs in on Recent
Supreme Court Rulings." *Globe and Mail* (27 December).

Drydyk, Julia. 2021. "Sex Trafficking Is a Game Where the 'Romeo Pimps'
Always Win, and That Has to End." Globe and Mail: *Opinion* (22 February).

Hamilton Spectator. 2011. "Jail Escapee Faces Hamilton Human-Trafficking
Charge." *Hamilton Spectator* (7 December), https://www.thespec.com
/news-story/2225110-jail-escapee-faces-hamilton-human-trafficking
-charge/.

Herhalt, Chris. 2015. "Police Rescue 20 Trafficked Sex Workers in Raids
across Canada." *CP24* (22 October), https://www.cp24.com/news/police
-rescue-20-trafficked-sex-workers-in-raids-across-canada-1.2622471.

Mandel, Michael. 2013. "Woman's Pimping Charges Dropped but Allegation
Scars Remain." *Toronto Sun* (17 September), https://torontosun.com
/2013/09/17/womans-pimping-charges-dropped-but-allegation-scars
-remain.

Miller, Adam, and David Shum. 2017. "Police Arrest 104 Men in Massive
Multi-year Child Prostitution Investigation in Ontario." *Global News* (21
April), https://globalnews.ca/news/3394952/police-arrest-104-men
-find-85-child-prostitutes-in-multi-year-investigation-in-ontario/.

Mitchell, Jeff. 2017. "Human Trafficking Suspect Accused of Exploiting
Girls as Young as 14 Arrested in Bowmanville." DurhamRegion.com
(14 March), https://www.durhamregion.com/news-story/9222408
-human-trafficking-suspect-accused-of-exploiting-girls-as-young
-as-14-arrested-in-bowmanville/.

Quinn, Jennifer, and Robert Crib. 2013. "Inside the World of Human Sex
Trafficking." *Toronto Star* (5 October), https://www.thestar.com/news
/gta/2013/10/05/inside_the_world_of_human_sex_trafficking.html.

Syers, Naomi. 2017. "Canada 150 and the Decriminalization of Indigenous
Sex Workers." AWID (30 June), https://www.awid.org/news-and-analysis
/canada-150-and-decriminalization-indigenous-sex-workers.

Toronto Sun. 2017. "Human Trafficking Awareness Campaign Launched
in Toronto." *Toronto Sun* (1 August), https://torontosun.com/2017
/08/01/human-trafficking-awareness-campaign-launched-in
-toronto/wcm/0be19f97-7947-400f-8e90-7f1a999c38d5.

Zangouei, Aileen. 2020. "6 York Region Residents Charged as Police
Dismantle Sex Trade Organization Criminal Activities Saw Victims Rotated
to Apartments around Ontario to Perform Sexual Services." Toronto.com
(17 July), https://www.yorkregion.com/news-story/10078956-6-york
-region-residents-charged-as-police-dismantle-sex-trade-organization/.

Index

Note: Page numbers in *italics* indicate figures and tables.